THE PAGEANT OF CUBA

By the same author
THE STORY OF BERMUDA

BY HUDSON STRODE

THE
PAGEANT
OF
CUBA

RANDOM HOUSE · NEW YORK

Second Printing, September, 1936
Copyright, 1934, by Hudson Strode
Printed in the United States of America
by Quinn and Boden Co., Inc.

For
THÉRÈSE

A thousand tongues would not suffice to describe the things of novelty and beauty I saw, for it was all like a scene of enchantment.

Christopher Columbus, writing from Baracoa,
on his first voyage to Cuba, in 1492.

Man cannot be more perfect than the sun. The sun burns with the same ray that warms. The sun has spots. The unfortunate speak only of the spots. The fortunate speak of the light.

José Martí.

CONTENTS

ix

PART III

The Spanish-American War and Leonard Wood

PART IV

The Republic

PART V

Only Yesterday and Today

ILLUSTRATIONS

FOREWORD

ONCE when Voltaire presented to a friend a copy of a work of his in two volumes he apologized for not having had the time to write it in one volume. After several years of research and documentation—I began to gather material for this book in Cuba in 1928—and after two years of writing, cutting, revising, I have the temerity to offer in one volume a history of Cuba and the Cuban people, covering some four centuries and four decades, beginning in that last mild-tempered week of October 1492 when Christopher Columbus first set eyes on the island and was so amazed by its beauties that he professed he could not find words golden enough with which to pen his praise. A two-volume work on the subject would indeed have been easier. Dr. Chapman in the introduction to his excellent six hundred page *History of the Cuban Republic* confesses that he found such voluminous material on Cuban affairs from 1900 to 1928 that he could easily have made each of his twenty-seven chapters into twenty-seven different books. Because of the necessity for condensation, I am aware that I stand peculiarly vulnerable to charges of specialists in every field of Cuban life—political, economical, social—for having slighted their specialties. I make no claim to competition with such fully realized treatments of particular periods, like Dr. Chapman's, or like Miss I. A. Wright's profoundly valuable *Early History of Cuba* (to 1586), gathered from original documents in the archives of Seville, or like Walter Millis's brilliant, satirical account of the Spanish-American War or French Ensor Chadwick's solid two-volume record of the same period.

Bearing in mind, however, that the highly developed ancient Indians of Mexico and Central America considered any falsification of history a crime deserving the death penalty, I have attempted wherever possible to double-check my sources and information and even the sight of my own eyes. If in some small detail I should prove to have been unwittingly inaccurate, I hope to be forgiven on the ground that never by even the slightest tipping of the scales have I intentionally through any preconceived prejudice given false color to "the spirit" of Cuban history. But, of course, from the bulk of perhaps some thirty thousand printed pages which I examined in research, I have selected my material according to my individual inclination as to what seemed significant and interesting to me personally; and I have put special emphasis and detail of color on those sections of the chronicle which I believed worth special pause and remembrance.

The immediate object of this work then is two-fold: to give pleasure and to convey historical information. Not relaxing the strictest fidelity to history, I have endeavored to present material without the stiffness of historical patterns, and yet to throw such illumination on the dramatis personæ as would release them from the puppet limitations of printed chronicles. I have endeavored, also, not to base persuasion on too keen a sharpening of the matter's novelty. I have tried to give the reader a sense of Cuba as much a matter of being as of doing. By this process, the account, in a sense, becomes an emotional and spiritual history of Cuba as well as factual. Objectively, *The Pageant of Cuba* turns out to be the presentation of a blood-stained cavalcade, beginning in 1492 with bravely caparisoned adventurers, and traversing four hundred and forty-two years of cruelty, romance, greed, hope, struggle, ecstasy, retribution—the spectacle interspersed with music and humorous interludes. The title of the book might well be *The Island of Expiation.*

Some years before chance sent me to Bermuda to live I had

become infatuated with Cuba and had begun to gather material for writing about it. After telling the brief story of quaint little Bermuda, where virtually nothing has ever happened, I returned to write a history of the exciting island of my first attachment. *The Story of Bermuda* was written for those who needed rest— those for whom onrushing life should pause, catch its breath, stand still awhile in a remote, peaceful Anglo-Saxon community, where life has seemingly stood still for a very long time. *The Pageant of Cuba* is written for those who yearn for the stimulation of the different, a place where the sights, traditions, rhythms, language are distinctly foreign. In Bermuda you *exist,* so pleasantly. In Cuba you *live,* tasting and digesting life with sharp appetite. One has few emotions in Bermuda; there are few activities to touch the emotions. In Cuba life is so keyed that, strangely, even while you are relaxed, you are vibrantly alive. You know with your brain that the pursuit of living really matters little; you know with your heart that it is a glorious adventure full of pulse-racing experiments. You sit at ease wrapped in an assuring philosophical languor and know at the same time that your nerve fibers are tingling joyously in the mere excitement of possessing life.

During 1933 and 1934 newspaper readers have focused more attention on Cuba than at any period since the Spanish-American War. The villainies of Machado, the graft scandals over the construction of the National Highway and the Capitol, the formation of the powerful secret organization called ABC, the bomb-throwing of students, the general strike, the massacre of August fifth, the flight of the tyrant, the revolt of the army sergeants, the siege of the Hotel National—these recent sensational events have served to throw a most lurid and unflattering light on the neighbor island. The resultant publicity has drawn a share of the world's contempt, which it is ever ready to hurl at a country distraught in estate. What manner of men are these Cubans that they keep their house in such disorder? the reading public demands a bit disdainfully. Americans hardly pause to consider that the better class of Cubans and the sturdy small farmers are no more responsible for the scandals of their politics than the clergy of Chicago are responsible for that city's municipal corruption and gangster depredations.

The average American has only the foggiest notion of Cuban character. He generally holds some tenuous impression that the composite Cuban is romantic, over-sexed, dance-loving, quick-to-fight, smooth-mannered, absolutely untrustworthy, with a dash of the tar brush. There is unquestionably a scintilla of truth in the picture, but the whole is no more justly conclusive than to say that Americans are compounded of brag, babbitry, and passion for baseball. José Martí, Cuba's martyred patriot, once wrote, "Man cannot be more perfect than the sun. The sun has spots. It burns with the same rays with which it gives light. The unfortunate speak only of the spots, the fortunate of the light." Only those who are fortunate enough to know Cubans intimately learn to recognize the excellence of their qualities.

Sir William Van Horne in 1905 called the Cubans "an intelligent, well-behaved, and kindly people." Twenty years later Dwight Morrow summarized them as "an able, alert, and sensitive people." These were the judgments of great-hearted, intellectual, and worldly-successful gentlemen. The average American promoter goes almost mad with exasperation at Cuban business methods. The truth is the majority of Cubans have little more desire to fit into an economic machine than had the aboriginal Indians who breathed the same climatic atmosphere centuries ago. Cubans are blessed with a joyous sensitivity to those aspects of life which have no market value. It is that peculiar trait in them which business men naturally loathe most. Where the American knows the price of things, the Cuban knows the value —at least to himself. He dislikes to be pinned down; he often breaks appointments with gayest nonchalance if the notion strikes him, or if something more pleasurable comes up. He will promise you anything, to be polite, without much thought of performing the promise. On the other hand, if he likes you, he will give up hours of time and go to endless trouble to be of service. He is lavish in spending money, careless about paying bills. Despite the occasional flare-ups of animosities, the gun-play, the sudden hates and name-callings, Cubans at heart are easy-going, ease-doting, easily contented. Their revolutions are sometimes no more than "a proud boy's play"—mere episodes in the pageant.

In temperament the Cubans themselves say they are like their own climate with its tropical storms. The hurricane comes with black clouds, fierce thunders, terrifying winds. It devastates the country-side and passes on. After the lull, the sun shines—and nature with miraculous ingenuity and prodigality rectifies the damages, and the landscape soon blossoms again with loveliness and peace. The Cubans are like that. They say they quickly forget to hate—and to thank.

Their women set a different value on life from American women. For the most part, even in this preternaturally flushed and ambitious modern world, Cuban ladies seem pleased to pass their lives in fountained patios or on marble balconies illuminated by stars and varying moons. They know only the natural mysteries of being, the birth of love, the birth of children, death as it makes its haphazard selections. They are not concerned with masculine goings-out by the front door, only with the comings-in. They are admired, respected, comfortable, safe. The routine of similar days and nights does not seem monotonous to them. They have no ambition to achieve honors for themselves. They smile languorously at American women agitating for personal careers. They cannot comprehend the Anglo-Saxon feminist who yearns to sit in the seats of men. The majority are too content with their long mirrors, their own wicker rockers, their lace and ivory fans. They dote on the prattle of children as much as on their husbands' caresses. It is in the security of being women whom men provide for and protect that they find the drug of the lotus. It is true that a few are emerging from limitations of the home. A most civilized divorce law, by which they do not even have to present grounds, has made them free to fend for themselves if they choose. Very, very few choose.

There is much in the Cuban's attitude to life that Americans might regard with profit. Without ever having been exposed to studies of Hellenic culture, Cubans in general have learned of themselves the old Greek acceptance of fate. Except for young girls undone by unrequited love who drench themselves in gasoline and make of themselves a burning sacrifice to their unhappiness, superiority to adverse fortune seems to come as naturally to most Cubans as changing moons to the heavens. In spite of his tragical history, the Cuban is not a man who mourns long. His attitude towards death is fatalistic. That primal element of sunshine gives him a basic joyousness that will not be suppressed. A fundamental content dwells easily in his breast. It is that quality which brings to mind much that Carlyle found in Robert Burns, who lived in land and climate so remote from the Antilles, but who had the same sort of warm song in his heart. The Cuban shakes off sorrow as gallantly as his own battling gamecock shakes blood out of his eyes. If the fist of tyranny is not oppressing him, he too, like the Scotch singer, is gay of speech, full of frolic, in the midst of abject poverty. For one Cuban who can stand prosperity with dignity, a thousand can stand adversity with grace.

Perhaps the Cubans' most charming quality is their inherent desire of pleasing. They are the most delightful of companions. They take pride in making the person in their company happy. There is a genuine warmth about them that unfailingly wins a foreigner's affection.

In the enjoyment of life they are artists, be it some ardent form of love dalliance, martyrdom for an ideal, or merely the sipping of strained pineapple juice. They dote on the pleasurable waste of Time, who is no stern enemy to them as he is to the ambitious Northerner. About themselves they are frank, humorous, and even caustically critical. They have a quick, original, sometimes almost grotesque sense of humor. They might be called realistic romantics, for they well know how to make use of their cool, inherent vein of satire to check romantic excesses of passionate feeling.

The unlettered *gaujiros* with their rough genuineness possess many of those attributes that lend dignity to human life: hospitality to the wayfarer, kindly consideration, self-sufficiency, the honest simplicity of strength and patient industry, paradoxically combined with an Olympian inertia and that serene disregard of time's flight. Cuban plowmen are as long-patienced as the slow-motioned oxen they prod. The peasants' "damned wantlessness"—using the immortal phrase coined by a disgusted German peddler —serves for many reasoned or emotional philosophies.

Threads of the foregoing characteristics of Cuban temperament are perforce woven in the warp and woof of the crowded chronicle along with darker elements of cruelty and dishonesty. Perhaps it may seem that the tragic happenings have been overstressed in this book, yet certainly no detail has been exaggerated. But since a miraculous story must be ballasted with facts to be miraculous, so a pageant full of beauty and wonder should possess foils of pity and terror. And if, as Stephen Crane maintained, great art is born only out of great pain and suffering, Cuba, the island of expiation, which has paid unto the twelfth and thirteenth generations for the sins of her ancestors, has come rightfully by all the beauty that belongs to her.

HUDSON STRODE

"Ingleside"
Stockbridge, Massachusetts
August 26, 1934

PART I

From Christopher Columbus to 1800

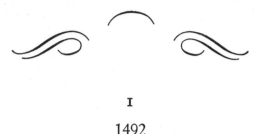

I

1492

AT the time that the precocious Cristoforo, eldest son of the Genoese wool-comber Colombo, entered the University of Pavia at the age of ten, the branches of learning for which that institution was distinguished were "natural philosophy, geography and astrology." During the boy's three years' attendance, we may believe that he neglected the first study because of an absorbing interest in the second, which was to lead later to the appellation of "the cosmographer." But it is also extremely likely that, with a temperament such as his, given to strange conceits and thirst for far-reaching adventure, he took a thrilling delight in the hieroglyphics of the stars, not only for their potential aid in navigation, but because of a personal advantage thought to be gained from the study of planetary movements in relation to individual nativities. Whether his quick mind had gleaned from the learned doctors all he deemed needful, or whether the call of the world fired his young blood to an uncontrollable fever that only sea-voyaging could assuage, he bolted from academic halls at the age of thirteen, signed up as a cabin-boy on a vessel lying in the port of Genoa, and set out to test the romantic truth of his first studies in sea-charts and the geography of far-off lands. Along with his scientific knowledge of star positions, orbits, and eclipses, he may have carried tucked away in a special pigeon-hole of that remarkably shrewd, practical, and oddly mystical brain of his, the belief that Friday was his lucky day. For so it proved in a series of phenomenal subsequent events.

The prologue to the pageant of Cuba should be set to represent the Spanish scene on a momentous last Friday of the year 1491. On that day, December the thirtieth, the crescent banners of the Moors, which had floated in the orange-scented breezes of Southern Spain for seven hundred and seventy-eight years, were taken down from the ramparts of the fortresses and the turrets of the famed Alhambra, as the Moorish government made formal surrender to emissaries of Ferdinand and Isabella. When the flags of Aragon and Castile bearing Christian crosses were lifted and unfurled, the greatest victory destiny ever accorded to the Catholic faith was crystallized in that dramatic hour. In the colorful spectacle, Christopher Columbus (called in Spain Cristóbal Colón) played the part of an unconsidered supernumerary, standing in drab garb, holding to the halter of the half-dead mule on which he had come an exhausting journey over icy mountain trails from the hospitable monastery of La Rabida. The future Admiral stood grave, silent; but his heart within was voluble, pounding prophetically as he speculated on the significance to him and his aspirations of the event taking place before his dream-haunted eyes.

Three days later in the same setting, Columbus witnessed an after-scene less climactic, but far more replete with splendor and emotional drama. Boabdil, the Moorish king, ceremoniously handed to the Spanish sovereigns, in the presence of their regally caparisoned entourage, the keys to the ancient city. Bowing his head in subjection, with the curse of his aged mother stabbing his ears, Boabdil went out of Granada's gate and started winding down the hills to his humiliating exile, followed slowly by a cavalcade of heartbroken, proud subjects.

The rejoicings of Spain were accompanied by picturesque pomp and the celebration of elaborate Masses. Before the triumphal festivities were concluded, while the hymns of thanksgiving were still being chanted, the happy Queen, adorned in some of the jewels she was to offer to pawn, granted an audience to Columbus.

Isabella was impressed. The "internal grandeur" of the man showed through his haggard exterior. His inflexibility strengthened her faith. When persons of confidence, courtiers and archbishops, came to negotiate with this impoverished navigator, who for years had been considered hardly more than a needy applicant for bread, shadowing corners of court antechambers, they were astounded at the princely conditions he set. Indeed his stipulations were scaled to stupefy the courtiers into incoherence and to make the bishops belch with indignation. The following were the principal items of his lofty requirements from the Crowns of Aragon and Castile: "he should be made Viceroy, Governor-General of the Islands and *terra firma* he would discover; the title of Grand Admiral of the Atlantic Ocean should be immediately bestowed upon him; his dignities should descend hereditarily in his family, by right of primogeniture; and he should be entitled to reserve for himself one-tenth of all the precious stones, pearls, diamonds, gold, silver, perfumes, spices, fruits, and other productions in whatsoever manner discovered in, or exported from the regions submitted to his authority." After eighteen years of rebuffs in diverse attempts to gain backing for his schemes, he would not derogate one jot his demands—what he considered "the dignity of his rights."

The shocked commissioners scoffed, argued themselves almost into apoplexy, and at length pronounced the terms fantastic. Then Luis de Santangel, receiver of ecclesiastical dues, besought the Queen and represented to her how much the enterprise merited her protection because of the probable "grand results for the glory of Jesus, the triumph of the church, and the posterity of her kingdoms." At the conclusion of the interview "God opened her understanding." But there were still delays and disappointments, and seven months later Columbus packed his few belongings and started for France to plead his case. Just in the nick of time messengers from the Queen caught him and brought him back. In the end the adventurer got a pledged agreement to every one of his demands. The title of Grand Admiral was straightway conferred upon him.

On Friday, the third of August, 1492, about three o'clock in the morning in the awed little sea-port of Palos, Columbus waked "to the rustling of the pines," and after hoisting the flag of the *Santa Maria,* which bore the image of the Savior nailed to the cross, he commanded the sails to be unfurled. Soon the caravel, with its two smaller companions the *Pinta* and the *Niña,* was gliding out of the harbor on its history-making voyage. The *Pinta* was commanded by an extremely able navigator named Martín Alonzo Pinzón, who is believed by a few historian-scholars to have been the master mind behind the momentous undertaking, and even to have crossed the Atlantic previously. Certainly the *Pinta* did keep the lead in the present adventure. The *Niña* was captained by Pinzón's brother.

Before the foreboding lamentations and half-hearted huzzas of the populace were out of ear-shot, Columbus had made the first entry in his journal. It was dated Friday, August the third, 1492.

The journal, which he proposed to keep in the manner of Cæsar's *Commentaries,* and which has become one of the world's most valued documents, attests to the series of happy-omened Fridays.

On the ninth of September, after the tag-end of Ferro, the last of the Canary Islands, had faded from the horizon and the three caravels had really struck out into perilous regions of discovery, the crew grew terror-stricken. Columbus sought to inspire them with the glory of the venture, painted pictures of magnificent lands overflowing with gold and jewels, and in the evening tried to soothe their misgivings by leading them in hymns honoring "Mary, the Ocean Star." Nothing availed to quiet their muttering distress. But on Friday, September the fourteenth, the first signs of the New World were seen when the sailors on the *Niña* espied a royal tern and a long-tailed tropic bird. All the crew took heart, erroneously believing that these birds never flew far from land.

A few days of hope, and then the intensely superstitious sailors became more clamorous in their apprehensions. They repeated oft-told tales about the *Mare Tenebrosum* found on the charts of some cosmographers, where were reputed to live horrible sea-serpents, griffins, and "other prodigies of nature run riot with monstrosities." At dawn on the following Friday, the twenty-first of September, they saw drifting from the west a quantity of weeds and herbs so vast that the sea appeared to be covered with it. And later in the day they rejoiced to sight a whale—"a sign that they were very near land, because they always keep near a shore."

After another respite of a day or two from fright, the crew once again gave over to their fancies, repicturing the most fear-some things that might lie beyond the weed. With soft words and prudent reasoning, Columbus endeavored to dispel their dark presages, appealing to their avarice by promises of rich re-wards. On the third of October, however, because he would not turn back, the crew began to stir up a mutiny. "The disagreement would have gone farther," says Las Casas, "if God had not stretched out his arms as he was wont, showing immediately new signs of their being near land." On Friday, the fifth of October, as if with a tremendous sigh of relief from wrestling with chaotic fears of the sailors, who "persevered in plots and complaints," Columbus wrote in his journal, "To God be many thanks given, the air being pleasant and temperate, with no weed, many sand pipers, and flying fish coming on the deck in numbers."

The following Wednesday the situation again became critical. The men fed on each other's discontent, and finally roused to a community outburst of fiery Spanish temperament, they plotted to throw Columbus overboard. After consultations, the captains—despite infallible signs of their being near land—declared they would go on "three days longer and not another hour." Oviedo in his *Historia de las Indias* does not say whether the Admiral acquiesced in this arrangement, but he graphically related the terrors of the situation, which in one more day might have proved mortal to Columbus and his monumental hopes.

Again the fateful Friday approached. On Thursday afternoon the Admiral predicted that before morning land would be reached. He charged them all to be particularly watchful. And to encourage them and to add a sharp incentive to their vigilance, he promised a fine velvet doublet to that man who should first cry out that he saw land—this in addition to the pension of 10,000 *maravedis* offered by the Queen. Excitement coursed through the pulses of the ships' company like heated quicksilver. The men now entirely forgot their fears. The *Pinta,* being a superior sailer, pushed on considerably in the lead.

That evening the Admiral from the poop of the *Santa Maria* watched with feverish intensity. About ten o'clock his sea-captain's eyes, accustomed to searching distances, beheld a light "like a wax candle rising and falling." At least so Columbus half-believed. He called a gentleman of the King's bedchamber to give his opinion. The answer was tentatively affirmative. A third man, being asked if he saw a moving light, declared he could see nothing. Columbus was too uncertain to affirm it was land. But he ordered sails shortened. Yet wind and current sent the ships forward at good speed. Every nerve and sinew on board were tautened to the snapping point. Midnight passed. Thursday had merged into Friday.

At two o'clock in the morning of this Friday, the twelfth of October, with the waning moon at 39° above the horizon and shining brightly on the sands of an island a few miles ahead, a sailor on the *Pinta* named Juan Rodriguez Bermejo saw the first land of the New World and cried out in a tremendous triumph, "Light! Land!"

A cannon shot from the *Pinta* proclaimed the discovery. Fully conscious of the glory "durable as the world itself" which he had secured, Columbus dropped down on his knees and gave thanks to God for his share in the great fortune. Raising his hands to heaven he began to intone the *Te Deum Laudamus,* while the conscience-smitten crew pressed about him and sang the responses in a delirium of joy. The vessels were hove to, waiting for daylight; but there was no sleeping on board any of the three caravels between the hour of two and dawn.

As the Admiral impatiently awaited the morning light, fancifully wondering what kind of land day would reveal—whether spice groves or some gold-towered city—he fitted on a suit of polished armor and arranged a scarlet mantle about his shoulders.

When dawn came he saw, rimming the turquoise water, stretches of an island—known now to be Watling Island of the Bahamas, but called then by its inhabitants Guanahani. A gentle surf lapped cream-colored sands. Flowery green groves yielded a fragrance like incense. Issuing from among the trees and crowding to the beaches, agitated with awe, were sun-browned people, as naked as the day their mothers bore them. Columbus commanded the small boats to be manned and armed. Clothed in the rich raiment which had been provided in anticipation of his meeting with the Grand Khan of Tartary, he took his place in the bow of the first yawl, and gave orders to his armored rowers. With one hand he held aloft the standard of Jesus. In the other, conqueror-like, he bore a glistening sword.

According to a whimsical legend, the first man to leap ashore, carrying the line to make fast the boat, was an Irishman named Billy Rice. This fellow was listed in the ship's book of the *Santa Maria* as Guillemia Ires; and sometimes he is accorded his place in the chronicle as merely "William of Galway." How he and an Englishman passing as Tallerte de Lajes—most likely named Allard—found themselves at Palos at the time of the expedition is unknown. But they sailed together on the flagship, as the only British-born members of the crew.

Before the astonished eyes of the marveling throng, Columbus planted in the yielding sands the standards of Christ and the Spanish sovereigns, and solemnly took possession of the natives' land for the Crown of Castile.

In compliment to the Savior he named the place San Salvador, and believing it to be an outlying island of India, he called the inhabitants Indians.

With some such expression as "Taino! Taino!", meaning "Peace! We are friends," the gentle savages timidly approached the men they conceived to have come from heaven. With an awed delight in everything about the visitors—the whiteness of their skin, their beards, their metal garments—they manifested an especial curiosity in Columbus's unsheathed sword. Except for their wooden lances, they were not knowledgeable in "the properties of weaponry," and innocently took the sword by the blade and cut themselves. Sudden and profuse blood spilt on the cream-colored sands. It was portentous. "The wild man and his destroyer had met."

The natives were not resentful. They smiled at the mishap, and offered presents of parrots, cotton yarn, cakes of cassava bread. The Spaniards in return gave strings of glass beads, red caps, and hawk's bells. It was a cordial and innocent enough first exchange. But the next day the sailors were palming off worthless bits of broken pottery, which the untutored Indians gladly accepted for the supernatural virtue of anything belonging to these celestial strangers. "It would have been happy," writes Sir Frederick Treves, "if the bartering had ended with balls of cotton yarn and hawk's bells; but it soon became a traffic in which the only goods that were marketable were human lives."

On that same Friday, a day disastrously ill-augured for the Indians, Columbus entered in his journal his desire "to free the friendly, simple people and convert them to the holy faith." "To see them free," says Filson Young, in ironic understatement; "they who were as free as seabirds!" A few years later the first colossal foreign mission organization had begun its work, starting at Haiti. And when the souls of the Haitians had been saved and their bodies cruelly destroyed with overwork and there was immediate need of fresh slaves, then the Spaniards turned to these Bahamas in their spurious missionary zeal. "Here they captured the docile islanders, without having to murder very many of them, baptized the survivors, and sent them to the mines to rot."

For the time, Columbus held his religious crusading in abatement, so propelling was his desire that "the Lord in His mercy would direct him to find gold."

Finding no gold in a fortnight's lingering among the keys and lagoons of the Bahamas, he decided to sail for a country to the southwest called Cuba, which he understood from the gesticulations of the natives to be very marvelous, with great ships and many skillful navigators. His eager imagination fancied this place to be the Cipango of Marco Polo, that island of gold and pearls and spices, lying at the outer edge of the Indian Sea. So convinced was he of the fact that he wrote in his journal, "On the spheres that I saw and on the paintings of the world-maps it is this region."

Taking with him several natives of Guanahani to act as decoys and, in time, interpreters, the Admiral gave orders for the caravels to take a S.S.W. course. On the morning of October the twenty-eighth, they came in sight of Cuba in the district of the bay of Nuevitas, and entered a very lovely tree-bordered river, where the water was transparently clear and free from shoals. But here no eager natives rushed to greet him. As the ships cast anchor, two paddlers in canoes sped away in swift, silent terror.

Arrayed in full regalia, the Admiral landed. In the presence of his men, with the tall trees as the only other witnesses, he took ceremonious possession of the land of the Cubeños. He named it Juana, in honor of the young Prince Juan.

The ritual over, Columbus inspected two thatched huts from which the inhabitants had fled like fowls. He found several hearths and fishing nets of palm-fiber, horn fish-hooks and harpoons of bone. In one of the houses was a kind of dog that did not bark—undoubtedly a domesticated opossum-like *jutía,* one of the two indigenous quadrupeds of Cuba.

Returning to his boat, he proceeded up the river and was enchanted by the scenery. The herbage was as thick as in Andalusia during May. There were abundant palm trees, different from those of Spain and Guinea, with naked trunks and very large leaves. The ardent air was sweet with the scent of strange flowers and the song of bright-plumaged birds unlike those of Spain. Humming birds darted among the blossoms "like animated particles of the rainbow." The distant mountains reminded him of Sicilian landscapes. That night he wrote of Cuba in his journal, "It is the most beautiful land human eyes have ever beheld, full of good harbors and profound rivers."

The next morning anchors were weighed and the caravels steered westward, where Columbus was told, by the Indians he had brought from the Bahamas, there was a king. At sunset, coming to another large river, which he named Rio de Los Mares, he saw villages by the bank. He sent two boats to communicate. Again men, women, and children fled to the woods. The Admiral gave orders that nothing should be disturbed and went personally to inspect the houses. He found them superior to the others he had seen. Fashioned of palm leaves in the shape of booths or pavilions, they were not laid out along streets, but scattered here and there about a grove like tents in a camp. The cleanly swept interiors were well supplied with fishing gear, and some contained wooden images "in the shape of females" and many masks, or as Las Casas says, "heads well carved from wood." Outside, near the huts, slung between the trunks of trees, were swinging couches of netting which the Indians called "hamacs." With a quick enthusiasm, the sailors took to these unfamiliar devices for sleeping; and thus began an affinity which has not abated after centuries.

At sunrise the caravels left Rio de los Mares and steered northwest, for the Indians on board the *Pinta* said that beyond a cape there was a river, and from there it was a four days' journey to Cubanacan, a great city. By this expression they designated a district in the center or the interior of Cuba. Columbus, fancifully excited by the name's resemblance to Kublai Khan, decided that the Indians must be speaking in some wise of the Tartar potentate. Believing the prince of this immediate neighboring region to be a man of some consequence, he got presents ready, which he was to send along with letters from the Spanish sovereigns. By now the self-deluded Admiral, wrapped in a tissue of gilded misconceptions, was in complete confusion as to whether he had reached the island of Cipango or the mainland of Asia. After a day's sailing he arrived at a palm-crested cape surrounded by sunken rocks which made procedure dangerous; and being thwarted by unpropitious winds, he gave orders to turn back to Rio de los Mares.

On their arrival he sent one of his decoy Indians to make friends with the people on shore. When the Cubeños had been reassured that the strangers were good men, who had given fine gifts in the many islands they had visited, they came in sixteen canoes to the anchored caravels, with hamacs and skeins of cotton yarn to barter. But the Admiral ordered that nothing should be taken from them except gold. Alas, they possessed none; and of silver Columbus saw only one worked piece adorning a native's nose. Yet they told of great merchants in the interior, at Cubanacan, who would come and buy the Spaniards' goods. The next day Columbus commissioned Rodrigo de Jerez and a converted Jew linguist named Luis de Torres, "who spoke Hebrew, Chaldean and a little Arabic," to go with two Indians to establish communications with the people of Cubanacan. Provided with glass beads with which to buy their entertainment and carrying specimens of spices and drugs to see if the like were to be found, they set off through a virgin Cuban forest to seek a fabulous city of Cathay.

When the emissaries had disappeared into the green tangle, Columbus careened his ships to make repairs. From the odor of the burning wood, in heating tar for the caulking, mastic was discovered. Columbus conjured up visions of a great exploitation of this precious gum, and shortly became excited over reports of the finding of nutmeg and rhubarb. But these proved fallacious. Martín Alonzo Pinzón, master of the *Pinta,* believed he had found cinnamon trees, brought his Admiral two pieces, and said a Portuguese sailor "had seen Indians carrying two very large bundles of it." Columbus, much excited, hurried to examine the trees; but he found they were not cinnamon.

Although disappointed in his quest for spices, he took delight in regarding the amenities of the surrounding country. Again he wrote that all he saw was so beautiful that "his eyes could never tire of gazing at such loveliness." He climbed an eminence and looked upon mountains as lofty as Peña de las Enamoradas near Granada, and one of them had "another little hill on its summit like a graceful mosque." He saw much cotton growing unculti-vated, some pods empty, others full, and flowers all on one plant. He found purslane and wild amaranth and honey and "fruits of a thousand kinds." An infinity of birds unlike those of Spain fascinated him. Three breeds were familiar: "partridges, geese, of which there are many, and singing nightingales." (Perhaps what he mistook for a nightingale may have been a Southern mock-ing-bird or a Cuban *solitaire*.) The songs of the birds and the chirping of crickets throughout the tropic night lulled him to rest, "while the November air was soft and healthy, tempered like the month of May." Along the shore he collected specimens of large, unfamiliar shells and kept an eye out for pearls. Specu-latively, he showed to the natives pearls and gold he had brought with him. He was flatteringly rewarded by tales certain old men told of a place called Bohio, to the southeast, where the people wore gold on their necks, ears, arms, and even legs. He under-stood them to say that there were many merchant ships in the great harbors of that country, and that much farther off there were cannibals that beheaded their captured enemies, sucked their blood, and cut off their private parts. When some added they had heard that the people of Bohio gathered gold on the beaches at night by torch flare, the credulous Admiral determined to seek that brave land as soon as his ambassadors returned. They came that night. The members of the crew pressed about them, eager for golden tidings. But it was a meager tale they heard, one which did not enrich their ears.

After walking about twelve leagues they had come to a village of fifty houses and about a thousand inhabitants. The Israelite "turned his tongue to all his vocabularies without profit." Through the Indian from the Bahamas, however, he had it given out that the white men came from heaven. The people of Cubanacan marveled at the strangers; some kissed their hands and their feet. They offered them vegetables and fruit. They placed them in seats of honor and grouped themselves on the floor to listen to the messages from the sky. All were naked except a few matrons who wore clouts about their middles. The same idyllic poverty seemed to exist here as in the other islands. No native could recall ever having heard of Kublai Khan. They regretted cinnamon did not grow in their regions. Of gold they had faint knowledge. But they courteously urged the white men to remain as their guests for at least five days. The envoys, however, thinking to profit little by remaining, soon took their departure. On their way back they met many men and women with a half-burnt weed in their hands, "being the dry herb they are accustomed to smoke." Las Casas thus describes the process: "The dry herbs are placed in a certain leaf, also dry like the paper muskets (or blow-pipes) which boys make at Easter time. Having lighted one end of it, they suck at the other end, draw in with the breath that smoke with which they make themselves drowsy, and in that way they say they cease to feel fatigue. These muskets . . . they call *tobacos.*"

At the disappointing report of a primitive and simple society, when they had expected an opulent Arabian Night's tale, the sailors groaned disgustedly. The only portion that interested them at all was that amusing bit about the "apparently naseous indulgence" of tobacco-smoking.

The report of the envoys put an end to many gorgeous imaginings of Columbus about an oriental prince and his gilded capital. But incorrigibly optimistic, he wrote up a cheerful account of the trip, praising the fertility of the soil his men had passed over, estimating the *quintals* of cotton that could be exported from the region. He closed his entry: "Today I got the ship afloat, and prepared to depart Thursday, in the name of God, and to steer S.E. in search of gold and spices, and to discover land."

From November the twelfth, however, to December the fifth, he coasted about the northern and eastern shores of Cuba, discovering ports, naming capes, planting crosses, and ever extolling the magnificence and charms of the scenery which surpassed that of all other places "as the day doth the night in lustre." He thought he found some stones "with gold in them," and hearing more fomenting phrases about the wealth of the sands of Bohio, he finally tore himself away from the Island. His last act was to name the extreme eastern point Alpha and Omega, "believing that this cape was the end of the mainland in the Orient."

On the morning of December the sixth he found himself before a port of a mountainous, verdant island, the Bohio of the Indians, which he named La Española—the Haiti of today. Six days after their arrival, the Spaniards captured a naked Indian woman, who made a great stir among them because she had a piece of gold in her nose, "which showed there was gold on the island." Shortly they established communications with a tribal king, a *cacique,* named Guacanagari. In a state visit to Columbus, the *cacique* presented him with a carved wooden head with eyes, nose, and tongue of beaten gold. His followers told of mines in the deep interior to which they would conduct the white men. At last the Spaniards seemed to be within grasp of what they had come to seek.

Like oil to flame, the news fired their avarice. But the tropical winter having arrived with bad weather, plans were temporarily halted; and an accident occurred in the first hour of Christmas Day which caused the sanguine complexion of their hopes to blanch. The *Santa Maria* ran into a sandbank, while the Admiral was taking some rest. Though he did everything in his power to save her, "her side fell across the sea, the timbers opened and the ship was lost."

The *Pinta* having deserted a fortnight before they quit Cuba, the Admiral now determined to return immediately to Spain; for if the *Niña* should get out of commission, no news of his achievement might ever reach Europe. As he stood gazing at his flagship—the proud little vessel that had made the most famous voyage in history—lying awkwardly on her side, derelict and captainless, his emotion for the moment overpowered him. But with that quick practicality of his, he conceived the idea of using some of the timbers of the gaping ship to build a fort as a memorial and a safe-guarding pledge of his return. He said he knew the Lord had caused the ship to stop there that a settlement might be formed. With the diligent help of the natives, a block house and tower were constructed in ten days, and the *Santa Maria's* cannon was recovered and mounted to complete the equipment. The place he named Villa de la Navidad—the City of Christmas—commemorating the Holy Nativity and the day on which the disaster occurred. Forty-two men consented to remain, some unwilling to suffer the discomfort of cramped quarters on the return trip, some having been lust-smitten for the unconcealed charms of the Indian maidens. Among those who chose to stay were Allard, the Englishman, and the Irish William.

Having secured the safety of the colonists, Columbus impressed upon them in a moving farewell their responsibilities and the tact they should assume with the natives, who had received them with such warm and generous hospitality. He left behind all the merchandise he had provided for bartering—that they might trade for gold. He left also the ship's boat, and seeds for sowing, and a carpenter, a cooper, a physician, and a tailor.

On Wednesday, the second of January, 1493, Columbus bade farewell to Guacanagari. The chief gave him a dinner. In return for the courtesy he gave the *cacique* one of his shirts. Thursday, the sea being rather rough, he decided to wait for more auspicious weather the next day. At sunrise, on the fateful Friday, he weighed anchor and commenced his homeward voyage to Spain.

On the sixth of January, the *Niña* met the deserting *Pinta*. The Admiral diplomatically pretended to believe in Martín Pinzón's excuses; and the two boats crossed the ocean in close company. Although their voyage was slow-paced, because of the neglect of Pinzón to repair his main mast, which was broken during his desertion, the weather remained propitious until a terrific storm assailed them on Tuesday, February the twelfth. Ferdinand Columbus in his life of his father quotes the entry in the journal on that black Thursday following, when the Admiral gave up all hope of saving the ships. He hurriedly sketched on parchment the accomplishments of his voyage, wrapped the precious document in wax, sealed it in a water-tight cask, addressed it to the Queen of Castile, with a superscription promising a reward of a thousand ducats to whoever delivered it unopened. Then he dropped it into the sea, praying God to send currents which would carry the barrel to some friendly shore. But the ships were not lost, for on Friday the sky cleared perceptibly, and they found they had reached an island of the Azores.

Again on the fourth of March at night they were exposed to an even more terrible tempest. Each despairing moment they expected to be overwhelmed by the cross-seas, while "the wind seemed to raise the caravels into the air." "But God preserved them." And at last on the fifteenth of March, on a rising tide about noon, the wind, fluttering through the tattered sails of the *Niña,* bore the limping storm-broken ship into the harbor of Palos. The triumphant date fell on Friday.

Never since the Frenchman Godfrey de Bouillon had delivered the Holy Sepulcher from the Infidels—on a Friday—were such plaudits rendered a mortal for his achievement. The glory of Columbus was proclaimed in pomp and processions. And in the midst of the adulation and showering honors, the Admiral did the meanest act of his life: he claimed and received from the Queen the trifling money award promised to the first man who should descry land. There is no record that he even had the grace to give to Juan Rodriguez Bermejo a velvet doublet. The mariner was so furious at the injustice that he forswore Spain and Christianity and went over to Africa and became a Mohammedan. Columbus throughout his life received the annuity—about $66— which the Crown levied from the butcher shops of Seville.

Before the tumult and fanfare of his triumph subsided, the hero was occupied with new dreams of exploration; and soon Spain was in the throes of vast preparations for conquest and colonization. In a half-year all was ready. The flotilla departed toward the end of September 1493, the Admiral in command, his eyes gold-thirsty, his lips speaking fervently of Christian conversions.

Coming into the port of La Navidad on an evening late in November, Columbus ordered a cannon fired to announce to the garrison the joyous return. No response came from the fort. Apprehensive of the hollow silence, they waited until morning. With the first stirring of dawn the new arrivals set out in boats to greet their fellow countrymen. The fort was in charred ruins. About the scene of desolation lay relics of Spanish garments, and in the rank grass were rotted Spanish bodies.

Believing that some survivors might still be alive in hiding, the men went through the forest shooting guns, blowing trumpets, calling out to their countrymen. But only the stark echoes of their own frantic noise answered them. The Admiral realized that all had perished. The destruction was so complete that the remains of the Englishman, Allard, and of Irish William could not be distinguished from those of Spaniards.

When some natives he had known, with expressions indubitably innocent of any wrongdoings, came and looked into Columbus's face, he knew that the garrison had not fallen "a sacrifice to the perfidy of the natives." Oviedo vividly recounts the story of the mimic empire that wrought its own quick destruction. No sooner had the Admiral departed than avarice and sensuality began to stalk rampant. The men sought gold ornaments from the natives by foul means; and not content with two wives allowed to each man by Guacanagari, they made seductions at will. They brawled among themselves over ill-gotten valuables and the charms of Indian women. Many left the fortress and gathered in factions, scheming one against another. With painful astonishment, the natives beheld these celestial men, whom they had worshiped, debauched with the most brutal earthly passions. Still complete havoc might not have been visited on them if they had stayed within the limits of the friendly Guacanagari's domain; but they sought the gold mines of the interior regions ruled by Caonabo, a Carib by birth, who possessed the enterprise and fierceness of his race. When the Spaniards tried their high-handed tricks in his territory, this *cacique* made short work of them. For their impudence, he killed the intruders at hand, and to finish off the job, he set out with warlike execution for La Navidad. Here he massacred the rest of the white men, burned the fortress; and for good measure, to show his intolerance at any such nonsense, he set flames to the village of Guacanagari for befriending the new-comers.

Outwardly undaunted by these dismal disclosures, the Admiral now faced the leaden realities of establishing a settlement. Hard labor was required. The men chafed at the toil and became seditious in their disappointment. Columbus began to awake to the harsh conditions and was filled with anxiety at the lurking perfidy in his men. But the dreamer in him refused to let his intelligence acknowledge what was plain, and pursuing his golden *ignis fatuus* he turned again to Cuba.

At the first port the friendly natives told him there was much gold in islands to the south; so he set out for what is now Jamaica. Finding the natives there unfriendly and seeing no indications of gold, he returned to Cuba to cruise the south coast and discover if it were an island or a continent. The Indians he visited said it was an island, but so vast that none of them had ever seen the end of it.

When he resumed his course on the nineteenth of May, a violent tempest swept his ships among keys and sandbanks. For leagues the surrounding sea was studded with a labyrinth of small islands, some low and barren, others thick with tropical vegetation. The archipelago he named The Gardens of the Queen, and recalling that Marco Polo had recounted that the coast of Asia was fringed with thousands of islands, he took fresh heart at the prospect of meeting Kublai Khan.

He steered for a mountainous part of Cuba, and was hospitably received there, for everywhere the rumors had spread about the men who had descended from the sky. He was feasted on stock-doves, which had such a peculiarly delicious flavor that he ordered some freshly killed ones to be opened before him, and in their craws he thought he detected oriental spices. Hearing of an adjacent district called Mangon, Columbus's ready ears caught the sound to signify Mangi, a rich coastal province of Cathay. And willingly he understood them to say that the people of Mangon had tails which they concealed by garments, just as Mandeville had related. For two days the ships sailed leisurely along the coast, and suddenly came to water which was the color of milk—caused by the white, powder-fine sand agitated from the sea-floor by certain currents. They were again in another labyrinth of small islands. When they had cleared them, they reached the bay of Batabanó and anchored by a grove of palm trees. An archer, going into the woods for game, returned swiftly, terror-stricken, and declared he had encountered a man in a long white robe like that of a white friar. Two others, he said, followed with white tunics reaching to their knees, and in the background among the trees he had seen some thirty more.

Columbus rejoiced in the story, and concluding these were white-robed inhabitants of Mangi, he believed he had at last reached the borders of a great civilization. But in the next days scouting parties could find no trace of the white-clothed people. Doubtless they were cranes the archer had seen; for in passing through a forest with meadows opening upon parts of it, the party saw flocks of white cranes "twice the size of those of Europe." At a certain angle from a shadowy distance they might

conceivably have looked like a convocation of holy men about
to make an ascension.

Perplexed, but still following his gleam, Columbus sailed on.
And before long he had reached a territory where his interpreter
could not understand the dialect. So the Admiral himself interpreted the signs and gestures of the natives to indicate a mountainous empire to the west ruled over by a saintly potentate that
suggested Prester John. Progress was retarded by a new bewilder-
ing maze of sandbanks and keys. One day they would sail among
acres of swimming tortoises. The following day flights of cor-
morants and wood-pigeons would hide the sun, and the atmosphere would be brilliant with butterflies.

Steering tediously and cautiously in the intricate channels, the
Admiral sent his dream-conjuring imagination roving before him,
while the sailors grew emaciated from their reduced rations of
a pound of soggy bread and a small measure of unmellow wine.
In the midst of the general doubt and discontent, in one final
flare of soaring ambition he thought of circumnavigating the
globe. His followers did not encourage him in his supreme bid
for glory. They pointed out the inadequacy of his ships, and he
himself on cool reflection admitted the truth of their objections.
So he decided to content himself with their statements sworn
before a notary that he had discovered a continent. They readily
agreed, for they had sailed—including all the courses and various
tacks—three hundred and thirty-five leagues along the southern
coast, and were sincerely convinced of the fact. A legal document
was drawn up, and every man on board signed. At that very
place of the turning back "a ship-boy from the mast-head might
have overlooked the islands to the south, and beheld the open
sea beyond." Two days' further sailing would have proved Cuba
to be an island. But Columbus died in the conviction that he
had reached the Asiatic continent.

Turning to the southeast, on the thirteenth of June, he discovered the Isle of Pines, and on the twenty-fifth he steered through
the milk-white sea that had appalled his crew. The men breathed

happily when they had reached the fragrant shores of Cuba, and the Admiral fancied in the atmosphere, odoriferous with blossoms and honey and the woodfires of the Indians, that he smelt storax, a resin valuable for perfumery.

Exhausted, famished, they anchored on July the seventh, in the mouth of a beautiful river. Here Columbus and his men were tendered their last banquet by the Indians of Cuba. The *cacique* provided a feast of roasted pigeons, cassava bread, and rare fruits. After the Spaniards had gorged their shrunken, sea-toughened bellies, Columbus ceremoniously planted a cross on the river bank and took formal possession of the *cacique's* domain. To be sure, why not? As he wrote to Luis de Santangel, "Of anything they have, if it be asked for, they never say no, but do rather invite the person to accept it, and show as much loving-ness as though they would give their hearts."

The day being Sunday, Columbus ordered a celebration of the Mass in a grove. With reverential awe, the crowd of Indians watched the procedure—the movements and intonations of the priest, the lighted candles, the smoking censors, the genuflections and cross-signings of the Spaniards. At the conclusion of the service, an aged counselor, a favorite of the *cacique,* stepped forward and made a speech. "I understand," he said to Columbus, "that you have been rendering thanks to God for his blessings. That is well. Lately you have come to these lands with a mighty force, you have subdued many countries, it is said, and spread great fear among the people. But be not, therefore, vainglorious. According to our belief the souls of men have two journeys to perform after they have departed from the body. One to a noisome, dismal place full of darkness, made for those who have been unjust and cruel to their fellow-mortals; the other pleasant and delightful, for such as have promoted peace among men. Beware then if thou art mortal and expect to die, of wrongfully doing injury to any-body, nor do harm to those who have done no harm to thee."

While the interpreter translated the words, the red man gazed steadily and profoundly into the white man's eyes. Columbus was

uncomfortably stirred by the challenging eloquence of the unlettered savage. He turned to glance at the leashed-animal visages
of some of his own adopted countrymen and then regarded the
defenseless innocence of the Indians' expressions. "These people,"
he murmured, vaguely troubled, "are very gentle, not knowing
what is evil nor the sins of murder and theft."

Farewells to Cuba were spoken quietly. As the Spaniards got
into their boats, clanking their heavy weapons harshly against
armor, the natives stood on the shore tinkling their hawk's bells
in child-like delight. After a scant fifty years had passed, there
was never heard again in Cuba the sound of a hawk's bell, nor
was there an Indian left alive to turn one between his fingers.
Not only had Spanish greed taken their possessions, but Spanish
cruelty had stilled forever the beating of their hearts, which
Columbus had said they seemed generous enough to give away.

2

UTOPIA

Destiny granted the Cubeños only a brief span of years in which
to continue an idyllic existence in their God-given garden.
Columbus had found them in that blissful, simple state which
many ancient philosophers have pictured as the most enviable
on earth. As naturally as day follows night these primitive people
had achieved an Utopia which countless complex minds conceive
but scarcely believe realizeable. It might have been a pattern for
a goal of Rousseau, a hobby of Voltaire, a millennial dream of
H. G. Wells. Better than all other commentators the erudite
Peter Martyr described the Cubeños' mode of living—a con-
fraternity of interest which has never existed among any so-called
Christian people, a common brotherhood like that with which

Soviet Russia is iron-heartedly experimenting. "It is certain," wrote the court scholar, "that the land among these people is as common as the sun and water; and that 'mine and thine,' the seeds of all mischief, have no place in them. They are content with so little, that in so large a country they have rather super-fluity than scarceness; so that they seem to live in a golden world, without toil, living in open gardens; not intrenched with dykes, divided with hedges, or defended with walls. They deal truly one with another, without laws, without books, and without judges. They take him for an evil man, who taketh pleasure in doing hurt to another; and albeit they delight not in superfluities, yet they make provision for the increase of such roots whereof they make their bread, contented with such simple diet, whereby health is preserved and disease avoided."

In this state of Eden-like felicity, for unrecorded ages the Cubeños had fed on such lotus as the climate bred and their own gentle dispositions craved. Although there were no statutes, they looked up to a patriarchal leader—a *cacique*—whom they revered for his superior wisdom. They accorded him the best house in the village and allowed him twenty wives, if he chose, to insure the multiplication of the finest seed of the race. They honored him with quick strangulation when his death seemed inevitable, so that he would not have to linger in vulgar worldly pain.

Dr. Fewkes, in his studies for the Smithsonian, has designated the inhabitants of Cuba "Tainans," the original Antillan race. They are distinguished from the raiding Caribs, an energetic, fiery people, who came from the mainland of South America and for the most part inhabited the Lesser Antilles. As Columbus soon discovered, they were greatly feared by all the peace-loving tribes of the Greater Antilles. It seems that the Tainans of Cuba (meaning good men—as Caribs means cannibals) were an off-shoot of the Arawaks of Haiti. According to some anthropologists the name Arawak signified meal-eater. Regardless of scientific nomenclature, let it suffice that we know the Indians Columbus found in Cuba for a comely, well-statured, light-copper-skinned people, "not so dark as Canary Islanders," with purplish-black eyes and straight black hair. They were constitutionally indolent, but they were not a stupid people. Although they had no written language and did not paint their chronicles on cloth or bark or stone, they were not ignorant. They had good memories, and Columbus said "wished to see everything, and asked the use of what they saw." They knew how to navigate the seas. They possessed various-sized canoes; some made of a single log of timber were long enough to hold seventy men. They were such swift rowers that "their motion was a thing beyond belief."

In disposition they were incredibly amiable. Unknowingly they lived by the Chinese Golden Rule. Or as Columbus said, "They love their neighbors as themselves, and their speech is the sweetest and gentlest in the world, and always with a smile." Nor did they lack dignity. Their *caciques* were men "of remarkable presence, with a certain self-contained manner, that was a pleasure to see."

The women were not made work-animals like the North American squaws, but had a dignified and respected position, virtually equal to that of the men. They did women's work. They kept neat the circular, pavilion-like houses built of bamboo and thatched with palm branches. Although all except the older matrons went in unashamed nakedness, they knew how to weave cotton into cloth. They wove hammocks and made some baskets and carved pestles. Both men and women loved to dance, were excellent swimmers, and delighted in fishing. Together men and women cultivated the kind of crops that rural Cuba does today: yams, corn, beans, squash, peppers. Except for fish and birds, the Cubeños were almost completely vegetarians, the only animal flesh they occasionally ate being that of the iguana and the *jutia* (or wood-rat).

Whatever warlike and treacherous propensities they may have possessed in previous ages, when Columbus found them they were certainly guileless and the antithesis of aggressive. The extent of their weapons virtually ended with fishing harpoons and wooden lances fire-hardened. "They have no iron or steel, nor any weapons," the Admiral wrote to Santangel, "nor are they fit thereunto; not because they be not a well formed people and of fair stature, but that they are most wondrously timid. They have no other weapons than the stems of reeds in their seedling state, on the end of which they fix sharpened stakes. Even these, they dare not use; for many times has it happened that I sent two or three men ashore to some village to parley, and countless numbers of them sallied forth, but as soon as they saw those approach, they fled in such wise that even a father would not wait for his son."

In their simple religious ceremonies tobacco was the incense they burned before whatever shrine they had, and the weed as a narcotic played a significant part in the rituals. They believed vaguely in a supernatural being and life after death, and that somehow power and goodness were in the sky.

In every-day intercourse it seems they practiced the religion of that philosophical Nazarene, of whom they had not heard until Columbus spoke of Him. He told them that his was the true religion, and that he had been sent among them by his sovereigns to tell them about it. And he said he would send priests to teach its glorious blessings, and "to protect them from harm and injury." True to his sincere but ironical promise, eighteen years later the Christians came, bringing "the light of a religion that had just evolved the Inquisition." With an unmitigated rigor Spaniards began to save the Indians "from the darkness of their happy innocence."

3

DEATH DANCE OF THE CUBEÑOS

On the arrival of Diego de Velasquez with his colonizing mission in 1511, a pall-like cloud began to gather and darken the scene of the Cuban pageant. On the stage, personifications of the naked modesty and gentle-spirited manners of the natives were grouped in contrast to the calculating avarice, lust, perfidy, and bigotry of the Spaniards—products of a civilization which supposedly had been nurtured on the forces of literature, art, and religion for an accumulation of centuries. In the vanguard of the Spanish armed force fluttered banners of Christ. Beneath them, the club and the lash urged the true faith upon the bewildered natives—who knew so little Spanish and no Latin. "Wherever the Host was consecrated," says Filson Young, "hideous cries of agony and suffering broke forth." In payment for the heathen blood that spilt on Cuban soil, the Spaniards offered the offices of the Church: the Trinity, the catechism, the doctrine of transubstantiation.

The spread of the Gospel had been delayed in reaching Cuba because of the gold mines opened up in La Española. But when the Indians there were about decimated, the crusade began among the Cubeños. Of course, it was not exclusively religious in its purport. Diego de Velasquez was a man of business, who had got rich in La Española. Conversion was, in fact, a subsidiary or byproduct of the great work of colonization, the hunt for gold, and the exploitation of everything and anything of mercenary value. These enterprising affairs cried out more avidly for laborers than for converts, and though slavery had been forbidden by the Queen, indentured labor was not; so by this twist the Indians were made slaves. Thus two fine birds were killed with one stone slung with impeccable sophistry; as fast as the natives were baptized, they were saved from demoralizing idleness, and the souls of their bruised and lacerated bodies received due instructions in the proper form of address to their Maker and His honored saints.

From La Española exuberant deceptive letters reporting the vast number of salvations had been sent the truly pious and tender-hearted Queen—she did not know that often the saved were dead by the time the communications reached her. The thought of the religious work her colonizing armies were to accomplish in Cuba brought her much consolation on her death-bed.

"Bestow upon benighted people the blessings of civilization!" the Spanish prelates and statesmen chorused. And like a very echo from the Spain of 1500, President Coolidge, at his first inaugural ceremonies four and a quarter centuries later, solemnly declared that our American soldiers "go out not armed with guns but with the cross!" "We extended our domains over distant islands," spoke the man noted for golden silences, "in order to safe-guard our own interests, and accepted the consequent obligations to bestow opportunity and liberty upon less favored people." Such inspiring, canny words might well have been composed by Christopher Columbus himself, who had died in 1506.

Commissioned by Don Diego Colón, Governor of La Española and son of the great discoverer, Diego de Velasquez gathered together in 1511 three hundred recruits for the colonizing of Cuba and for conferring blessings on its people. Velasquez had accompanied the Admiral on his second voyage and had proved himself an able fellow under three subsequent governors, attaining a prominent position and acquiring considerable private fortune, some of which he staked in the equipment of the expedition. With his commanding figure just beginning to take on corpulency, and his strong handsome face set off by gold-colored hair, Velasquez was admired for his authority and liked for his amiability. But he was more of an administrator, a level-headed man-of-affairs, than a swash-buckler or a plumed-and-armored conquistador. No man in the New World was better equipped by temperament, experience, and means for the arduous task of colonizing "300 leagues of territory containing 200,000 natives assembled in 31 provinces." Having faced realities—the hardships and fevers of La Española—there was no muzzy dreaming in Velasquez's calculations. He did not look for the romance and splendor of an Asiatic City in its prime glory as had Columbus. Nor did he have that eye to publicity and the dramatic effect which the Admiral possessed. Idle luxuries did not go into the cargo of his ships, which were laden to the gunwales with horses, cattle, seeds, farming utensils, tools for building, and the precious gear for gold-mining. But a few gentlemen who volunteered to accompany him clung to their soiled silken doublets, their ribbons, and golden chains; and a young fellow in his late twenties named Hernando Cortés, who had set his heart on high fame, brought with him a secret relish for a bit of pomp and strut, as well as an obvious hardihood and fearlessness. Besides the *hidalgo* adventurers, priests, and minor officials, the band of 300 colonizers contained a large proportion of criminals, who had been liberated from the prisons of Spain on the promise of freedom if they would remain two years in the colonies. In November 1511, Velasquez assembled his oddly mixed followers in four caravels and sailed to the northeast coast of Cuba. As well as he could, he restrained his crew from folderol and trumpet-blowing.

The settlement was established at Baracoa, which possessed a circular land-locked harbor and was overlooked by the anvil-shaped Yunque mountain towering with its scarped sides to a height of 2,000 feet. A fort was built, and houses for sheltering the men. Doubtless the shacks were *bohios* of bamboo and palm boards or wattle huts with thatched roofs. The Spaniards contemptuously described their dwellings as being "of straw." The nascent municipal government had hardly begun to function when there was an abrupt pause to make a ceremony of the burning-at-the-stake of an Indian who did not choose to accept the blessings of enlightenment and slavery.

In the years immediately preceding Velasquez's arrival in Cuba, the conditions of the Indians in La Española had become so intolerable that many of those who had not died under Spanish cruelty, or had not committed suicide, had escaped to Cuba. Among those wretched fugitives who haunted the eastern woods was a *cacique* named Hatuey. He was the first to reveal to the Cubeños the true character of these Christians. He told what they had done to the natives of his island. Before an assembled band he made a speech inciting them not to receive the strangers hospitably but to resist their advances. Las Casas set down the speech as best he could from one who had listened to Hatuey. "You know the report is spread abroad that the Spaniards are ready to invade this island, and you are not ignorant of the ill-usage our friends and countrymen have met with at their hands, and the cruelties they have committed at Haiti. They are now coming hither with a design to exercise the same outrages and persecutions upon us. We know not upon what account they come hither, but we know they are a very wicked and cruel people. I'll tell you then that these Europeans worship a very covetous sort of God, so that it is difficult to satisfy him; to perform the worship they render to this idol, they will exact immense treasures of us, and will use their utmost endeavors to reduce us to a miserable state of slavery, or else put us to death." Then he took up a box full of gold and jewels and held it up to their view. "Here," he said, "is the God of the Spaniards. If we keep this God till he is taken away from us, he will certainly cause our lives to be taken away, and therefore I am of the opinion it will be best to cast him into the river." They approved of his advice and went with him to the river and watched him throw the symbolical God into the deep water.

The Spaniards were surprised to encounter resistance instead of the docility Columbus had led them to expect. Hatuey's rebellious propaganda was disclosed. He was betrayed and captured. Velasquez ordered him burned alive.

As the wretch stood in the midst of flames, a certain well-intentioned friar took upon himself to speak to Hatuey of God, explaining some Articles of Catholic Faith, promising him Eternal Life if he would believe, and threatening him with Eternal Torment if he continued obstinate in his infidelity. Hatuey, reflecting on the matter "as much as the Place and Condition in which he was would permit," inquired if Heaven's gate was open to Spaniards. When told it was, the *cacique* replied he would choose Hell rather than go to a place where he would ever meet again such cruel and wicked people as Christians.

The flames of Hatuey's execution pile lighted lugubriously the first movement of that tragic *danse macabre,* in which the Cubeños made their final exit from the world. Fortunately it was finished swiftly—as history reckons time.

At Velasquez's command the paroled prisoners and hot-blooded adventurers returned from the mountains, whither they had chased the Indians like stricken deer. He set them to planting seed and making wine from the wild grapes growing in profusion. He ordered some to pan the nearby rivers for gold. For the time, while he broke his men into the new conditions, he postponed putting into operation the King's compliant means of reimbursing himself at the expense of the natives' potential slave value. Finding merely "interesting returns" from the river pannings and no gold in negotiable quantities, he determined to send an exploring expedition to hack its way through the jungle and forest. At the head of the party of a hundred infantry and eight men on horseback, he placed a lusty, red-headed young chap named Panfilo de Narvaez. This debonair leader had followed Velasquez, to whom he was staunchly devoted, from Jamaica with thirty skilled crossbowmen. The force set off westward and entered the district of Bayamo. The attitude of the natives being hostile, Narvaez called for reënforcements of forty foot-men and ten cavalry-men. Narvaez had been instructed by Velasquez to reassure the natives that no harm was intended, that they were merely having a look at the country, and he hoped to convert them to the Catholic faith.

"Between the letter of Narvaez's instructions and his execution of them," says Miss Irene Wright in her valuable *Early History of Cuba,* "there was the usual discrepancy." The Spaniards made certain demands of entertainment, of course, and became less well received the farther they penetrated. One night, as they slept in a village, the Indians descended upon them with ear-splitting yells, seized many of their clothes for which they had taken a childish passion, and dashed away without doing any more serious bodily damage than to bowl Narvaez over with a stone **in**

the pit of his stomach. When he caught his breath, the young
commander, thoroughly aroused, jumped bareback on his horse,
which was stabled in the room with him, and throwing a string
of bells across his beast's withers, he galloped forth clad only in
his shirt, creating the most fearful excitement among the natives,
who fled wildly before the clattering hoofs and jangling bells.

At best, horses were wondrous and fearful objects to the
Indians, who had never seen a quadruped larger than a wood-rat
until the Spaniards came. It was not unnatural that natives had
the daylights scared out of them by a warlike charge at night with
bells making a hellish noise. Cortés, noting the effectiveness of
Narvaez's horse-tactics, later used the knowledge to intimidate
the more sophisticated Indians in Mexico; he had a mare picketed
among a delegation of chiefs and then at a signal he had a stallion
brought from among his own forces, where the beast could catch
the scent of the mare. When the stallion began to take on might-
ily, pawing the ground and snorting, the frightened chiefs
thought the animal was roaring at them.

Shortly Narvaez reported to Velasquez that he could not avoid
fighting the natives, and after "the careless leader" had killed
about a hundred, Velasquez decided to go in person to Bayamo
to reassure the Indians of the invaders' honorable intentions.
Narvaez he sent to pursue those who had fled with their few
belongings farther westward into Camagüey. The fiery young
man spread terror on every side. Because of the general unrest,
crops had been neglected and the hungry fugitives from Bayamo
found an unwonted inhospitality among the Camagüey folk who
had hardly enough food for themselves. Faced with starvation,
the natives of Bayamo began to creep submissively back to their
abandoned homes, offering placatingly as gifts to the Spaniards
their bone necklaces, which they loved above all their possessions.

Velasquez had left in Bayamo as adviser and soothing mediary
a learned priest named Bartolomé de Las Casas. This *clerigo,*
who had been ordained only two years before in La Española,
came to be known as the Protector of the Indians. Throughout

his life he had an active devotion to them, which had begun early when he was a student at the University of Salamanca, where he had owned an Indian slave. He is the famous commentator of the times, and he described in detail Narvaez's expedition, which now began deliberately to scour for gold. As they set out west again, Las Casas was sent ahead to prevent trouble and to arrange accommodations for the armed party following. The natives were asked to vacate one-half of the villages for quartering the soldiers and to prepare food in advance.

The Indians loved and trusted Las Casas, but not always was he able to prevent the blood-thirsty instincts of the Spaniards from breaking bonds. At a village one quiet evening, as a thousand or so natives squatted about in the village-square marveling at the horses, and while Las Casas was watching the soldiers pass out the supper rations, a certain Spaniard on a crazy whim drew his sword and made a villainous pass at an Indian. Quick as a reflex-nerve-action the Christians jumped to bare their weapons and began to slaughter the naked throng. In vain Las Casas frantically pled with them to desist. He went from place to place trying to stop the killings, which were now occurring madly in the houses and the bush. He came upon Narvaez on his mare, coldly watching the proceedings and doing nothing to prevent the holocaust. The priest consigned him to the devil with hot contempt and hurried on, shouting to make himself heard above the hideous din. Presently there was a lull, and Las Casas, entering a house, persuaded a well-set young Indian to come down from his hiding place in the rafters, telling him that the slaughter was over. A few minutes later the young man had his stomach ripped open, and rushing to find the priest, who had passed on in his errands of mercy, held out to him his entrails dangling from his hands. Grieved to the heart at this ultimate gesture, which so far surpassed the offerings of bone necklaces, Las Casas tendered the wretch profound pity and the consolations of religion, as he fell dead at the priest's feet.

It is a dreadful chronicle of his fellow countrymen that Las

Casas records in his *General History of the Indies*—so horrible, in fact, that he ordered the manuscript not to be printed until forty years after his death. When the gold-seekers quitted the blood-soaked town and pressed on westward, they found the country deserted. Las Casas was hard put to reassure the natives. It was weeks before he could establish communications with them. But presently they returned—"men and women like sheep," he writes, "each with his little bundle of poverty upon his back"— and, as always, bearing gifts for the invaders.

Perhaps it would have been far better if Las Casas had not given the Indians his comfort and his reassurances. For all too soon they were made slaves and put to working from first dawn to dark, forced by whip-handed task-makers to labor relentlessly at tasks beyond their strength, delving with pickaxes and standing twelve hours at a stretch in rivers washing the sands for gold. And more barbarous and most unbelievably cruel, a repulsive practice arose among the Spaniards of supplying meat for their bloodhounds by feeding them Indians. In their conquests they had quickly discovered that ferocious dogs made formidable allies; for the Indians, who had never seen dogs before the Europeans brought them, had a consuming terror of the beasts which were set on them in raids. "It was a fairly common sight," wrote Las Casas, "to see armies accompanied by processions of slaves chained together like droves of pigs to furnish food for the dogs. The more humane of the captains killed them first, but others turned the hungry dogs loose upon the terrified living naked victims." As Marcel Brion comments—after recording how the Spaniards took pleasure in roasting their captives wrapped in straw at a slow fire—"A sort of habit in evil had its climax in letting them consider the most horrible tortures as entirely natural."

In their general despair many Indians strangled themselves and ate the poison squeezed from the yucca roots which also provided their bread. The savage women bitterly resented the uncivil attacks upon their persons by the Spaniards. And even when left among their own men, child-bearing all but ceased; uneasy conceptions developed into vague miscarriages, and many abortions were deliberate. Parents hanged their children that they might escape the misery, and then ended their own tribulations.

And as if to make the Cubeños' death-dance more consuming in its fast fury, a Pandora's box of European disease germs was opened, for which the Indians had no immunity. With all their skill as herbalists the aborigines had no medicinal specifics that protected them from the ravages of smallpox, measles, and scarlet fever. Germs proved as devastating to the Cubeños as the musket-balls, saber-cuts, and gun-powder of the invaders, and their own self-inflicted deaths.

Of course, the entire aboriginal population was not wiped out within a year, but by 1521 it had thinned to such negligible numbers that black-slavery was introduced to help fill the awful gap made in red-slavery. However, the story of African slavery belongs to another chapter, and in the dozen years between Baracoa's settlement and the forced introduction of Negroes, the most significant events of Cuba's history transpired.

4

CORTÉS SAILS FOR MEXICO

In 1514 and 1515 Velasquez established settlements at Santiago, Sancti Spiritus, Camagüey, Trinidad, and San Cristóbal de la Havana (on the south coast of the present Batabanó, removed within a few years to the present site of Havana). Early in 1513 the governor had paused from the trials of colonization to prepare for a colorful interlude, in which his marriage was celebrated. Doña Maria, the daughter of Cristóbal de Cuellar, who was appointed the King's Treasurer in Cuba, accompanied her father

to Baracoa and remained to become Velasquez's bride. With all
the flourish and style which the struggling, squalid village could
muster, and with finery dug out of the Cuellar's chests and trunks,
the celebration proceeded bravely. Soldier-criminals, bursting with
boasts of their exploits, returned jovially from the interior, their
weapons glistening like silver, for they had paused long enough
to scour away the bloodstains with river-sand. But the echoes
of the feasting and dancing had hardly died away, when on the
Saturday following, the governor-groom became a widower. The
general sadness and mourning were said to have far exceeded the
rejoicing. With naïve shrewdness an early chronicle comments
on the unhappy episode: "It seemed God desired that Lady for
Himself, for they say that she was most virtuous, and by untimely death saved her perhaps from time and prosperity which
might have altered her admirable character." The loss of a bride
was merely one of the unlucky circumstances in a career which
earned Velasquez wealth and respect, but which was to end in
green bitterness.

Velasquez really tried to do what he could to keep from making the lot of the natives intolerable. But because he had at first
refused to institute in Cuba the *repartimiento* system of La
Española—in which groups of Indians were "commended" and
parceled out to the Spaniards, to be instructed in the faith and
worked to death—he was confronted with the disaffection of his
followers, who had little taste for the drudgery of building up
towns. This disaffection, headed by one Morales, grew into hatred
and open defiance of his orders. Prominent among the disloyals
was discovered young Cortés, Velasquez's own secretary and the
future conqueror of Mexico. The governor pondered over hanging him; thought better of the matter, pardoned him, and soon
began to bestow new favors. Finally to still the grumblings,
Velasquez somewhat reluctantly permitted the *repartimiento* system to have its tentative beginnings. And shortly afterwards he
made Cortés *alcalde,* or "judge and mayor," of Santiago. From
that time on the young man, who had boldly proclaimed at seven-

teen that he had come to the New World "to get gold, not to till the soil like a peasant," was fortune's favorite child.

The luster of Velasquez's practical abilities has been dimmed to posterity by the romantic splendor of Cortés's conquest. But had Velasquez not possessed the foresight to arrange first of all that his men had food, thereby insisting on the cultivation of the indigenous food crops and hog- and cattle-raising from imported stock, Cortés could not have commandeered the supplies necessary to ballast his undertaking. Velasquez saw to it too, as soon as possible, that permanent habitations of stone were erected to replace *bohios*. He built churches and warehouses as well as forts and houses, and wisely considering the advantages of Santiago—its harbor, its impregnable position and its nearness to Jamaica—he had the customs house and the smelting plant moved there, and made the settlement the seat of government.

Commerce began to flourish. Into the picturesque harbor of Santiago great vessels out of Seville came loaded with silks and fine stuffs, resplendent cloaks and fashionable footwear. The foreign ships brought gayly painted carts, and the Cubeños were astonished to see, for the first time, wheels—a simple device produced by the Chinese about 2700 B.C., and introduced into Egypt by the Hyksos less than four centuries later, but one which the American Indians had no need to invent since they had no animals suitable for drawing vehicles. The ships brought, too, personal knick-knacks for the Indians, which the Spaniards doled out to cheer their miserable discontent: mirrors and combs and glass beads and gaudy headkerchiefs. The priests distributed clothes: trousers and shirts for the men, yellow and red petticoats for the women. With the gift of clothes, the Indians received instruction in the sins of immodesty, and severe penalties were imposed on any indecent exposure.

Venturesome, fatalistic grandees came with their families, their furniture, their musical instruments; high-bred dogs and chickens; jars of oil and casks of vintage wines; scented soaps, and innumerable expensive fripperies. They brought with them as well what Hume calls that "false standard of honor and conduct, and an exaggerated notion of their own qualities." And with their heads stuffed full of fancies of knight-errantry, they strove in Cuba "to dress and live up to the stilted romantic ideal."

The Spaniard of this period was above all a soldier by preference, and although many of them became successful, affluent cattlemen, the majority were ready enough to pursue the rôle of adventurer—to join any treasure-seeking or slave-hunting expedition organized. When in 1518 the Crown gave Velasquez authority to explore and acquire new territory at his own expense, there was a superfluity of eager volunteers. In that year Juan de Grijalva, the governor's nephew, took formal possession of Yucatan and sailed along the lower coast of Mexico. On his return to Santiago with opulent tidings and substantial samples of gold and silver, Velasquez began preparations for a major prospecting enterprise. The purported objective was to found a Christian colony in the mainland to the west. Of course, everyone knew that gold was the magnetic needle that drew the undertaking. No one was more frank in his local admissions than Cortés, who found himself made captain-general of the venture; and with refreshing humor he confessed to Aztec chiefs in Mexico that Spaniards suffered from a heart disease for which gold was the only specific remedy.

Velasquez's choice of a coadjutor-commander was intelligent, but it was not shrewd. He was certain Cortés would bother little with conversions and that he would get the gold if it was to be got. But he did not thoroughly take in Cortés's oddly complex character—the good humor, the boyish enthusiasm, the playacting spirit, the personal magnetism, mingled with absolute fearlessness, an iron-clad will, inordinate greed, and super-craftiness. Least of all did he gauge Cortés's ruling passion for enduring fame. Velasquez liked power and wanted his own high place in history, but he was not a showy fellow; and he underestimated the younger man's pleasure in demonstration, his flamboyant signature, his occasional dressing in a "velvet cloak trimmed with knots of gold" with which he wore plumes and a woven gold chain about his neck. These manifestations he discounted as tricks of youth, and he counted on his lieutenant's loyalty up to the hour the ten small ships, assembled with his own private fortune, were being prepared for sailing. Then a sudden flare of suspicion that Cortés might claim all the glory and keep all the gold for himself made him decide to oust him from the command. But Cortés, hearing whispers, quickly slipped out of Santiago harbor on November the eighteenth, 1518, with the flotilla only half requisitioned. Learning of the hasty departure, Velasquez rushed to the shore too late and impotently commanded him to return. Cortés saluted nonchalantly and sailed on in audacious defiance. At Trinidad he stopped for supplies and volunteers. The latter were enthusiastically furnished; the supplies were rendered grudgingly, for Cortés paid only a fraction of their value, or nothing. Making final halt at the south shore port of what had been Havana (now Batabanó), he took on more supplies and the flower of the young manhood of the district. The Governor of Havana, Pedro de Barba, on orders from Velasquez, attempted to arrest Cortés, who snapped his fingers in the worthy's face and demanded whatever horses were in the neighborhood. On the tenth of February, 1519, the conquistador left Havana, with eleven ships (having seized a trading vessel on the way). The boats were loaded to the gunwales with the best provisions of the island. The personnel numbered 633 men—100 mariners and 533 soldier-adventurers, well seasoned with paroled criminals. Their equipment for conquest consisted of sixteen horses, thirty-two crossbows, thirteen muskets and four falconets. Such was the full strength of the force with which Cortés expected to conquer a vast country with a population of millions and a civilization so ancient that Castile was a *parvenu* compared to it. When he reached Yucatan, to prevent any possibility of return to Cuba before he won his goal, Cortés, with an ultimate gesture of do or die, burned Velasquez's ships in the harbor. For his nerve, fortune was to grant him one of the supreme victories of all times.

Waving aside all allegiance and obligation, he formally resigned his commission under Velasquez. In a naturally indignant rage at such trickery, the governor prepared an expedition of thirteen vessels and a thousand men under Narvaez to "recall" his lieutenant. Whole hog ranches were commandeered to supply food for the undertaking, the inhabitants suffering great want in consequence. Like manna from heaven, the entire expedition fell into Cortés's hands as welcome reënforcements. And instead of exulting over the return of a humiliated ingrate, Velasquez was informed that ships from Mexico "ballasted with gold" were passing the Cuban shores on their way to Spain. He knew that Cortés had found his way to the king's heart. But vainly he set about to equip another expedition, even willing, if necessary, to depopulate the island and to reduce the food supply to near famine. In his bitter obsession to punish Cortés he undid much of the splendid colonizing work he had done for Cuba. On October twenty-second, 1522, the Crown made Cortés Governor of Mexico; and in the May of 1523 a town-crier proclaimed about the streets of Santiago that the king ordered Velasquez not to go in person or to send any further expedition to annoy the great conquistador—the fellow who had been his servant and secretary, but who was now raised to the nobility with the title of Marquis del Valle. From his corner windows giving on the plaza and the cathedral, Velasquez heard the royal proclamation vociferated, taken up by the citizenry and reëchoed from house-wall to house-wall. This clamor was the bitter end to Diego de Velasquez's ruin. Before a year had passed, he had died. Cortés's brilliant lucky star so bedimmed the fine accomplishment of Cuba's first governor and the conquering founder of her first seven cities, that even today there is not on Cuban soil a single monument to his memory.

5

DE SOTO'S CAVALCADE

From the death of Velasquez in 1524 until the coming of de Soto in 1538, activities in Cuba were more or less humdrum and unprogressive, largely consumed with lawsuits and personal squabbles between governors, *alcaldes* and their successors. The mad lure of Mexico drew the best high-spirited blood of the country to fill the gaps made by swift deaths from malignant fevers and incredible hardships. The less stout-hearted of the Spanish malcontents, who had had their thirsts for adventure satiated, settled down with some relief and much profit to raise cattle and to supply rations for gold- and silver-gatherers in Mexico. A few stayed in Cuba to mine the more meager gold there (about 25,000 *pesos* were smelted annually in Santiago).

In 1530 copper was discovered within ten miles of the capital, and shortly afterwards new rich veins of gold were found in the Jobabo mines at Cueyba, which yielded 50,000 *pesos* within the first five months, a considerable amount for those days, but diminutive when compared with the treasure houses of Mexico and Peru. The Indians, who loathed mining above all their sufferings, but who were made to labor for unconscionable hours at Jobabo, began the practice of eating quartz sand as a form of slow death. Although the manager of the mines had all the workers who were caught eating the sand castrated as a deterrent punishment, they persisted, until within a year or two not one was left alive. Negroes replaced them. (The first shipload of 300 African slaves had been brought to Cuba as early as 1521.) Even the blacks, who were doubly as hardy as the Indians, could not stand the cruel rigors of the Jobabo mines and revolted in November 1533. A troop under Esteban de Lagos came from Bayamo to quell the uprising. The four black leaders fought to the death. Their battered and broken heads were hacked from their bodies and displayed on pikes as grim evidence of the defeat of the first Negro rebellion in Cuba.

In the early part of April 1538, throughout Spain the word *Cuba* was excitingly enunciated. The country in which foreign interest had languished for almost two decades revived marvelously when Hernando de Soto, who had won romantic fame and fortune fighting with Pizarro in Peru, sailed for Santiago de Cuba from Santa Lucar with the most brilliant armada that had ever cleared from any Spanish port. Accompanying his own fleet were ten merchantmen bound for Mexico. De Soto bore commissions as Governor of Cuba—the first ever so appointed directly by the Crown—and as *adelantado* (military-governor) of Florida. Cuba was to be the base for expeditions setting out to conquer Florida and other new provinces and kingdoms stretching to the unknown north and west. When the citizens of Spain had learned that de Soto, not satisfied with the golden returns of his South American adventures, was staking his enormous private fortune on the new objective, and when the terms of the division of the spoils were made public, and the words "precious metals, diamonds, emeralds, pearls" were tossed about like copper coins, from all parts of the Peninsula came men pleading to join the expedition: bored old hidalgos, quick-pulsed young nobles, seasoned soldiers, and adventure-bitten shop-keepers and farmers avid to buy estates and the rank of gentlemen. They turned their castles or their farmhouses, their camp or household gods into cash, and thence to armor, weapons, and resplendent raiment. Many fashionable ladies came with their husbands, purposing to domicile in Santiago or Havana while their men were conquesting in the northern continent. De Soto's wife, the beautiful and intellectual Lady Isabella de Bobadilla, whose wifely devotion and executive abilities won for her first place among the women in the New World annals and legends, accompanied her husband, attended by three white slave girls.

In June de Soto's squadron arrived at the narrow entrance of Santiago harbor beneath the watch-tower crowning the precipitous headland. Mistaking it at first for an enemy fleet, because only a fortnight previously French corsairs had thrown the people into a fright, a watcher gave the flagship *San Cristóbal* false orders to bear to the left. Before the mistake could be rectified, the vessel ground raspingly against the submerged rocks of a key. In a few minutes the ship's pumps were disgorging honey and wine along with bilge, for most of the bottled cargo was smashed. Several panicky young gallants unacquainted with sea-perils tried to save themselves by grabbing the first places in lifeboats, even before the Lady Isabella and her attendants could be cared for. Their agitation was ill-timed, however; no real damage was done to the ship, as it was soon extricated from the unfortunate position. And when at the head of the fleet the flagship sailed into the port four miles up the bay to the drumbeating and clamor of a welcoming populace, the shamefaced, too-hasty gallants had lost their zest for swagger. They slunk ashore, and in the days of festivities that followed they were the butt of ridicule. Poor, ill-fated, scarce-bearded hopefuls—they still thought to retrieve their reputation gloriously, ten-fold, in romantic conquest! And they did expiate their unpremeditated little act of cowardice a hundred times over, not as they had expected, but through sweat and blood, fever germs and gangrenous wounds in Florida marshes and Mississippi swamps.

The people of Santiago had quickly bedecked the village and themselves in gala attire to greet Cuba's new governor. A whole string of days was given over to continuous entertainment. Settlers from the surrounding districts came with their troops of fine horses. Lowing herds of cattle crowned with garlands were brought into the city daily to be slaughtered for the feasts. The best wine the colony afforded was drawn from casks without thought of tomorrow. Races and bull-fights were the principal amusements in the daytime; dances and amateur dramatics, by torch flare, in the nights. Prizes of jewels and rich fabrics were awarded for feats of arms and for poetic compositions.

These cheering tributes of good will the urbane de Soto accepted with his most charming grace, while he retained some three hundred of the best horses for his Florida expedition. A hundred fellows joined his ranks, including some wealthy old cattle-men who had become irked with ranch life and security and who felt the call to exercise their fighting muscles. In August, two months after his arrival, de Soto despatched his fleet to Havana, bearing the Lady Isabella, the other ladies, and his infantry. The cavalry, led by himself, set out overland. In the departure, again there was multifold fanfare and pageantry. Then the inhabitants settled down to neglect and small rations and idle gossip, not to be stirred until pirates bombarded them from their apathy.

By the New Year, 1539, all the detachments had met in Havana, and de Soto had purchased several estates in the vicinity and was supervising work on a fort to guard against a recurrence of the piratical sacking which had occurred in 1537. The low, quadrilateral, double-walled fortress, with a square tower constructed as a look-out for corsairs, was built not far from where La Fuerza now stands. It was completed in seven months, and Isabella was left in charge. She was also proclaimed acting-governor for the space of her husband's absence. On the twelfth of May, 1539, "the noblest body of Spanish chivalry that ever set foot in our Western hemisphere" sailed from the Havana harbor in an expedition more magnificent than any that had ever before cleared from a New World port. The gorgeousness of the cavalcade almost matched the incredible expectancy of dazzling success. The fact that Florida had proved only a death-breathing false-fire, and that the smaller parties which had previously attempted its conquest had been virtually obliterated, did not cast even a shadow of foreboding. That farewells were said not far from the place where Florida's discoverer, Ponce de León, romantic seeker after perpetual life, had returned to die of an arrow wound which no fountain of youth could have cleansed into health, did not daunt the intrepid hopefuls. Music of drum and flute played as the company of 900 foot soldiers and 350 horsemen boarded the eleven big ships, drawn up alongside brigantines and barges laden with arms and provision. Arquebusiers; doughty crossbowmen; toughened soldiers in protective doublets of quilted cotton; young courtiers in azure and salmon silk hose, who had spent half their inheritance in princely trappings for their steeds; armored knights with steel casques and waving plumes dyed yellow, green, crimson—all setting forth in high-colored gayety with the assured bearing of conquerors. Never was an ambitious company more radiantly sanguine; never were any adventurers destined to a blacker despair.

Before long, some of the older men returned to Cuba, fed-up with Florida miasmas, insects, and sneaking attacks of hostile Indians. Progress had been so beset with difficulties that a year was consumed in getting the troop from Tampa to Pensacola. Not a nugget of gold had been seen, not a precious stone. Men died like flies of fevers and wounds. De Soto commanded reën-forcements and food supplies—eight shiploads full. The few remaining Cubeños, beholding the island stripped of its fighting men, leaving only the "infirm and spiritless, rejoiced in song and dance that Spanish domination in Cuba was approaching its end."

After some months dark news was brought that de Soto and his men could not be traced. For three years loyal lieutenants searched the coast from Mobile to Vera Cruz. It did not seem possible that a whole army should have been swallowed up as if in quicksand, without leaving even a rumor. Day after day, month after month, the anxious Lady Isabella mounted the steps of the fort's tower and strained her eyes to the northern horizon, des-perately determined to catch sight of her husband's returning sails.

At last in October 1543—four years and five months after the gallant departure from Havana—news came from the Mexican capital destroying all hope. About three hundred tattered stragglers—empty-handed, emaciated, ill, "full of scurvy"—had reached Mexico City after a heroic and torturous march southwest through Louisiana, Texas, and Mexico. They were the only living relics of de Soto's débâcle. Their leader they had left behind, sunk beneath the waters of the great river he had discovered, buried in a leaden casket made of melted bullets. He had been dead of swamp fever for more than two years when the survivors reached Havana. According to early chroniclers, the news of her husband's ruin and death broke the heart of the Lady Isabella, who died before the year had passed. The news also broke the spirit of Cuba, which had poured its best blood and the bulk of its resources, first into treasure-yielding Mexico, and then with tragic futility into the swamps and forests of the northern continent where no silver mines could be found.

6

DRAKE, THE DRAGON

The succeeding governors between de Soto and Dr. Angulo, who came in 1550, left no records except those of dreary lawsuits and libel suits. Their enemies accused them of various thefts and crimes, and managed to get one of them sent back to Spain in chains. The honor of being governor in Cuba in the middle period of the sixteenth century was indeed thankless, and even perilous.

The first act of Dr. Angulo on arrival in Santiago was to proclaim the "entire liberty" of the last Cubeños. In July of the same year, to the towering indignation of the Santiagoans, he removed from the capital to Havana, and made that place his permanent residence. As Miss Wright explains, the removal was more or less imperative, for Havana had become the rendezvous for shipping

from Mexico and Terra Firma, and here foregathered merchantmen and armadas sent to convoy the bullion ships to Spain.
Havana had to supply fresh water and provisions, and in her harbor the captains careened their ships and made repairs, just as
Sebastian Ocampo had done when first he circumnavigated the
island in 1508 and named the port Carenas. Angulo straightway
began work on a masonry church, built an abattoir, and had a
window cut in the jail so that prisoners "might enjoy the view."

In the fall of 1553, Cuba was notified of the renewal of hostilities between France and Spain and cautioned to be on guard.
The next year profoundly disquieting news came from Santiago:
the heretic Lutheran corsairs under the notorious Jacques de Sores
had looted the place with such thoroughness that "men had not
a coat to their backs nor women a chemise." The whole population of Havana was in a fearful tenseness of anticipation. The
fighting force of Havana settlers at this time numbered no more
than sixteen cavalry and some sixty-odd other fighting men indif-
ferently equipped. At last in the dawn of July tenth, 1555, a signal
from Morro announced suspicious sails, and within a few hours
Havana was in possession of the dreaded de Sores. The warden of
La Fuerza, Juan de Lobera, put up a spirited defense and three
times refused to surrender, even after the gate in the walls of the
fort had been burnt, and "the cords on the cross-bows broken
beyond repair." Instead of the great treasure the corsair was expecting, there was nothing in the fortress worth having except
Lobera's emerald ring. An act of treachery which involved the
death of a cousin so enraged de Sores that he stabbed to death all
his prisoners except Lobera, whose pluck he admired. Then he
burned the local craft in the harbor, allowed his men to knock
the sacred images from their altars; and after laying hands on
whatever he wanted, he set fire to the town itself. At last, satisfied with his work, the Lutheran sailed away from the settlement
on the night of August fifth, the light of a full moon gleaming
on the rich satin of coats his corsairs had fashioned from holy
vestments pillaged in the church. The appalled citizens cast their

eyes from their desolation questionably towards the throne of
God. What had happened to the Catholic Deity that he would
suffer such profanation from the heretics?

The word *corsair* originally meant nothing more deadly than
courser, cruiser or rover; and sometimes the fellows were merely
peaceable traders, who resented Spain's decree that all foreign
trade with her colonies was contraband. Spain's arbitrary policy
was in a large measure responsible, first, for the smuggling; next,
for a forcing of goods with compelled payment; and finally, for
out and out plunder of towns and seizure of treasure galleons.
Many settlers along remote inlets and unwatched bamboo-shaded
rivers were not averse to dealing secretly with the rovers. Readily
they bartered hides, hogs, and bread for silks, trinkets, and household gear. Sometimes merchantmen from Seville would be
months behind schedule in arriving at Cuban ports, and very
necessity forced the settlers to buy from the first ship that came to
supply their needs. The southern and eastern coast towns especially became guilty of illicit trade with foreign ships, not only
those of the French, who sold silks and linens and shoes, but
Genoese and Portuguese merchantmen, which brought slaves,
oils, and wines. In 1565 it was declared that only two of the ships
which cleared from Bayamo and Manzanillo with cargoes of
cabinet woods and hides went to Spain. Prominent officials in
Santiago were accused of entertaining French traders in their
homes. Spain expended a large sum in sending investigating committees from Santo Domingo to put a stop to the unlawful commerce. The Cubans claimed the investigators were more corrupt
than corsairs

Because of the super-excellence of its harbor and its key position, Havana soon became an important shipping center. It was
the stop-over station for the plate fleets from Vera Cruz and the
Isthmus, and galleons from Seville and the Canary Islands. In
1574, almost half a century before the Pilgrims arrived at Massachusetts and thirty-six years before the English landed at Bermuda, the waterfront of Havana was buzzing with colorful activi-

ties. Two hundred and sixteen ships entered its harbors in that one year. Thousands of persons—traders and sailors—crowded the town. The citizens began to pile up money from sale of food stuffs. Under the stimulus of inflated prices, forests within a fifty mile radius about Havana were felled and vast plantations put into cultivation. African slaves were imported in great quantities to till the soil. The value of sugar cane crops just now began to be slightly appreciated. Town houses were remodeled or rebuilt. Adobe walls took the place of palm boards, and tile roofs those of thatch. The king lent his own Negroes as a holy offering to rebuild the two monasteries that had been little more substantial than native huts. New images and rich vestments embellished the church. Private fortunes waxed, Miss Wright tells, until certain individuals counted among their assets not only series of houses and extensive estates with slaves, herds, crops, but complete silver table services and gold-handled daggers and swords.

In the flush times, immigration was encouraged and met hearty response. By 1582 the population of Havana and its environs had passed the 20,000 mark. As Cuba augmented in prosperity and international importance, foes of Spain grew covetous and piratical attacks became more frequent. The waters of the Caribbean were said to be "caked with corsairs." Holland and England joined in a common enmity to harry ports of the Indies. Francis Drake began wreaking havoc in various Spanish colonial possessions.

This dreaded Drake was reputed to be more formidable than ten de Sores. The most swarthy Spaniards paled at mention of his name—they called him Red Beard and the Dragon. He had had his training from the age of twenty under that horny-handed old slave-dealer John Hawkins, who captured Negroes on the Guinea coast and sold them in Santo Domingo. Hawkins (afterwards Sir John) purported to believe that he operated under the beneficent protection of God. The largest of his slave-ships was named *Jesus*. In its log one of Hawkins's characteristically devout and cautious entrances, following a tempest in which he and all his black cargo were nearly drowned, reads thus: "The Almighty God, who never suffereth his elect to perish, sent us on the 16th of February the ordinary breeze." Drake was with him in Vera Cruz when his fleet was treacherously attacked by Spaniards who had granted him permission to make repairs. Only one vessel escaped, with the commander and Drake aboard. Then and there the youth conceived an undying hatred for Spaniards, on whom he resolved to be revenged a hundred-fold. Shortly England's canny queen gave him full and legitimate opportunity by placing in his hands letters of marque and reprisal, with coy hints of ardent gratitude for all villainies he would perpetrate against her Spanish brother-in-law. Avidly Drake took up the royal Virgin's cause: shooting, ramming, slashing, looting, and burning his way to victories and favor extraordinary.

For three years Havana, continually receiving disquieting messages of the Englishman's depredations, waited in feverish anticipation for a major attack. Then came the awful news of his crowning exploit of January 1586: he had taken Santo Domingo, the pride of Spain's Caribbean possessions. The inhabitants of Havana were stunned. The import of the message was ominous, not only to the colonies in themselves, but to the very structure of the Spanish empire.

Preparations for resistance were pushed with relentless vigor. Leading dignitaries and aristocrats stripped off their doublets and wielded pickaxes and shovels side by side with sweating loin-breeched blacks. Plump priests tucked their shirts about their middles and took orders from those whom they were accustomed to confess. Barricades were thrown up, trenches dug, and pits sunk in false roads. A gigantic chain of wooden blocks was slung across the harbor's mouth just beneath the water's surface. The viceroy of Mexico sent four ships with three hundred men, ammunition, and provisions. Volunteer fighters from every corner of the island came overland by horseback and afoot to the city's defense. The halt and infirm stood their watches at the lookouts. A ship fleeing Cartagena brought word that Drake had possessed the treasure-stored city and was giving it a thorough looting. The suspense of waiting became almost unendurable. On May the twenty-ninth the first six of the thirty English vessels appeared, chasing a ship loaded with dye-woods, which escaped into the safety of the harbor. Cannon shots from Punta Fortress sent the enemy back. The whole town stayed awake throughout the rainy summer night, waiting. With the silver light of dawn, watchers on the coast beheld the full thirty ships at anchor silhouetted blackly against the platinum-colored sky and water. The sight was stirring in its beauty and dreadful potentialities. Nerves in trenches tautened. Citizens not on duty spoke in hoarse whispers as if in church. No dog gave tongue, and infants were strangely hushed.

In the strained atmosphere, weary eyes were deceived into seeing many things: one night exhausted groups of watchers thought they saw a number of barges making landings. The alarm was sounded and the town thrown into a turmoil, as a result of this illusion. But four days passed and nothing had happened. On June the fourth, to the people's incredible astonishment, the vessels weighed anchors and hoisted sails. Silently they glided away, disappearing one by one into the northeastern horizon. The people crossed themselves and stared at each other wonderingly. Had the whole affair been some fantastic dream?

As sinews relaxed with relief, the Spaniards professed themselves to be grossly disappointed that the English had not tasted of their valor and their revenge. For the life of them they could not imagine why Drake had not attacked. There were two main reasons: first, he was already rich (his ships were virtually ballasted with treasure); and second, a plague had broken out among his crew before he had reached Cuba. While he was at anchor his sailors and prisoners were dying by small-boatloads and daily being dropped into the sea.

Drake's victories throughout the Indies—after passing up Havana he paid a visit to St. Augustine and demolished it—convinced Spain that she could no longer depend on her own naval strength for the protection of her colonies. With no more delay she sent the renowned engineer, Baptista de Antonelli, to design comprehensive and expert fortifications. At Havana work was soon begun on Morro fortress and the new Punta. In 1592 Philip II put his seal on the royal decree granting Havana the title of city (Ciudad). On the shield were emblazoned three silver towers (Morro, La Punta, and La Fuerza) against a blue field (the Gulf of Mexico). A golden key signified the city's strategic position.

In 1597 Morro was completed. The work was so well done that for one hundred and sixty-five years Havana was able to resist successfully all attacks of her enemies. By 1634 the city was flourishing not merely as "a wayport of empire," but in her own prosperous right. Agriculture had been established on a firm basis; sugar mills had sprung up along the Almendares River; shipbuilding had become a leading industry; copper mining, which had languished, had been brought to life again; a considerable export business in cabinet woods was being carried on. Mother Spain now beamed with rosy favor on the daughter she had so long treated like a Cinderella. The crown conferred on Havana a proudful title: Key of the New World and Bulwark of the West Indies.

7
THE BUCCANEERS

In the next century Cuba reflected in some measure the political turmoil of Europe, and gradually she began to develop a sharp sense of insular nationality, as the throne of the Spanish empire tottered and lost its grip financially and morally. The climax of Spain's glory had been reached before August 1588, when Philip's grand armada was mortally defeated by that new rising seapower, Elizabeth's England. With the shattering of her maritime supremacy, Spain's last good act for her colonies was to provide them with fortifications. Having done this the old despot betook herself to a stuffy, prolonged sick-bed, and more or less left Cuba and the others to fend for themselves.

The only liveliness known to slow-moving seventeenth-century Cuba was furnished by the buccaneers, originally a tatterdemalion group of husky meat-curers, who introduced another blood-congealing period of piracy under a different name. First the wilder parts of Haiti and then the formidable Island of Tortuga, which lay just off the northwest point of Haiti, became the nursery, the refuge, and the seat of government of an odd assortment of men, banded together by the call of the wild and cemented by a vendetta against Spain. English, French, and Dutch joined the jungle brotherhood. This heterogeneous bunch was made up of wanton fortune-seekers, fleers from justice, souls who thrived on bloody hazards, and strange, restless spirits who chafed under conventions and the laws of church and court. From Haitian natives they learned a process of preserving meat by drying it and smoking it over a fire of green leaves and branches. The rack on which the meat was laid was called a *boucan* or *buccan*. Those who prepared and sold the meat were called *boucaniers* or buc-caneers. As these fellows smoked meat and tanned hides for sale, they browned and toughened their own skins under the parching sun and steaming tropical rains, and in the process they schooled their consciences callous. When their band augmented in strength, and meat-curing grew monotonous and Spain's enmity became too forbidding, they took to haphazard pirating. At first they operated modestly, trickily, with the long canoes of the natives. Making a few successful captures of vessels, arms, and ammunition, they began larger ventures. Before long the West Indies and the Spanish Main were put into a fever of unrest by their bold depredations. The general apprehension lasted almost to the very end of the century, when the Treaty of Ryswick in 1697 broke up the buccaneers as a banded power.

These seventeenth-century marauders were a wild and colorful gang. Their formidable, picturesque leaders were sometimes French, sometimes English, but all scarred-face villains of amazing enterprise, iron-clad courage, and with an inspired gift for blasphemy. The costume of the buccaneers was generally reduced to one garment and a gaudy rag about their heads. Above the waist they wore nothing but their own mahogany-colored hide, often tattooed with the blue naked body of a woman curving between their chests and bellies. Below the belt they wore coarse linen pantaloons, stiffened and dyed with bullock's blood. The pantaloons were held about their middle by a rawhide belt bristling with pistols and cutlasses in shark-skin sheaths. On their feet they wore rough pig-skin boots without stockings. Sometimes their hair was matted under a greasy net, sometimes plaited into a pig-tail wrapped in bunting. Their faces were generally dark-flushed with rum, their ears pierced with gold rings. Now and then little silver crucifixes on slender chains—pilfered with a jest from nuns—hung about their bull-necks and heaved boisterously when the cutthroats bawled songs of bawdy. Occasionally the marauders would dress themselves in fine clothes they had stripped from cadavers of gentlemen. Even the least foppish might swagger among their half-naked brethren in emerald silk coats with waistcoats of cherry-colored velvet and breeches of yellow satin. In their hats they often affected the perfumed blossom of the logwood tree.

By no means, however, were all these illegitimate seafarers either chronically boisterous or vicious. They counted among their numbers: shy apothecary's apprentices, who had run away to escape the shut-in boredom of bottling compounds; students of geography; and disillusioned divinity students, who would now and again seek "to relieve the tedium of bivouac by translating aloud from the Greek testament." There were map-makers among them who took little delight in clouting bewildered victims over the head, but who scrupulously kept their maps and their journals in joints of bamboo sealed water-proof with wax. Some who scorned their share of pieces-of-eight were quick to defend with their lives rare specimens of natural history they had collected. No matter how much one made sport of another's curious predilections, a strange savage loyalty bound them stoutly together, as if with hoops of those Jamaican rum casks, from which many chose to drink themselves to a howling, happy death.

In 1654, when Spain took Tortuga, the buccaneers helped England capture Jamaica, and as a reward were allowed to establish headquarters at Port Royal. England, France, and Holland connived with the outlaws to the extent of furnishing them with letters of marque authorizing the seizure of enemy vessels in West Indian and South American waters. Operating from Port Royal with outposts in The Virgin Islands, Campeche Bay, and The Isle of Pines, where they hid their loot in caves, they did not confine their activities to the high seas, but raped the Cuban coast towns at intervals. And not content with mere coastal harrying, they made forced marches into the interior, spreading terror with a kind of sadistic glee.

The roster of notorious buccaneers who preyed upon Cuba in the seventeenth century is long, and the history of many individuals has been recorded by their contemporaries. Captain William Dampier, "Pirate and Hydrographer," and John Esquemeling have left exciting histories of leaders and raids. Esquemeling, who sailed with Henry Morgan, printed in Amsterdam in 1678 his story of this most famous of the pillagers.

Morgan, who was a native of Wales, was kidnaped when a boy and sold to slavery in Barbados. Escaping to Jamaica, he subsequently turned pirate with gusto. A violent and fearless fighter, Morgan fought largely for the fun of the thing, and he was much put out when his enemies failed to offer stubborn resistance. When in 1662 he sacked Santiago with too much ease—because the inhabitants fled and hid in the hills—out of spite he robbed the cathedral of its bells and blew up the stronghold of Morro, declaring contemptuously that he alone could have defended such a fort with one gun and a dog.

Not satisfied with nibbling at the Cuban coast, Morgan enlivened his activities with inland forays. Esquemeling gives us an account of the perturbations and distress of the prosperous town of Puerto Principe (now Camagüey) which could not escape the aggressions of Morgan, even by the town's removal and reëstablishment fifty miles inland.

In March 1668, Morgan, very much irritated on finding that Puerto Principe had bodily left the sea-side to prevent a second sacking at his hand, set out to teach the people a lesson for their inhospitality. "As soon as the Pyrates had possessed themselves of the Town, they closed all the Spaniards, Men, Women and Children and Slaves in the several churches and pillaged all the Goods they could set their hands on. Then they searched through the Country round about, daily bringing in many Goods and Prisoners with much Provision. With this in hand they set to making great Cheer after their custom without remembering their poor Prisoners whom they left to starve in the Churches; though they tormented them daily and inhumanely, to cause them to confess wherein they had hid their Treasure; though of a fact little or nothing was left to them, not sparing the Women and little Children, giving them no food to eat and whereby the greater part miserably perished." At last having thoroughly exhausted the resources of the city and obtained all available goods and money, they killed many of the inhabitants and left for the coast and their ships, driving with them over 500 head of cattle and many prisoners, who were compelled to slaughter and dress the beeves for provisioning the ships.

Morgan's last act on Cuban territory was to bring there the million dollars in booty he had looted from Puerto Bello and divide it before returning to Jamaica. On reaching Jamaica, puffed with glory and heavy with gold, he was surprised with arrest. Since the sacking of Panama had taken place after the treaty with Spain, England was forced to make some show of bringing the ravager to trial. Arriving in England an apprehensive prisoner, Morgan presently found himself a popular hero. And England, ever attuned to the affections of her people, forgave him. Furthermore, as had been a custom since the golden days of the shrewd Virgin, her king knighted the pirate, who had on a score of counts deserved the gallows. As a crowning gesture, before the year was passed, Morgan was sent back to the scene of his robust villainies as deputy-governor of Jamaica. When Cuba inquired into heaven's ultimate vengeance on her chief plague and up-setter of the period, she learned that Sir Henry's end had been peaceful in an atmosphere of sedate British authority which he had established, and that his death was mourned by the entire British Empire and more locally by some hundred-odd natural offspring, the fruit of his old cavalier custom of "marrying" his female captives.

After Morgan's metamorphosis into respectability, Cuba suf-fered little from the piratical enemies of Spain. But the century ended with Spanish trade in the West Indies almost killed. How-ever, the cessation of Spanish rule by the Hapsburg dynasty in 1700 and the ascension of the Bourbon, boded somewhat better for the West Indian colonies.

8

SWEETNESS AND LIGHT

By the dawn of the eighteenth century most of the Creoles em-phatically considered themselves Cubans rather than Spaniards. In 1717 they revealed their attitude in concerted gestures by opposing an attempt of Captain-General Roja to enforce a government monopoly of tobacco. In the riots, Roja found it expedient to withdraw hastily from the island. This was the first bloody protest against the insular government. Except for fur-ther insignificant tobacco revolts in 1721 and 1723 there were no other overt uprisings against Spain for another hundred years—until in 1823 the colony made an abortive bid for freedom, with

Herédia, Cuba's foremost lyricist of all time, among its inspirers.

In 1723, like relief from drought, a new prosperity came with the establishment of the present Navy Yard in Havana, during the constructive governorship of Martinez de la Vega. Here the navy of Spain was replenished. For many a decade vari-shaped vessels were built and set afloat, vessels of a dozen classifications with brave type-names like ships-of-the-line, corvettes, brigantines, three-deckers. With the freshening activity that echoed the harbor noises of ship-building up to the city's center, an institution of higher learning was founded and designated the University of Havana (1728). Under the governorship of de la Vega's able successor, Field Marshal Don Juan Güemes, a post office was established. The cultivation of tobacco and sugar was encouraged as cordially as commerce and shipping. At the middle of the century Havana was as busy a seaport as any in the New World. But Spain's myopic policy of drastic restrictions on foreign trade retarded the country's full development, clogged the Cubans' native enterprise, and annoyed all Europe. Especially aggrieved was aggressive England, who at this time was particularly well stocked with merchandise, merchantships, and free-trade principles. This resentment, augmenting a political upheaval caused by the Seven Years' War then in progress, helped to bring about a declaration of war against Spain in 1762.

By June the 70,000 inhabitants of Havana, of whom only about 3,000 were well armed, were daily expecting a British attack. On the sixth, the forerunners of an overwhelming fleet of almost 200 vessels including warships and transports reached Cuban waters. The flotilla was commanded by Admiral George Pocock and bore 14,000 fighting men with Lord Albemarle at their head. Havana's women, children, nuns from the convents, and aged and ailing males were hurried beyond the city walls, as the citizens prepared to put up an obstinate fight against the tremendous odds. The English did not delay the attack. They divided their land forces, and on the second day were in possession of suburbs to the east and west of Havana. By the eleventh of July Cabaña Heights had been gained. From this advantageous point Albemarle conducted a withering rain of shot on Morro Castle and the besieged city. In all their history Cubans never fought more heroically. Albemarle was forced to draw continuous reënforcements from Jamaica. There were no troops to come to the Cubans' aid. For allies, they possessed only the brain-baking sun, which confounded the alien Britishers, and a malignant epidemic of "black vomit," or yellow fever, which carried off a hundred of the enemy a day. On July twenty-eighth over 3,000 Americans arrived to help the British, among them Lieutenant-Colonel Putnam, who was to gain a larger fame in another war on a contrary side. Two days later Morro fell, when a mine breached its wall. For the first and only time an enemy flag was hoisted over its citadel. The loss of life had been terrific, the English losses twice as heavy as the Spanish. But still, Havana itself had not been captured. Albemarle fought his way around the city over hills contested yard by yard. Finally he had the place completely surrounded with cannon. On August eleventh, 6,000 shells fell shattering into Havana. Had the early Spaniards not built soundly, for permanent duration, nothing would have been left but crumbs of stone and mortar. At length the punishment went beyond human endurance and the Cubans gave up. The British were very kindly in their personal treatment of the gallantly defeated. But the terms of the capitulation (August thirteenth) were severe on the Spanish Crown. Besides territory, battleships, frigates, and a vast quantity of naval and military stores, the British demanded fifteen million milled dollars. Not only did Admiral Pocock and Lord Albemarle become rich as rajahs for their pains, but the soldiers were recompensed for wounds and fevers to the tune of three-and-a-half million dollars distributed among them.

For ten months and twenty-four days Cuba remained a British possession—the one brief interlude in four centuries' destiny when she was not under the control of Spain. In that short interval, British rule proved so astute and sound that Cuba prospered no end. The benefits incurred from British occupation copiously made up for the excessive ransom. Lord Albemarle first gave the city a thorough cleaning. Next he opened the eyes of Cuba and the eyes of the world to the island's potential wealth. Then he threw wide the commercial gates and invited the trade of all nations.

By the treaty which terminated the Seven Years' War, England relinquished opulent Cuba and accepted the grant of empty Florida, a short-sighted exchange of salmon's head for salmon's tail. In the acquisition of Havana had been combined all the advantages that could be procured in war. As a military victory the conquest was of first magnitude. Having cost Spain the loss of a whole fleet as a prize, it was equivalent to a great naval victory. Had England not given back this strategic possession to the Spaniards, she could easily have maintained her ascendancy in West Indian seas. And in the War of American Independence Havana could not have become a formidable center against England, from whence expeditions were sent to recapture Florida, attack Nassau, harass Jamaica, and consequently to distract her forces from a concerted invasion of the Thirteen Colonies.

England's brief stirring of the pot of Cuban affairs proved so seasonable and wholesome that even the torpor of Spain could not discredit the resultant fine savor, and she found it exceedingly difficult to reëstablish the old trade restrictions after England had withdrawn. Finally in 1783, Spain reluctantly declared Havana and Santiago open to free world trade. The new decree lasted until 1809, when foreign commerce with Spanish-American ports was again prohibited. In the interim Cuba waxed rich and the population increased with the flush years. French immigrants arrived from Martinique and introduced the cultivation of coffee. These Frenchmen understood, too, bee culture; and honey and wax became articles of export. Laughing peasants from Andalusia came with their love of dancing, their holy images and their guitars; taciturn peasants from the Basque districts came with their farm gear, their sturdy self-discipline and quiet industry. Hidalgos extended their estates, gave more time and energy to their cane fields and tobacco crops, and purchased African slaves in lordly quantities.

The preponderant majority of governors sent out from Spain had done next to nothing for the improvement of the colonials. Their interest lay only in the spoils of office to be enjoyed on their return home. They tendered the people little besides the opportunity of gaping at elegance, when the gilded state coaches paraded through the rutted streets, or the elaborate state barges, bedecked with flowers and pennants, glided magnificently like painted swans in the foul-smelling, shark-haunted harbor. But with the arrival in 1790 of Governor Luis de las Casas, for once an envoy of Spain did not govern Cuba wholly for the benefits of Spain and Spaniards.

Las Casas was a cultured man of enlightenment, vision, and broad humanity. His first significant act was to institute a lighting system for Havana. Hitherto the undependable moon and occasional lanterns placed by some inhabitants before their individual doors were the capital's only nocturnal illumination. This higgledy-piggledy system was now supplanted by street lamps set at prominent corners. In giving the people light, Las Casas brought them some security in walking abroad, by reducing the dangers of assassination that had been all too bold and frequent in darker administrations. And by the sincerity of his energetic inquiry into his people's needs and natures, by the example of his innate gentle breeding, by his intuitive sympathy with all cultural inclinations, and by his establishment of a small court of good manners and charm, he brought sweetness to Cuba as well as light.

A diplomat with an intelligent sense of humor, Las Casas managed to please the pompous landholders with their dreary notions of social prestige by instituting functions on certain afternoons when the captain-general's hand might be kissed formally. But he also contrived to insinuate into his parties an informality freed from the moldy etiquette which customarily stifled all vice-regal courts. Whenever possible, he moved his entertainments from the high-ceilinged rooms with their rows of stiff-backed chairs into the gardens of the summer palace. And here in an unwonted freedom, men and women strolled or paused on marble seats, under the rustling palm trees, and talked liberally with vivacity and sometimes with wit. The quick tapping of a lady's ivory-stick fan against the jewels of her bodice punctuated the murmur of conversation which mingled with the music of stringed instruments and the insidious trickle of fountain water. It was all so agreeable and charming that even the ice-coated hearts of *duennas* and Moorish-notioned *papas* thawed miraculously.

Other hidalgos followed the court example and extended the practice of giving *tertulias,* as evening gatherings of high society were called. To these *tertulias* were invited foreign gentlemen, traveling scientists, and recent Oxford graduates of means, who, scorning the customary continental grand tour, sought the variety of the tropics. The young princes of the House of Orleans, the Duc de Orleans, the Duc de Montpelier, and the Count de Beaujolie, after visiting the United States (descending the Ohio and Mississippi rivers to New Orleans) honored Havana. Here they were so pleased with the society that they remained a year.

Under Las Casas's régime Cubans became less conscious of both their sense of inferiority and their protective snobbery, as they ceased to be reminded of their provincialism. In January 1796, when the warship *Lorenzo* arrived in Havana harbor bearing the supposed bones of Christopher Columbus which had been removed from Santo Domingo because of the French occupation, the Cubans took as prominent a part as did the Spaniards of the nobility and military in the mundane and ecclesiastical *fiestas* which celebrated the occasion. And after the distinguished bones were encrypted in the almost completed cathedral, Spaniards and Cubans began going there to each other's weddings and christenings in most friendly wise.

As the embryonic nineteenth century neared the period of its birth, and the influence of Paris touched the minds of the people, new fashions came to light with the new ideas. Men began to put their eighteenth century knee-breeches into cedar chests or to pass them on to lackeys. The parsimonious surreptitiously snipped their silk hose into socks, and offered the dingy, gorgeous lace stripped from their sleeves to pretty servant girls for favors. Tailors with their apprentices pondered the new fashions perplexedly and spoiled much fine material in attempting to get the correct smartness into the long, narrow trousers with the Spanish flare at the ankles. The new models with their tight-fitting sashes were very trying to caballeros who did not possess firm flat bellies, and tailors were haughtily upbraided for faults caused by a patron's own injudicious diet. For ladies' dressmakers the change in fashions was not so upsetting. Anyhow, it was not the eighteenth century brocades and hoops, or any special style of gown, that had given the Spanish woman her distinction. It was her accessories. And now that styles were simpler, the accessories became duly more significant. The cut and gleam of evening slippers mirrored in the polished ebony floors of ball rooms became as important as silver-inlaid ivory combs reflecting the flickering candles of crystal chandeliers. The mantillas became finer in texture and design; the fans, more exquisite in workmanship. And to complement the skill of the artisans the ladies carried to the ultimate triumph of perfection the art of employing these dual-natured appurtenances—for the mantilla and the fan possessed the fascination of serving both as a lady's defense and allurement. The graceful fall of gossamer lace or the troubled unfurling of a painted fan inspired many a serenade that drew Las Casas's tolerant smile, and occasionally provoked a duel that made him frown, but not severely.

By no means did Las Casas confine his energies merely to improving the tone of Havana's society. He established schools for the poor and an orphans' asylum. He built bridges and endeavored to improve roads. He founded the first newspaper. But surrounded as he was by so many ignoramuses, rascals, and lazy incompetents, he had a superhuman job instilling civic pride into the inhabitants. Because he chose to administer by persuasion and not by compulsion, his police force was scarce, casual, languid. In consequence, walking in the streets was still rather full of vexations and humiliations to the end of his term. A pedestrian suffered from the verbal rudeness, as well as the physical jostling, of porters balancing baskets on their heads. The drivers of drays laden with boxes of sugar considered themselves monarchs of the narrow ways. Wandering bulls parading through the principal thoroughfares gave many a lady the vapors, when she drove out in her frail two-wheeled carriage, which seemed so unprotected with the driver sitting far in front on the horse's back. And the scent on her handkerchief and the perfume of potted flowers on iron balconies were completely routed by the strong offensive odor of *tasajo,* or salted meat, which drifted through the iron-barred windows into the sun-stricken street and polluted the lower air.

In the face of the general Caribbean apathy regarding a bettering of conditions, Las Casas on the whole did a remarkable work for Cuba. The principal evil, burdensome taxation, however, he was unable to relieve; for in considerations of finance he was shackled by the Crown. Of course, there were enemies to blame him severely because he was powerless to reduce taxes. But on his retirement his name was revered throughout the island, and still is, if not with such ardor as goes to the Father de las Casas of almost three centuries earlier, at least with the gratitude that goes to the most admirable of all governors sent out by Spain.

With uniquely empty pockets, Las Casas said farewell to Cuban shores in 1796, leaving the hearts of the citizens lifted. 1800 came, and people in diverse parts of the island remarked how beautifully serene the nights were that year. Then suddenly one night the islanders held their breaths with awe as the sky became ablaze with an incalculable number of falling stars. When they breathed again they were living in the turbulent nineteenth century.

PART II

The Nineteenth Century

I

TACÓN

AS Providence bunched England's most exciting fires and plagues in the last forty years of one century, the seventeenth, so she sent Cuba hers in the first forty years of the nineteenth. The earliest significant event of the new era occurred in 1802, when Havana was blessed by her great fire which destroyed almost 200 houses. In the rebuilding, the city enjoyed a grateful general cleaning. Finer houses were erected on the old sites, and the city's area considerably extended. Along the water-front a promenade known as the Alameda Paula was constructed. And promenading—where one could be seen and also see—ever being a sacred rite to Cubans, this new parade ground assumed a focal position in the social by-play of the 1800's.

Here under God's most beneficent sky, the high and low in estate would pause in their nods and bows and snubs to watch the keenly constructed "blackbirds" slither into the harbor and unload their freight of ebony males and females, uprooted from the Guinea Coast or Mozambique and dumped cowering and confused on Cuba's civilized soil. In the decade from 1811 to 1820 alone, 116,000 of these transplanted wretches were entered legally at the Havana custom-house, and some 60,000 more were smuggled in by traders who were squeamish about duties on human flesh.

Humboldt, the great German naturalist, who visited Cuba at the beginning of the century, made notes on the slavery situation, and commented on man's inhumanity to man, which had lightened so little since the first Europeans three centuries before began their brutal destruction of the Indians. And as evidence of another kind of bloodsport men relished, Humboldt recounts a story of bird-slaughter indulged in purely for the lust of killing, which occurred among his own sailors.

On the south coast of Cuba, which exhaled an extraordinary fragrance of flowers and honey, while he and his men were employed "in herborizing," their sailors went searching among the rocks for lobsters. Disappointed at not finding any, they avenged themselves by climbing on the mangrove trees and making a dreadful slaughter of the young alcatras (brown swan-tailed pelicans) grouped in pairs on their nests. The young birds defended themselves valiantly with their enormous beaks, which are some six inches long; the old ones hovered over the sailors' heads, making hoarse and plaintive cries. Blood streamed from the tops of the trees, for the sailors were armed with great sticks and cutlasses. The ground was covered with wounded birds struggling in death.

"In vain we reproved them for their cruelty," writes the naturalist. "Condemned to long obedience in the solitude of the seas, this class of men feel pleasure in exercising a cruel tyranny over animals, when occasion offers. At our arrival a profound calm had prevailed in this secluded spot; now everything seemed to say: Man has passed this way."

In 1803, Frenchmen seeking refuge from the slave uprising in Santo Domingo arrived somewhat helter-skelter in eastern Cuba. They received a sympathetic welcome, however, and with their coming the cultivation of coffee was given a new impetus. They settled mostly in the Yateras Mountains northeast of Santiago, the locality thence becoming known as the Coffee Mountain District. By 1827, on 2,067 "colorful and inviting estates," coffee was grown in the shade of fruit-bearing trees. In 1833, 2,328 coffee plantations were taxed, and that year exports reached their maximum with 64,150,000 pounds. The principal market for Cuban coffee, which brought high prices, was Vienna, Havana's rival as a coffee-drinking city. Due to wealth from coffee export and the aristocratic lineage of many French families, a charming high-bred civilization gave tone to Oriente for half a century. The dawn-arrival of mules pack-laden with coffee berries and adorned with little bells on silken ribbons was a picturesque sight in Santiago. Trade reprisals against Spain's discriminatory commercial policy, together with the lowering of prices by Brazil, the new value found in sugar cane, and finally the vandalistic destructions of the revolt of 1868-1878 ruined the coffee plantations and virtually obliterated the piquant culture the aliens contributed. The coffee plantations shrank to two hundred small farms. Cuba began to import coffee. The French moved away, were absorbed, died out. Little trace of them remains.

1808 found the colony on the most friendly terms with the mother country. In that year Cuba won her famous epithet "Ever Faithful Isle" because the provincial council had taken an oath of fidelity to the "legitimate sovereign" as a defiance to Napoleon who had dispensed with the dynasty in Spain. But in the next year Cuba's sweet loyalty went sour, for foreign commerce was again prohibited. In the face of a lowering aspect of disaffection, Spain—having lost all her American colonies except Cuba and Puerto Rico by 1818—made an effort to regain the heart of her faithful isle by establishing a new system of foreign trade. The tariff, however, was so absurdly discriminating in favor of Spanish merchandise that goods wanted from the United States had to be shipped to Spain and reshipped to Cuba. And besides, Spain's policy of internal taxation continued to be so "excessive, arbitrary and unscientific," that bribery was the only protection against unreasonable assessments. At last Cuba, which had been phenomenally patient and long-suffering under Spain's blundering selfishness, turned like the sluggish worm and fixed her sight on the goal of freedom.

In 1823, with the arrival of the incompetent Dionisio Vives as governor, general disorder prevailed, and several secret societies were organized for fomenting a revolt against Spanish authority. The most noteworthy of these conspiring bands was known as *Soles y Rayos de Bolivar* (Suns and Rays of Bolivar), inspired by the example of the patriotic deliverer of Venezuela. An uprising was planned for August sixteenth; but on that day the leader José Francisco Lemus and many of his associates were arrested and imprisoned. For his participation in the treason, José María Herédia, the twenty-year-old poet, was sentenced to perpetual exile.

The government shortly became even more despotic. In 1825 a royal decree conferred on the Cuban governor an absolute authority. The position of captain-general—it had been established in 1589—had always in effect been that of a military ruler, but with the new autocracy he became head of the ecclesiastic jurisdiction as well as that of the military and civil. The governor being responsible only to the king himself, the extent of tyranny and corruption to which the Cubans were now submitted depended entirely on the character of each appointee. He had the power of life and death and liberty in his hands. He could by arbitrary will or whim send any citizen of any rank into exile. He could suspend all laws and ordinances. He could destroy and confiscate property.

The petty Vives remained in office until 1832, considerably bewildered by so much power. He did nothing constructive, and all in all he was so ineffectual that he is scarcely remembered for anything but his nonchalant advice to his people: "Don't go out at night and you won't be robbed."

The year after Vives's departure came the great plague. Cholera with its loathsome breath enveloped Havana and carried off over 8,000 people within two months. Flights and groans and huggermugger burials consumed the horrifying days and nights. In one single day 435 gave up the ghost. When the enterprising Miguel Tacón arrived the next year (1834) to seize the reins of government in his firm, relentless fingers, he found his capital still enjoying a profound Latin mourning.

Tacón's vigorous, orderly, and executive mind made an alert survey of his romantic capital. It did not take him a week to learn that every judge was corruptible and that every malefactor who had silver for bribes was secure. Disgusted with the manifold evidences of tropical disintegration he observed or smelt out, he sent an official letter to Madrid, written in impatient ink, giving his impressions. "Assassins, burglars and sneak thieves," he began his unsavory report, "roam the streets of the city, wounding and robbing not only at night but in broad daylight. So great is the terror inspired by these highwaymen that clerks in commercial houses dare not go out to make collections without an armed escort. There exist also companies of wicked men ready to murder anyone for a conventional price. There are 12,000 persons in the capital without honest occupation, many of them vagabonds who will bear false witness or engage in any sort of rascality for a small stipend. Judges and others squeeze merchants so mercilessly that when a man is robbed he keeps silent about it rather than expose himself to further loss by reporting it to the police. At any time during the day, the cry of 'ladrones' causes the merchants to lock and bar their doors until the danger is past. The streets are filled with homeless and hungry dogs which make life a burden by their continuous howlings. Carriages dash through the narrow thoroughfares at reckless speed, to the constant danger of the pedestrian, who oftentimes is maliciously run down if he is not agile enough to get out of the way! The groups of negro slaves who pass boxes of sugar, fruit, etc., in and out of warehouses, make their count in stentorian voices, to the constant molestation of nerve-racked dwellers in the vicinity. Fathers of families and timorous persons deplore the custom practiced by colored people who employ the filthiest language on the streets, near church entrances, etc. The plazas contain mountains of filth and rubbish; the nastiness of the streets is horrifying, and laziness, excess, and dissipation are the paramount attributes of many of the people." This disorganization of Cuban society in which neither life, property, nor social rights seemed to have any protection,

Tacón zestfully attacked with the directness of a falcon darting at prey.

The four years of Tacón's rule, 1834-1838, began and ended with a thundering activity. No Cuban administrator ever accomplished more materially for his people, and few have ever been more feared or hated. Though historians diversely deal with Tacón in extremes of vituperation or hearty praise, all admit his strength. Obviously he lacked the warmth of heart, the charm, the finesse of Las Casas, the gentleman. In fact, except for a whimsical and sometimes theatrical gift of humor he had few characteristics calculated to gain a people's affections. But he possessed an uncompromising sense of justice, a forthright materialism, and ruthless constructive abilities of the quality that erected the pyramids.

His first care was to visit the prisons. He ascertained from each prisoner the cause of his incarceration. Some had been rotting away, forgotten for ten or twenty years, their only offense having been to incur the enmity or the indebtedness of a person of means. One of the wretches had been major-domo to the Count de Philameno who, to avoid paying him six thousand dollars he owed for services, had had him thrown into jail on a trumped-up pretext. Tacón, ordering the man's release, almost frightened the wits out of the nobleman and forced the immediate cash payment of the six thousand dollars. Many of the nobility who had hitherto enjoyed blissful immunity in their wrongs to the lower classes quaked with apprehension and sullen fury at Tacón's attitude, as he encouraged the people to make all their wrongs known to him.

Next, he tackled the problem of professional murderers, who were a terrifying instrument in the hands of the wealthy classes for the uses of gain or revenge. Backed by his assurance that no harm would come to informers, the citizens exposed the hired assassins, and Tacón dealt with them with zealous finality.

On his first drive out into the country, the governor was puzzled to see posted on conspicuous trees placards bearing the legend

"Money or mutilation." When he learned that the most fre-
quented of his highways were infested with bands of brigands,
and that travelers did not dare stir abroad without tributary gold
in their pockets, his indignation was volcanic. Returning speedily
to his palace, he hastily prepared charts, dividing anew the territory into *partidos* or police districts. Placing the most energetic
and courageous of his captains in charge of armed forces in the
various posts, he commanded them to rid the country of the audacious banditry with celerity and whatever bloody thoroughness
was necessary. "Like King Alfred," he is said to have cried, "I
promise the Cubans they shall be able to leave their purses of
money on the highway without fear of having them stolen." His
officers, not daring to risk Tacón's sarcastic scorn for failure, vigorously hunted the ruffians down in every part of the island. Soon
squads of robbers chained together were being passed from one
partido to another until they reached Havana, where the law
took its unbribed course. Those outlaws who escaped capture were
perforce driven into some useful occupation and made honest
men willy-nilly.

That he would tolerate no petty revolts against the government
Tacón demonstrated grimly by squashing an uprising of blacks
with concentrated direction. The instigators and leaders were
condemned to the garrote. After a partial strangulation, they were
uncollared, and their heads struck off with an ax. The dumb
black heads were then imprisoned in parrot cages and swung
lugubriously on suburban bridges as voluble warnings to upset-
ters of the peace.

Within the city walls, Tacón ferreted the underworld denizens
out of their haunts, exposed them to the critical sunlight, sorted
out some for redemption, banished many, hanged many more, but
the majority he set to useful work paving the streets with stone.

He laid out new thoroughfares and military roads to the fortresses. Beyond the walls he constructed a great parade ground.
He began the Prado and hinted at the Malecón. He erected municipal buildings and the vast sanitary fish market which bears

his name. Like a benevolent Renaissance tyrant he gave the people a series of convenient and ornamental public fountains. Outside the walls he built for them a sumptuous national theater. He outdid the tyrants by commanding benefit performances in the theater to provide marriage dowries for girls in the orphan asylums.

That he was not a reactionary out of tune with the scientific overtures of the nineteenth century he proved by encouraging the first line of Cuban railway to be laid. It ran between Havana and Güines (forty-seven miles) and caused great excitement and a flurry of derision. The latter was due to the fact that the English engineers in charge of the work had inadvisedly brought out locomotives which were too heavy. The first engines did not possess the speed of a donkey. With the most agonizing puffs and snortings they could not make the grades. On the extensive grazing lands through which the track lay, the bulls were more excited and indignant than the citizens. Enraged to madness at the monster-like invader of their fields, their chivalric natures overcame discretion and they charged the snorting sleek black rival with headlong fury. Passengers shivered at the impacts with the awful sound of crushing horns and bones. Then in the middle distance of the landscape, they remarked the soft-eyed cows that merely paused in their cud-chewing and swished their tails with interest, their preening gestures importing that favorite old slogan of jousts, "May the best man win." At length, when smaller engines were imported from the United States, all went well. People who had nowhere to go now became travelers for recreation. And the remaining bulls that had not killed themselves in mistaken valiancy grimly calmed their rage, when it had been demonstrated past a doubt that the locomotives meant no dishonor to their cows.

Before Tacón's coming, self-respecting girls of the people had little redress from the dishonorable intentions of high-born gentlemen. One bright morning Tacón, with a whimsical gesture that might have belonged to an all-wise caliph, threw the fear of heaven into unscrupulous roués and made virtue safe for those who cared to treasure it. The heroine of the story was a lovely

young Creole named Miralda Estralez. The girl kept a small tobacco shop in the Calle de Mercaderes and was engaged to marry
a stalwart young boatman called Pedro. They were both very
much in love and lived only for each other, while they worked
hard to earn money enough to marry. A certain Count Almonte,
a notorious Don Juan, who owned much rich land, became enam-
ored of this Miralda over the cigar counter. When she would not
succumb to his blandishments or accept his gifts of jewels, he had
her abducted by a ruse and brought to his country villa. There he
showered every luxury upon her in his efforts at wooing. But
whenever he approached, Miralda threatened to stab herself
through the heart. In the meantime, Pedro, frantic at her disappearance, guessed at the truth, manfully but unsuccessfully attempted a rescue, and then in desperation appealed to the governor. Tacón commanded the count to appear before him with
the girl. Pedro was called. A notary and a priest were ushered in.
The governor in judgment pretended to listen attentively to the
stories. To the dismay of the young lovers, he ordered that
Miralda and the count should be married immediately. But first
the count had to sign his testament, willing all his goods to his
widow at his death. The marriage ceremony was performed,
Miralda in tearful half-consciousness, Pedro grinding his teeth in
agony by the window. Before he could even kiss his bride at the
conclusion of the ceremony, Almonte was ordered to return to
his villa alone, leaving Miralda temporarily in the governor's cus-
tody. Pedro and the bride stood silent, paralyzed with misery.
The governor sat silent too, but smiling and expectant. The priest
remained, mumbling prayers in a corner. Less than a quarter of
an hour had passed when an attendant rushed in bearing the
news that Count Almonte had been shot dead in the streets.
Miralda was a widow. Tacón called Pedro to her side. He beckoned the priest. The marriage ceremony was again performed.
The notary deeded over all the count's possessions to Miralda.
The governor, giving the breathless couple his blessing, sent them
off to enjoy their love and new fortune.

The story spread with the swiftness of a hurricane. People exulted in their doorways—here was a champion of the poor! Chatter in society drawing-rooms reached a new crescendo. Casual and confirmed profligates in the company answered jests with jeering banter and bade good night with their usual gay bold humor. But out in the streets they watched their steps with unwonted caution.

It was not alone in these cases of differences in humble life that Tacón manifested his administrative ability. Jonathan Jenkins, a New Orleans miniature painter living in Cuba during these years, records a case in point revealing Tacón's shrewdness. In the difficulties arising during the disaffection of General Lorenzo, the governor displayed his accurate knowledge of Spanish character by ordering that his forces pursue a policy of "masterly inactivity." To arrest Lorenzo's movement, he sent three thousand men by land, and the fleet with transports of troops by sea. "They were to be always advancing, but to delay their actual meeting with Lorenzo as long as possible, so that his forces would be kept in constant apprehension and their new-born patriotism would have an opportunity to subside and leave not a trace behind. The whole matter ended with the escape of the general to Spain and the dispersal of his followers."

Although Tacón personally was little given to entertainment, being temperamentally too robust and abrupt to dawdle among drawing-room bric-a-brac either with any ease to himself or pleasure to others, Havana's social life in his régime was charming. Mr. Jenkins left in his papers an agreeable authentic picture. The society was not exactly sophisticated, and it was definitely limited, due in a measure to the governor's closing all the gambling houses, and allowing no one in and out the gates after eleven o'clock except when there was the presentation of a drama or a ball in the theater. People entertained each other at games and dancing in private mansions. Often the small evening parties consisted merely of smoking and making music. Practically all women smoked, from highborn hot-house beauties to tobacco-colored fishwives. When guests entered a home, cigars on a silver salver were handed around. If the guest was a favorite or an intimate friend, one of the young girls of the family lighted the cigar and gave it a few good draws to get it well started, and then gracefully presented it to him. When a guest played on the guitar, a girl sat at his side and kept his cigar lighted, and at each pause in the music she would hand it to him to catch a few puffs before proceeding. Throughout the evening drinks were served by Negroes in livery. The gentlemen drank absinthe and water, or the water of a green coconut flavored with gin. The young girls took a concoction of sweetened water and white of egg. The ladies sipped orchata, a drink white as milk, made from the juice of almonds. Occasionally literature was discussed and a show of erudition proffered. One lady of title made quite a stir by diligently pursuing the study of English in order to realize her life's ambition to translate *Paradise Lost* into Spanish.

The majority of ladies, however, had no such bluestocking predilections; in fact few of them had the slightest curiosity about the ciphers that lay between book covers. Their best energies were given over entirely to perfecting the grace of their dancing or to the study of the wardrobe. It was very bad form for young ladies of the wealthier class to wear the same dress twice; after one appearance the dress became the property of the mulatto maid. So most young ladies were content to be students of fashions and manners and the subtlest modes of flirting.

In the afternoons when the military band played "retreat" the *beaux* foregathered in the Plaza to await the *bellas,* who came driving in their graceful *volantes* and *quitrins* up the broad avenue with blackamoors in azure or crimson satins sitting on the horses' backs. The ladies, gowned in billowy silks, wore high combs and mantillas, with a gardenia or a rose in their lustrous black hair. Pausing in the park to listen to the music, they pressed lightly against the brocaded upholstery of their conveyances and toyed artfully with perfumed fans. And as the music swelled and the moon rose, Spanish bachelor officers in resplendent uniforms and exquisite young gentlemen wearing skin-tight trousers and incredibly tall hats would approach the carriages to pay brief court, extravagantly correct and correctly extravagant.

All young ladies, however, were not allowed the advanced privileges of being spoken to by gentlemen in the Plaza. Widowed fathers were notoriously careful of their daughters' upbringing. In the afternoons when girls went driving, the fathers rode on horseback by their side. In the morning they were accompanied by duennas. The girls were convent educated and knew nothing whatever of the "world." Their fathers and their confessors were the only men to whom they had ever spoken. Indeed, courtships even up to the betrothal were conducted without a spoken word. The following story about herself recounted forty years ago by a charming old lady is typical of the quaint courtships of that day.

One morning while seated at her window, a young girl saw riding up the street a young cavalier, superbly mounted, and wearing a broad-brimmed sombrero trimmed with silver-lace and a black riding cloak lined with scarlet. She thought never in her life had she seen so handsome a cavalier. In passing he caught sight of her, and turned and rode past again, taking off his sombrero and bowing. Trembling with excitement, she scarcely slept that night. Next morning, accompanying her *duenna* to Mass at the cathedral, she found the cavalier standing at the entrance. As she passed, his hand touched hers and a little note was placed between her fingers. Returning home she read and reread her first love letter. But alas, she had no means of answering it; for ink, pen, pencil, and paper were the four things denied strictly brought-up young ladies. Confide in her *duenna* she dared not. Yet so kind a note; so handsome a cavalier; it would be cruel to leave him without a reply. The ingenuity of an enlisted heart found a way. Desperately sacrificing her stack of saints' cards, with pictures of a saint or martyr and a prayer addressed to each underneath, she cut out the words she needed for the composition of an answer. Taking one of her handkerchiefs, she sewed the words in regular order. When the cavalier passed under her window next morning, she dropped the folded handkerchief like a ball at his feet. Having used up all the saints' cards, she began to mutilate the two books of sermons which composed her library.

In this manner, exchanging handkerchiefs and notes daily, either at her window or the cathedral door, the pair corresponded for two months. At last she wrote her cavalier in fair words cut from her holy books that she thought he should speak to her father. The next day he made formal proposal for her hand. His family proving to be of equal position with hers, his offer was accepted. For the first time the young lovers exchanged spoken words.

Up to Tacón's time, it was considered an advantage to capture a Spanish, rather than a colonial, husband, for the governors saw to it that the Spaniards, and consequently their wives, had precedence in everything. But when in 1837 Cuba's right of representation in the Spanish Cortes (granted in 1834, Tacón's first year) was taken away, the Cuban discontent grew so intense that many Creoles stopped speaking to the Spaniards, and the Spaniards in turn ostentatiously ignored them. Tacón's utter lack of tact intensified the situation. In his irritation he became increasingly arbitrary and vindictive.

Although at his retirement Tacón left Cuba more serviceable monuments to his forceful talents than any predecessor, unfortunately the chasm between the colonials and the Crown which Las Casas had so diplomatically bridged, if not cemented, Tacón had widened with his to-hell-with-it contempt. After him, as the decades passed, the rift deepened until any hope of ever filling up the breach became foolishly phantasmagoric.

PLACIDO, THE MULATTO POET

When the tyrant was gone, the citizens relaxed to enjoy the benefits he had imperiously thrust upon them. The island's population in 1838 had virtually reached the million mark, and the annual revenue amounted to ten million *pesos*. Spain smiled on Cuba and licked her lean chops. The office of captain-general loomed up as the richest plum in the Spanish political pie. Grandees gave up their lives to wire-pulling in order to gain the prize.

Leopoldo O'Donnell y Jovis, Count of Lucena, got the office in 1838 and held it for five years. He was to return to Spain with far more spoils than any of his predecessors. Queen Isabella became so envious of his wealth that she had him removed. The main source of this wealth came from the slave trade—the governor collecting a big fee on every African sent into the island—and from the proceeds of hiring out *emancipados* (Negroes captured en route by British cruisers). Another source was from the sale of niches O'Donnell built in the cemetery. A further lordly sum was derived from the cleaning of privies in the city. These last new monopolies were very annoying to the citizens' sensibilities. People complained they could neither die nor perform their natural functions without encountering the governor's demanding hand thrust at them for the privilege.

While the governor was in his counting room computing the odorous profits from sweating Negroes, backhouses and corpses, his lady was in the cellar gathering up the empty cobwebbed bottles from which former executives had furnished exhilaration for their banquets. These "dead soldiers" she sold for personal pin-money and not for sweet charity as one might suppose. But she was by no means uninterested in charitable institutions. She had a particular penchant for the orphan asylum. Her visits there were notoriously frequent. She was extravagantly enthusiastic about the young girls' needlework; she commanded them to sew and embroider for her such prodigious quantities of bedding that their eyes turned as bloodshot as if some strange epidemic had swept the gloomy halls. The rumor went that the good lady was having the beautiful work done to take back as presents to her friends in Spain. It was later reported that on her return she exhibited the sheets as samples of her useful instruction in Cuban orphan asylums—and then sold them.

The Irish and Spanish blood had not mingled graciously in O'Donnell's veins. He had not only all the instincts of a grafter and a thief, but he was also written down by his contemporaries as a bloodthirsty coward, who inflicted dreadful tortures on innocent as well as guilty. While deluging the island with African slaves for his gain, he grew fearful of the threatening black predominance and ordered some wholesale executions to keep the Negroes in their place. Placido, the inspiring mulatto poet of Mantanzas, was among the victims forced to stand before a firing squad. For every bullet hole his body received, hundreds of patriots were born out of pity and righteous resentment.

Beginning in Tacón's administration and continuing in O'Donnell's, a flourishing period of Cuban literature occurred, due largely to a literary circle which formed about the person of Domingo del Monte (1804-54). Del Monte, wealthy, cultured, instituted the custom of inviting poets to read their compositions in his home at evening parties. To these *tertulias* came Herrera, Milanes, and Gabriel de la Concepción Valdés, known to posterity by his pen name of Placido. In inspiration and imagination Placido was vastly superior to the others, and after the great Herédia, he is today the popular idol of poetry-loving Cubans. His bitter-sweet, plaintive lyrics, saturated with fervid Southern perception, have been translated into many languages.

Gabriel de la Concepción Valdés, whose name was derived

from the foundling asylum which had "sheltered his infancy," was a mulatto of illegitimate birth, born in 1809, the same year as the star-crossed Edgar Allan Poe. He was the son of a Spanish dancing girl and a mulatto hairdresser. He earned his living by fashioning tortoise-shell combs. Somebody taught him to read, acquaintances lent him books. A druggist, Francisco Placido, supplied him with writing materials and an opportunity to write in his shop. In gratitude he selected "Placido" as a pen name, when he found he had a gift for lyric verses.

To a sensitive, talented man in the low social position of Gabriel de la Concepción Valdés life seemed very bitter at times. He chafed too under the tyranny of Spain. "I made an altar of hard earth," he says, "in the shadow of a tree upon a hill top, at the outlet of a narrow valley, where a little silver stream invites me to drink of its waters. And then, stretching my hands to heaven, I swore to be the eternal enemy of the tyrant, and to bathe my garments in his blood, and to die, if need be, under the arm of executioner, that so I might break this yoke of slavery."

Bold and fearless in his verses, he went so far as to address the Queen Regent thus:

"Let them who fear be dumb, for not of them am I!"

As a prominent member of the African race and the author of pungent political criticisms circulating in manuscript, it was natural that Placido should fall under the suspicion of the authorities, when, in 1844, they scented a Negro uprising. He was thrown into prison where he spent his hours composing songs and exhortations, writing with peculiarly touching beauty to his mother. Stoutly defending his innocence of any complicity in sinister plotting, he expected eventually to be released. When, however, after a pretense of a trial, the sentence of death was announced to him, he replied: "I shall die singing like the Cuban nightingale."

On the morning of the twenty-eighth of June, with nineteen others, Placido was led to the execution place on the Plaza of

Mantanzas reciting his own verses. He passed to his death like a *cacique,* chanting for a death-song his own noble prayer.

Stay thou, O Lord, the oppressor's victory!

Forbid it, Lord, by that most free outpouring
Of thine own most precious blood for every brother
Of our lost race, and by thy Holy Mother,
So full of grief, so loving, so adoring,
Who clothed in sorrow followed thee afar,
Weeping thy death like a declining star.

But if this lot thy love ordains to me,
To yield to foes most cruel and unjust,
To die and leave my poor and senseless dust
The scoff and sport of their weak enmity,
Speak Thou, and then Thy purposes fulfill;
Lord of my life, work Thou Thy perfect will.

Selected the first to be executed, he stepped into the square and knelt with unbandaged eyes. He himself gave the signal to the soldiers to fire. When the smoke cleared, Placido was seen writhing in agony on the ground. A murmur of pity and horror ran through the crowd. Placido, slowly rising to his knees, drew up his body proudly, and cried in a broken voice: "Farewell, world! ever pitiless to me!" Then raising his hand to his temples he commanded, "Fire here!" This time they shot him dead.

Negro slavery in Cuba reached its peak about the middle of the nineteenth century, during the régimes of O'Donnell and his immediate successors. Due to the rapacity of captain-generals, a half-million Africans were illegally brought as slaves into Cuba after the nefarious traffic had been formally abolished by Spain in 1820. (Denmark had been the first country to declare slave trade unlawful, in 1792; Great Britain had followed suit in 1807; then France and Holland, with Spain, characteristically the die-hard, last.)

3

BLACK SLAVERY

In any period of history, in any locality, human slavery with its degrading manifestations is more than likely to spin a frightful tale. The Redmen of Cuba had vanished from its horrors with appalling swiftness. But the Negroes were made of stouter fiber. They could endure more. And if they did not endure, the fecund jungles of Africa were relentlessly breeding an incomputable supply.

It has often been repeated that Father Las Casas, out of overwhelming pity for the Indians, first suggested the scheme of substituting African slave labor for that of the aborigines. But Negro slavery, as Ballou makes clear, did not originate with the good priest. For a long time prior to Columbus's discovery of America, Spain was engaged in slave trade. Some of the first new settlers brought their black slaves with them when they came to Cuba, and King Ferdinand himself sent over fifty slaves to labor in the royal mines. Las Casas, to save the Indians, did plead for the further employment of Negroes; but he lived to be horrified at the consequences of his suggestion. Had Las Casas never have been born, the cloud of black slavery would have sullied the Cuban landscape just as inevitably.

The pernicious traffic in human beings is a crime with an extensive geography and a long drawn-out chronology. The English, fanatically crusading in their efforts to suppress slavery in the nineteenth century, were the most ardent and successful slave-traders through the sixteenth, seventeenth, and eighteenth centuries. Queen Elizabeth herself set an early example for her subjects by graciously condescending to accept her share of the emoluments of the business and by bestowing knighthood on the most affluent of her loyal slavers. For a long stretch of years the slave trade lagged somewhat, until in 1713 England purchased from Spain a monopoly on slave trade with Spain's colonies. England carried on her business with such aggressive British vigor that Cuba was kept constantly stocked with almost more slaves than she could manage. The governors of Cuba were very kindly disposed to the English traders. Every imported black meant a golden bonus.

Likewise in later days Boston drew immense wealth from this extensive slave trade. The Americans built the fastest ships in the world, and speed above all things was what the slaver wanted. Havana's harbor was crowded with these American clippers, which had been built on speculation and sold to the highest bidder. It was due largely to the Americans and their fast craft that the importation of African slaves increased so extensively in the first half of the nineteenth century. And then aping the conscience reversals of Mother England, the very descendants of these New England slave traders—who became aristocratic and independent through their inherited fortunes and who had no possible use themselves for cotton-choppers—turned the shrillest-voiced in subsequent abolitionist indignation. Spain at least had the grace not to be inconsistent.

Baron von Humboldt estimated the number of slaves brought into Cuba from 1521 to 1791—a period of 270 years—as something over 90,000. Thrasher, one of Humboldt's translators, gives the arrivals of imported slaves up to 1854 as 644,000. In the time of O'Donnell the colored population in Cuba outstripped the white by more than 170,000. In 1841 the census gave 589,333 colored against 418,291 whites.

The most vivid commentators on slave-life at the middle of the century are Mr. Jenkins, the miniature painter, and a gentleman from Philadelphia who calls himself the Yankee Traveler. As a point of interest, American tourists would be taken to see the slave-barracoons on the outskirts of Havana. Here the droves of dazed savages were confined, awaiting sale—as many as two hundred at a time. Either completely naked or almost so, their emaciated bodies, as well as their agonized faces, were stamped with the horrors of the ocean crossing. Their flesh was indented with the mark of planks where they had lain cramped in the stinking hold. Their hands had scarcely enough strength to worry the gnats and flies feasting on the sores made by the whip-lash. Half-perished with hunger and thirst, they sat mumbling to their heathen gods, speculating on the ultimate destiny of their dead companions whom they had seen raked out of the ship's bottom and dumped over the side like offal.

Cuban citizens and foreigners who came to visit the barracoons were moved to pity, or to jesting, according to their natures. But the majority remarked the Africans more as beasts than humans, even though the Catholic Church recognized them as baptizable human beings, which the English Church did not.

Once settled at the barracoons, the slaves were rather well treated—to be got into condition for sale. They were given plenty of rest and sufficient food. Simple expressions were taught them by a Negro teacher who passed before them, as they sat cross-legged in a row, and rewarded each with a sip of rum as encouragement to learning. When they were in proper condition, sugar planters from the interior and ladies in need of house servants would come to bid for laborers and wenches. The planter always made an examination of a Negro to ascertain his strength and his health. To gauge his disposition, he would slap him in the face. If the fellow smiled, and showed no resentment, the planter would buy him.

Out on plantations the new Africans were put in charge of an overseer, who generally went about armed with a *machete* and an orange wood stick used for flogging. On first arrival, the slaves were not worked too hard, because early discouragement had led many a black to commit suicide in the belief that he would thereby return to his native land. Planters had lost much money through these suicides. Sometimes there would be epidemics of self-killings on a plantation. To check the evil, overseers hit upon the idea of burning the bodies of suicides before the other assembled slaves and forcing them to scatter the ashes over the fields. This disorganizing process, so the Negroes believed, prevented the dead man's soul from returning to Africa.

Generally in Havana Province, the owner of a plantation did not live on his estate, but stayed in Havana where he and his family could enjoy official society. The entire management he turned over to his major-domo, and took little interest in his estate except to demand more and more profit to meet the exigencies of social life in the capital. The steward in turn ground the life out of the slaves trying to satisfy the owner and to increase his own percentage. The overseers and slave-drivers could flog, maim, or maltreat slaves with impunity. But if a slave showed violence towards his keeper, unmerciful torture or even death might be the penalty. Fiske says that "general burning alive, beginning at the feet, was a legal punishment on a second conviction for beating a white man."

Of course, all overseers were not vicious. And in Cuba abuses were not as insufferable as in other West Indian colonies. It is significant to note that in three and a half centuries of black slavery in Cuba there was never a really serious Negro uprising, not even with the diabolical example of Haiti just across the way. But the cruelties in Cuba were awful enough, though the black thunder cloud never did burst.

One striking fact Mr. Jenkins pointed out as attesting to the barbarous hardship of slave life was that children were seldom seen on the plantations. Men slaves were more valuable than females, and only a few women were allowed in a force of a hundred men. The labor the women had to undergo tended to prevent increase, and the few children born generally died early of neglect. Overseers argued that it was cheaper to replace deaths on the plantation by fresh importations of men than to provide for the rearing of children.

Yet the keep of slaves amounted to almost nothing. For clothing in the fields, they required only a straw hat and a loin cloth.

Slave children of both sexes up to the age of ten went entirely naked. For dress occasions a shirt and pantaloons of sheeting were given to the men and a calico gown to the women. At Christmas they received trinkets and sometimes a woolen jacket. For food they had plantains and sweet potatoes, and every morning a boiled corn meal mush was poured into a trough from which they ate their breakfast with wooden spoons or their fingers or their mouths, according to inclination. To vary the monotony of diet and to give them extra strength, a ration day was held once a week; the slaves were drawn up in long lines and a hunk of black South American beef was "thrown at the feet of each."

After sunset when the *oracion* was rung, the Negroes were free to enjoy themselves until *Ave Maria* was rung next morning shortly before sunrise, when they arose to prepare the oxen for the carts. At night they stuffed their pipes with the tobacco scraps distributed among them and smoked with slow draws. Some of them made music on the rude musical instruments they fashioned after remembered tribal models. They would sit in the moonlight for long unbroken hours and chant songs of Africa to the monotonous cadences of their subdued music. Occasionally they would dance themselves to a new exhaustion, performing ritualistic phallic dances of the jungles. The next day they would be flogged for weariness.

In the cities, too, the Negroes had their amusements peculiar to themselves, and on the Feast of the Epiphany (the twelfth of January) they were given the freedom to devote themselves to unconfined jollification. It was the day of the year they lived for. Mr. Jenkins has preserved a lively account of one of these "All Kings' Day" orgies that made pageantry in old Havana. "The negroes of many African tribes mingle in a grotesque saturnalia, marked by the utmost extravagance of costume, representing every device of bird, beast, or devil of which the barbarous imagination can conceive, accompanied by the most frantic cries and gestures. Thus are brought out in bold relief the wild spirit and savage customs of the Africans. The more subdued and civilized housemaids, loaded up with the utmost finery that their young mistresses place on them, will at first reject with disdain the proffered gallantries of their strapping and gaudy admirers; but their native character gradually asserts itself despite their prudery and veneer of civilization, and by night they may be seen mingling in the savage dance, as bold and barbaric as the wildest, making the most hideous grimaces, their finery reeking with dust and perspiration, and they themselves half-dead from excitement and exertion."

In many considerations the lot of house-bred town slaves was far from unenviable. Servants were kept sleck and well dressed not only as a matter of pride before neighbors, but often because of natural affection. Frequently little pickaninnies were reared as carefully as the mistress' own children. Some, pampered like pets, became demanding spoiled darlings. Beautiful octoroon girls lazed in a sweetmeat existence similar to that of the silken concubines of mandarins. Old negresses attained positions of dignity and authority in Havana households. Whites and blacks there were who would have fought and died for each other.

Yet poisoning by revengeful slaves in these days was common. For this evil no satisfactory remedy could be found. The owner of the slave did not care to disclose the guilt of an offender, as this course would certainly mean that he lost the money value of his slave either by capital punishment or imprisonment; for the public treasury declined to defray the worth of the criminal. The Yankee Traveler recounts a revealing case in point that was much talked of during his Cuban sojourn. "A widow lady whipped a negro boy, about 14 or 15. The same day she was attacked by dysentery, and no other cause could be assigned for it than a cup of coffee and milk that the negro had brought to her. She suspected, and having frightened him in order to obtain a confession, he acknowledged that he had put in her coffee some powders which a man passing by the street had given to him. This last was certainly false, as his other confessions showed, and he only made it, believing that he was thereby exculpated. The lady died the following day; she was buried without any inquest being held; the sons sent the negro to the plantation, and punished him by flogging; loaded him with irons, and condemned him to work always shackled. This punishment evinces that the owners believed in the guilt of the negro. They did not want, notwithstanding, to lose him, though their mother was the victim."

That gold-lusty objective which motivated the activities of the original Spaniards in Cuba descended to scions through direct or devious strains, corrupting the fabric of society piecemeal and wholesale. Out of phenomenal cheapness of slave labor and its unfeeling conditions, planters poured into the government treasury from twenty to twenty-four millions of dollars annually. Not only did the government and the captain-generals become rich from the inhuman traffic, but private individuals piled up notorious fortunes. A certain Joaquin Gómez, who came from Spain at the age of thirteen, ragged and penniless, lived to see his fortune from the slave business mount to $2,000,000 and to hear himself entitled Don.

When Concha came in 1851 as the new captain-general, his arrival was attended by pomp befitting the occasion of his salary's increase from $20,000 to $50,000 a year. This increase was supposed to be compensation for certain fees and privileges which were now taken away from the chief executive. The new governor had sworn to end the slave trade. But he merely winked at it, and held out his left hand obliquely to receive the illegitimate gold. With his augmented salary from the Crown filling one pocket and slave bounties filling the other, Concha became richer than O'Donnell. Twice more after his first term of office he gained the appointment of captain-general to Cuba, and battened grossly on the defenseless people. All of which naturally added more bitterness to the long brewing pot of colonial resentment.

LOPEZ DIES FOR CUBA

But although the disaffection was wide-scattered through the island during the middle decades the quality of the general unrest was decidedly lukewarm. Only in Narciso Lopez, a Venezuelan by birth, did patriotic feelings heat to the boiling point. Lopez had risen to the rank of general in the Spanish army. He was a man of spirit and intelligence, of peculiarly frank and unintimidated behavior. Once when he went to O'Donnell to plead for a cessation of his tyrannies, the governor did not ask him to be seated. Lopez seized a chair himself, and in placing it to face the governor, he set it down with such emphasis that it broke in pieces. Calmly kicking the fragments aside, he took another chair and sat down as if nothing had happened. O'Donnell, pale as death, listened to his case without interrupting—but the mission was not fruitful.

Definitely convinced that no redress for Spanish oppression would come from intelligent arguments and pleas, Lopez determined on deliberate revolt. Like José Antonio Saco, Cuba's distinguished thinker and historian, Lopez looked to annexation to the United States as the only salvation for Cuba's misery. In 1837 Saco had written: "I have always wished that Cuba might be only for the Cubans, but, now that perhaps that cannot be, we have no other recourse than to throw ourselves into the arms of the United States. That is the idea that it is best to diffuse and inculcate in the minds of all." And because of the threatening predominance of Negro over white population in the 1840's, Lopez himself did not wish an independent Cuba, for he feared it might become a Negro republic on the Haitian pattern.

Lopez's first conspiracy in 1847 was betrayed to the Spanish authorities and he was forced to flee to America. Here he represented the whole population as ready for revolt and annexation to the United States. In 1848 President Polk made an offer to purchase Cuba from Spain. The offer was declined. Lopez organized a filibustering expedition. President Taylor squashed it. Lopez, still assuring the people of the United States that all Cubans were armed and wanting for a leader, offered the command to Jefferson Davis and then to Robert E. Lee. When both of these soldiers declined, Lopez besought Governor Quitman of Mississippi. Quitman flirted with the idea, but ended by merely giving Lopez his moral support. So Lopez again headed his own rebellion.

The New York *Sun* encouraged Lopez through its presses and offered him the courtesy of its flagpole. Lopez accepted the honor; the new-created virgin flag of free Cuba was initiated in the swirling breezes of New York. The banner—with the three blue and two white stripes at the top of which a red field bore a single white star—is the selfsame standard that proclaims from Cuban flagpoles today the island's independence.

In the spring of 1850 Lopez sailed from Yucatan with some 600 men, including many sympathizing or adventurous Americans. The force landed at Cárdenas, expecting to be met by a great army of patriotic rebels. But the town emptied itself of its inhabitants, who fled to the country or hid themselves in the holds of vessels. Those who remained barred themselves in their houses and shops, leaving Lopez and his followers to deal with the Spanish detachment on its way to annihilate them. A handful of colored men modestly offered their services to the general. "The Cuban flag was hoisted, and waved majestically in the breeze, waiting the arrival of those who, wishing to be redeemed, would come to take shelter under it against the attacks of despotism and oppression. But nobody was seen coming with that end in view. The invaders considered that a strange occurrence; some time had elapsed and nothing notable had yet happened. Soon afterwards the soldiers began to reëmbark themselves without waiting their commander's orders. Lopez, accompanied by a few Cubans and Americans, remained on shore, but was at last persuaded to leave by boat."

As the ship steamed listlessly towards Key West, the general pensively stroked his long white beard. "What-in-hell's-matter with your Cubans?" the Americans demanded. Lopez gazed back at his beloved land, struck the deck table wearily with his fist, and said in a sorrowful voice: "Ah, Cubans!"

Despite his fiasco, in America the general was received like a hero. Not yet satisfied that his people did not yearn to be liberated, he gathered a new force the following year (1851). As unquenchably optimistic as Christopher Columbus, he sailed from Louisiana with 400 men. Four of them were "authentic Cubans"; most of them were Americans, including 150 soldiers under Colonel Crittenden of Kentucky. Complete disaster befell this third attempt. A landing was made near Bahía Honda, about fifty miles west of Havana. Again the Cubans failed to rise to throw off the yoke of repression. Those of the cities who sympathized with the invaders were still only faintly lukewarm in their sympathies. The suspicious country people, to whom the Spaniards had represented the invaders as robbers, harassed the gallant rebels and set their dogs upon them. A rain storm, which occurred shortly after their arrival, ruined most of their ammunition. With the few good bullets they had, however, they mowed down the first line of royalist troops and killed the Spanish general, Enna, who died shouting "Cowards!" at his own men.

By a strategical error, Lopez and Crittenden divided their forces, and the separate detachments were surrounded and captured. The Kentucky Colonel and his Americans were shot against a wall at Atares Fortress, above Havana. Lopez was taken to La Punta and garroted publicly.

The Yankee Traveler, much moved by the unhappy fate of Lopez, records his end thus: "Lopez, after being taken prisoner, walked several miles escorted by a few soldiers, and not even a dozen patriots endeavored to wrest him from the grasp of his murderers. This is more to be wondered at, when we consider that for doing this, it was not necessary to be a warm patriot; any person of humane feelings, and endowed with sentiments of gratitude, possessing besides some courage and dignity, would have made the attempt. Lopez was exhausted from weariness, hunger and thirst; he walked barefooted for a long distance, limping and bleeding from his lacerated feet; while the soldiers who guarded him embittered his sufferings by insulting and mocking words."

The Spaniards, especially the Catalonians, were savagely jubilant at Lopez's defeat. (The class of peasants and small shopkeepers who had immigrated to Cuba from Catalonia seemed of a peculiarly lower type that other immigrants and were particularly loathed by both Cubans and blacks.) The Catalonians celebrated the Kentucky Colonel's execution with cannibalistic glee. And on the morning of Lopez's death some of them in Havana invited guests to a feast. In the center of the table they placed a glass bowl. They intended to fill it with Lopez's blood—"to enjoy the smell!" However, they were cheated of full satisfaction. For that morning news was received that New Orleans was in a threatening uproar at the report of the killing of Crittenden and his followers. The Spaniards had to call off the intended celebration of dragging Lopez's body through the streets and cutting it up in pieces. At the execution, the Catalonians were not even permitted to pluck at the rebel's long rippling beard, which lay along his breast, like Chaucer's Frankelyn's, white as a daisy in the September sunshine.

A vague whisper had gone about that half a hundred well-armed young men were going to dash up a few moments before the execution and effect a rescue or die by the martyr's side. Two or three men, supposed rescuers, appeared near La Punta, hovered about as if waiting for others to arrive, then slunk away.

Lopez's martyr-lit eyes turned to right and left searching the crowd and the near landscape for sympathizers, for someone into whose hands he might pass the torch. "Ah, Cubans!" he

doubtless thought, as he died alone. His last audible words, however, were prophetic: "My death will not change the destinies
of Cuba!"

The behavior of the Cubans did not prove cowardice so much
as unconcern. They were temperamentally given to making themselves as comfortable as possible with whatever the gods sent.
The vast majority had no burning desire for liberty or independence. Their only wish was for easement and reform in the present system of government. They were not ready yet to bestir
themselves to rise against oppression. Only a comparative few
in scattered parts of the island allowed themselves to be deeply
moved by Lopez's martyrdom. When Captain-General Concha
gave his next ball, Havana ladies and gentlemen accepted his
invitation with accustomed grace. The dancing frocks and jewels
of the ladies were as gay and carefully thought out as ever. The
expressions on the faces of the men as they danced the *bolero*
did not belong to mourning. But down in Oriente Province, a
somewhat bookish young aristocrat named Carlos Manuel de
Céspedes was stung to the heart by the story of Lopez. The impression remained there like a living spark. Years later, in 1868,
on the tenth of October, just before dawn, de Céspedes marched
out of his house at Yara holding aloft a flaming torch. A hundred
and forty-six patriots rallied about him. All together they
"launched the shout" known as the *Grito de Yara,* the cry of
liberty, the call to active revolt against Spain. It marked the
turning point in Cuba's struggle for freedom.

5

GALA DAYS

In the seventeen years between the execution of Lopez, 1851,
and the beginning of the Ten Years' War, the Cubans lived more

sumptuously than at any time in their history. Private palaces were erected in Havana, Trinidad, Camagüey, decorated with superb Italian murals, rare French tapestries. The parlor furniture for the Aldama Palace in Havana, where the island's aristocracy came to pay court, cost $30,000. Señor Aldama traveled in state like a rajah, a dust-raising retinue of liveried servants and outriders accompanying him. The women of his family wore jewels and robes queens might envy. The elaborate state dinners and dazzling balls of Havana amazed European visitors, to whom existence in Cuba seemed an unbroken succession of luxurious pleasures, larded with hours of delicious ease. Ladies were pampered with comforts "such as only the most favored on earth have ever known." They never touched the earth with the soles of their dainty shoes. They entered silken upholstered carriages in the marble-paved courtyard of their homes. They shopped from their equipages in the Turkish fashion, never crossing the threshold of a shop. Silks, linens, laces, bric-a-brac were brought out on trays for their inspection. For supersensitive ladies, goods were brought to their own drawing-rooms for selection.

The country vied with the city in the magnificence of its living. At an estate in Santa Clara the mistress kept hundreds of servants to administer to her house guests and two hundred conveyances in her stables to fetch other guests to her entertainments. According to a pleasant country custom several families would go to a neighboring estate for a surprise party. With great abandonment, clatter and chatter, they would drive up beautiful avenues colonnaded with royal palms, which had been planted before "Old Wolfe Putnam" helped Lord Albemarle storm Morro Castle in 1762. Welcomed royally, they dined and danced, then bore off the host and his family with them, and proceeded to the next "picnic."

In provincial towns, tournaments were in vogue; cavaliers, dressed in knightly court garb with plumed hats, speared iron-rings hanging from gibbets and crowned ladies Queens of Love and Beauty. Humbler country folk doted on gander-pulls and bet high stakes on chosen contestants. From strong tree branches unfortunate ganders with tallow-greased necks would be tied by the feet to dangle head downward. At full speed, riders on horse-back would dash by and make a grab for the greasy neck. The gallant fellow who first succeeded in pulling off the gander's head was acclaimed the winner. Spanish governors encouraged the *guajiros* in the "innocent" pastime, for, as the Cuban gentry charged, "they liked everything which contributed to brutalize the people."

Though the Spaniards tried hard to stimulate enthusiasm for bull-fighting, the sport never really gained the people's affection—perhaps because it was so peculiarly identified with Spain. But in this third quarter of the century they made the most elaborate efforts to give éclat to the bull-run. Yet few Creole gentlemen appeared at these events, and no ladies. The crowds were made up mostly of Spaniards. The Creoles, who were on the side of the bull, went mainly to hiss the Spaniards' bad horsemanship and poor sportsmanship.

The spectacle was sickeningly brutal. The blindfolded horses were made to cavort disemboweled until they died in agony. The bull was not given half a chance. Just before his entrance he was crippled by being struck over the haunches with an iron bar, and further rendered less formidable by having been starved for twenty-four hours. When the bull was nearing exhaustion, four uncloaked men presented themselves bearing *banderillas* to stick into the creature's neck. The *banderillas* were yard-long wooden sticks decorated with colored paper and having an iron hook provided with percussion caps and firecrackers, which exploded, burning and tearing the flesh and lashing the bull into revived fury. The Catalonians always became rabidly joyous at this part of the spectacle and howled for the bull, which they called "the Yankee," to be killed. Here the killer entered; and, according to his performance, received plaudits and sombreros, or rinds and skins of melons and bananas on which the spectators had gorged themselves during the show.

Although the Cubans have never been noted for a superflux of piety, considering weddings, funerals, christenings merely as a background for social events, the wealth of the mid-century decades was reflected in the ostentation of the churches. In Trinidad, where the inhabitants revealed more fervor in their devotion, the celebrations of Holy Week were events of major interest to the island, and drew not only the population of neighboring districts but distinguished visitors from Havana and Santiago, and tobacco planters from far-off Pinar del Rio. The processions of Holy Thursday were an imitation of those famous magnificent and solemn spectacles of Seville. Life-sized effigies of the saints, clothed in rich satins, elaborately embroidered in gold and studded with jewels, were promenaded through the streets on the shoulders of prominent citizens. Leading families divided among themselves the care and attention of these images, and ruinous rivalry over the splendor and richness of the saints' and their bearers' apparel often cost the price of a dowry or a hundred slaves. Patios were robbed of blossoms and gardens stripped to cover the streets with flowers. Balconies were hung with banners, "mantones," tapestries. Citizens and visitors, dressed in their finest clothes, took positions in doorways and windows to watch the procession pass. A traditional itinerary was marked by tall stone crosses cut into the walls of houses, and known as stations of the Calvary. The way may be followed today, for the plan and architecture of Trinidad, most fascinating of all Cuban towns, has changed little in these last seven or eight decades.

City funerals of the wealthy were only slightly less well attended than the Holy Week Processions. When a death occurred, invitation cards were printed immediately, and female friends gathered to write the names and addresses of all acquaintances who possessed carriages. The longer the procession, the more successful the funeral. Well-to-do families kept several sets of livery with which to dress their slaves for these occasions. Friends lent their liveried Negroes in batches. The undertaker provided others, if still more were desired. The Negroes wore cocked hats with black cockade and tassel, silver-buckled knee-breeches, and long coats reaching to the ankles with heraldic escutcheons woven into a border of bright yarn fringe. Selected slaves performed as pallbearers. While the corpse remained in the house, all the Negroes formed a guard of honor. In the parlor the corpse lay on a raised bier surrounded by wax tapers in candlesticks six feet high, which were kept burning day and night. In a back room with walls, windows, and doors covered with black cloth, female relatives received condoling guests in silence. A midnight supper was served to the vast number of men and women who "watched" the dead. The talk in the parlor was merry, and in the relaxed intimacy of such nights many matches were made. The following day a dinner was served to almost anybody who cared to attend. When the body was removed to the church, priests and strings of acolytes bearing tall silver crosses and swinging incense-pots preceded the cortège. At the cemetery just before the body was lowered in the grave or stowed away in a niche, while the priests were chanting prayers, a friend of the deceased stepped forward with a long knife in his hand. In the presence of the company, he ostentatiously slit the dead man's burial clothes to ribbons. This finale was to prevent thieves from robbing the grave, a rank practice of those days.

Though the execution of Lopez and the Americans had made no great outward stir in Cuba, the incident aroused in citizens of the United States a new interest in Cuban affairs. An expedition of sympathizers headed by the Governor of Mississippi was formed for the purpose of avenging the executions. Had President Taylor not put his foot down on the venture, the United States might have been involved in a war with Spain half a century earlier than she was.

In the United States there were several Cuban juntas, or committees, and some Cuban newspapers that definitely favored annexation. But though Polk had made Spain an honorable offer of purchase, he had lent no encouragement to Lopez and he had frowned severely on promoters of violence.

The answer to Polk's offer had been that sooner than see the island transferred to any power, the Spaniards "would rather see it sunk in the ocean." American irritation for the past fifty years at the trade restrictions, the searching of American ships, the killing of American citizens, became acute when the steamer *Black Warrior* on its way to New York was detained in Havana on some uncleared duty charges, and a cargo of cotton worth $100,000 confiscated. The Cuban juntas used the incident to try to inflame the United States to take aggressive steps against Spain.

In October 1854 three leading American diplomats, the Ambassadors to England, France, and Spain (Buchanan, Mason, and Soulé), decided to take a simultaneous little holiday at Belgium's gay seaside resort, Ostend. There they "exchanged views" regarding the Cuban situation and drew up the amazing Ostend Manifesto. This curious document recommended to the state department that we should offer Spain $120,000,000 for Cuba. If the immediate acquisition was not accepted, and Spain's rule continued to endanger the internal peace and existence of our cherished nation, they declared, "By human and divine law we would be justified in wresting the island from Spain." The Democratic politicians lauded the manifesto, for Cuban annexation meant an extension of slave territory. The Republicans, cooling in their Cuban ardor because of the slave state situation, called it a "highwayman's plea." Spain continued indisposed to sell. But the United States did not declare war.

Disregarding entirely moral issues involved, it is not uninteresting, if idle, to speculate on what would have been the results had the United States fought Spain at that time. Because of the drain of a preceding war and the fighting side by side of American troops from various sections, the Civil War might never have come to pass, and Cuba would assuredly today be one of the richest and most prosperous states of the Union.

Various American statesmen had cast a covetous eye on Cuba as far back as 1807, when Thomas Jefferson remarked that in case of war with Spain Cuba might "add itself to our confederation." Madison saw the matter, "not that we desired Cuba for itself, but that we were afraid some European power might make a fulcrum of that position against the United States." It was largely John Quincy Adams's concern over Cuba that led to the composition of the document known as the Monroe Doctrine. In 1823 in writing to the minister in Spain, he said, "It is scarcely possible to resist the conviction that annexation of Cuba to our federal republic will be indispensable to the continuance and integrity of the Union itself." Jefferson in the same year said, "I have ever looked on Cuba as the most interesting addition which could be made to our system of states."

After 1860 America was too busy with her own internal differences to worry over the plight of Cuba. When the Civil War ended she was too sick of blood and hunger and burning to be much moved by the killing and devastation that shortly began in Cuba. At first, when the Ten Years' War commenced in 1868, there were the natural howls of resentment at the destruction of sugar estates involving loss to American capital. The American people in general sympathized with the Cuban patriots and ardently wished them success; but the long drawn-out decade of guerrilla fighting grew boring and America lost interest. Only in the storm raised by the *Virginius* episode was popular sentiment brought to seething talk of war.

6

THE TEN YEARS' WAR

Despite a prevailing opinion, Cuba prior to 1906 was not "a land of revolutions." The tenth of October, 1868, marked the first uprising in the history of the island "to be properly classed as a revolution." Before taking up the rifle and the machete, the Cubans had submitted reasonable and just demands to Spanish consideration. According to Señor Cabrera, what they asked was: "A constitutional system in place of the autocracy of the captain-general, freedom of the press, cessation of the exclusion of Cubans from public office, unrestricted industrial liberty, abolition of restrictions on the transfer of landed property, the right of assembly and of association, representation in the Cortes, and local self-government." Spain would accede to none of these demands, which were for the most part identical with the Thirteen Colonies' demands to England. And while Spain paradefully extolled the "ever faithfulness" of her colony before the world, she kept in Cuba a soldier under arms for every four white adults. The soldiers' board and keep she charged to Cuba's account.

Fate tied neatly together some significant threads in the Cuban tapestry by selecting the village of Yara for the launching of that war cry that was to reverberate through Spain's diplomatic halls and leave an empty echo presaging the loss of her last colonial jewel. It was in Yara (the Indian town of Jaxa) that the Cacique Hatuey, Cuba's first martyr in the cause of liberty, had been burned at the stake. Now three and a half centuries later near the spot of the Indian's agony, the fighting idealist, de Céspedes, having freed his own slaves and being supported by a few gentlemen who followed his example, took up the avenging torch that was to light the sacrificial way to end forever Spanish oppression in Cuba.

Before the gates of the de Céspedes plantation *Demajuga,* 147 men swore "Independence or Death." By the New Year, 26,000 patriots had been infected with the cause of liberty and added to the insurgent forces. A majority of these were slaves given their freedom in exchange for war services. On April twentieth, 1869, the Constitution of the Cuban Republic was drawn up and de Céspedes was selected President. Bayamo was made the provisional capital of the new republic. The people of Bayamo, along with those of Camagüey, Sancti Spiritus, Trinidad, and the surrounding districts, were the real aristocrats of Cuba. Old Creole families there could truthfully boast of having kept their Castilian strains undiluted, and point with reasonable pride to their gentle ancestry. Bayamo alone was the birthplace of a score of Cuba's most illustrious men. Among them were José Antonio Saco, the philosopher, educator, and patriot; Zenea and Fornaris, the distinguished poets; the patriot Carlos Manuel de Céspedes, who was the first president of that republic which died; and the patriot Tomás Estrada Palma, the first president of the republic which lived, and for which the United States stood sponsor at baptism in 1902. Bayamo thus was a fitting choice of a first capital. But the exigencies and hazards of war kept the government itself constantly on the move, and Bayamo was burned by the people late in 1869 to make it useless to the attacking Spaniards.

Señor Morales Nemus, as the newly appointed minister to the United States, was sent to ask recognition of the American government. President Grant in his message of December 6, 1869, while expressing his sympathies and warm feelings for the Cubans, declared the *de facto* political organization of the insurgents not sufficient to justify a recognition of belligerency. And indeed a United States envoy would have been hard put to follow the movements of the peripatetic capital, which was forced to change its seat on very short notice and to hide itself in mountain fastnesses, where the Spaniards themselves could not find the chiefs of office.

The activities of the Ten Years' War remained in the eastern provinces of the island. At no time was Havana threatened. The war was erratically supported by a Cuban junta in New York— "active in the established departments of propaganda, collections and gun running." The chief leader in the field was General Máximo Gómez, a Santo Domingan. The second fighter of importance was a young mulatto named Antonio Maceo. The Cuban troops were made up largely of blacks. No real battles were fought. It was pure guerrilla from first to last. The resident soldiery which joined sides with the Spaniards were known as Volunteers. They corresponded to the Tories in the American

Revolution, but they were a far more powerful group in Cuba than their counterparts were in America.

Count Valmasedo, the Spanish Commandant, to stop the hide-and-seek procedure of guerrilla activities, issued a proclamation from ruined Bayamo, saying: (1) "Every man from the age of fifteen years upward found away from his place of habitation will be shot. (2) Every unoccupied habitation will be burned by the troops. (3) Every habitation from which no white flag floats, as a signal that its occupants desire peace, will be reduced to ashes." Valeriano Weyler, a subordinate officer, later to become the most hated man ever in Cuba, gained his epithet "The Butcher" in carrying out these drastic orders.

The Cubans answered the proclamation by applying the torch to the houses of all Spanish sympathizers. General bloodthirsty distraction prevailed. Curses, recriminations, screams of terror and pain rent the towns with hideous bedlam. Both sides were guilty of horrible butcheries. Old people say it is a wonder the children of Santa Clara, Camagüey, and Oriente who first saw the light during that decade of confusions were not born idiots. A staccato turmoil so gripped the three eastern provinces that nowhere did there seem a safe and serene spot of ground. Only in the sky was there tranquillity, where scavenger buzzards wheeled in smug contentment.

On Hallowe'en, 1873, a free-lance filibuster named *Virginius* was captured twenty miles off the Jamaican coast by the Spanish gunboat *Tornado*. The *Virginius* had formerly been American-owned, but was now employed by Cuban sympathizers to carry supplies, and by means of forged papers she was still sailing under the protection of the American flag. Captain Joseph Frye and a crew of one hundred and forty-odd, made up largely of American citizens and a few Britishers, were taken into Santiago and imprisoned in a slaughterhouse. After a mockery of a trial, on November fourth at four o'clock in the afternoon, four of the men were lined up against the slaughterhouse wall and riddled with Spanish bullets. On the seventh, thirty-seven more, including

Captain Frye, were shot down. The next day eight more were slaughtered. The lives of the remaining ninety-odd were saved by a thrilling nick-of-time arrival of Sir Lambton Lorraine, Commander of the British sloop-of-war *Niobe,* who rushed his ship from Jamaica and threatened to bombard the city if the butchery was not stopped.

Excitement coursed through the pulses of America, as newspaper headlines grew tall and thick with hints of war. But the United States navy was in no condition to fight. And it was proved that the *Virginius* was unlawfully engaged in supplying munitions to the insurgents. So America merely cherished a stronger hatred for Spain, while the exhausted Cubans were inspired with new zeal.

As is usual in revolutionary war, it was the landed gentry who suffered most cruelly. Leading families of Camagüey, Sancti Spiritus, Bayamo, Trinidad, and Santiago sacrificed everything for the cause. The Romero family alone gave $200,000. To get funds for munitions ladies pawned their gorgeous harness and trappings with metallic decorations of solid gold and silver, which were the "wonder even of fashionable Parisians," whose harness was ornamented only with plated gold. The slaves had all to gain, nothing to lose. The *guajiros* possessed little besides palm-thatched houses, which could be replaced within a day. The great plantation homes of the gentlefolk were burned; their furniture, their heirlooms, their libraries, carried off by the Spanish soldiers. Wives and daughters of gentlemen revolutionaries were thrown into cramped prisons. Today in Sancti Spiritus or Trinidad, one meets prominent men and women with family trees spreading over three colonial centuries who were born in prisons or on roadsides, where their captive mothers had only raw Spanish recruits to act as midwives.

Don Alcides Betancourt, a distinguished lawyer of Camagüey, can remember when as a little boy of five he and his pregnant mother and older brothers and sisters were captured in the mountains, where his father, an insurgent general, had removed them

from their townhouse for safety. The Spaniards took them a two
days' journey back to Camagüey in a decrepit ox-cart, which
joggled unmercifully over the treacherous, rutted roads. When he
was not yelling from banging his head on the side of the cart,
little Alcides was enjoying the flash of fire from rifles—to him
they were jolly firecrackers. His mother, from the cruel jolting,
gave premature birth to another little brother along the route;
and because of lack of attention she died in agony of septic poisoning in prison four days later. The home in town was wrecked,
all the inherited possessions gone. Thousands of householders in
the towns suffered a fate similar to that of the Betancourts. On
the plantations it was the same—only stone walls of great houses
were left standing, blackened and empty; gardens were trampled;
cattle, hogs, horses, all gone; sugar cane burnt; slaves free, hungry,
insolent, and demanding.

As the war dragged on, it degenerated more and more into
banditry and pilfering—and finally settled into a deadlock. To
pacify the island, Spain at last sent her foremost military mind,
General Martínez Campos. By some tricky diplomacy full of fair
promises he beguiled the Cubans into a peace. On February tenth,
1878, in a war-wrecked farmhouse at Zanjón, a village in
Camagüey Province, the Pact of Zanjón was signed. The Cubans
turned in their arms. The Ten Years' War was over.

Over, too, were the days of lavish colonial entertaining in those
eastern districts. Only the great avenues of royal palms leading
from monumental entrance gateways to the ruins of plantation
houses remained as testimony of former grace and grandeur. The
owners—those who were left alive—and their families regarded
the ashes of their habitations ruefully. It was hard for any except
those made of unadulterated martyr fiber to thrill at the sacrifice.
On the surface, nothing had been accomplished except the freeing of their slaves. The upper classes themselves were still slaves
to Spain, but now completely impoverished, and filled with more
grief and bitterness than exaltation.

Yet the aristocratic idea was by no means dead. In the gala

days, even great wealth had been no lever to an exalted social position without the heritage of blood. And now, though poor, the thoroughbreds were still the thoroughbreds, and they loftily cut off social intercourse with the Spaniards. Not even the captain-general was admitted to the seclusion of a Cuban's home. Once a year only, at a national feast day, they paid haughty respect to him at public functions. Rarely now did Cuban women marry Spaniards—if they did, they were ostracized by Cuban aristocrats.

The Cuban losses in the decade of warfare had reached 50,000 dead; the Spanish, 208,000. The latter high figure was due to deaths from fevers. The cost in money had amounted to $300,-000,000. This sum was added to the Cuban debt, for Cuba was made to pay for the expenses of both sides.

Spain speedily began to break her promises. So in reality Cuba's sacrifices and sufferings had seemingly gained nothing—except an intangible sense of her potential power. But she had trained in endurance and skill young men who were to be her leaders in the fight of 1895. The seventeen years' interim was virtually no more than a truce. As Chapman, following Saco, so pertinently observes, the Ten Years' War had been a necessary preliminary to the winning of independence. Cubans needed "tradition of heroism and self-sacrifice upon which to rear a structure of patriotism that would embrace all elements of Cuban citizenry."

7

FROUDE AND HENRY ADAMS
VISIT THE ISLAND

The years from 1878 to 1895 were virtually a period of preparation for the next struggle for freedom. At least so a large number of the Creoles regarded them. The fields were planted anew and cultivated; fresh batches of children were begotten and reared;

trafficking and *fiesta* resumed their former prominent places in the pattern. Soon the mechanics and overtones of tropical, Spanish-blooded civilization seemed to move in their wonted ways, languorous, sensuous, inefficient, old-fashioned, fatalistic, charming. But beneath the surface of quieting routine, the obsession of freedom continued to gnaw vulture-like at the breasts of patriots, while the itch for political sinecures made less noble-purposed citizens claw at the air impatiently as they orated about freedom and honor.

The thinking Cubans were by no means at one in their hopes for the destiny of Cuba. A great number discredited the stability of their own people and did not consider themselves fitted to conduct a successful government. The inhabitants in general, they maintained, were almost totally unconcerned for the evils of their country; they did not read, had no interest in improving their characters, and had inherited from the Spanish ancestry a strong passion for obtaining political office, "a desire almost epidemic among Hispanic people." The thinkers distrusted the motives of many so-called patriots, whose object they declared was not to do good to the country, but to rise from nothingness into power. Imprudent and unlawful procedures of former revolutionary juntas in New York, which they investigated, forced them to confess they were doubtful if Creole citizens could properly carry out such an institution. The contributors to former juntas had supported it for financial gain—and "never were they heard to utter a liberal principle." These revolutionaries, they said, "manifest an unquenchable thirst for riches and privileges; and when they think of liberty they fancy the enjoyment of this blessing as intended exclusively for themselves, as if freedom did not require a reciprocal regard for everybody's rights."

Agreeing with these Cuban opinions and doubts about Cubans, intelligent Americans residing in Cuba—men like Atkins, the leading sugar planter—had little faith that Cubans were anywhere near being ready to take up the reins of government. And while little people talked and argued this way and that, Destiny, only semi-aware of men's voices, approached the hour of issue, which two immaculate patriots like Martí and Palma were hastening to bring about.

In the interim distinguished visitors came: among them, James Anthony Froude, the English critic, in 1887, and Henry Adams, the Bostonian world-traveler, in 1894. Before he relaxed and gave himself up to the seduction of Cuban life, Froude cast about him with a clinical eye and jotted down shrewd notes. With a quick-pointing finger he demonstrated that diseased spot, whence would ensue Cuba's chief future ills, after she attained her eventual freedom. "Official corruption," he wrote, "is engrained in the character and habits of the Spanish people. . . . Judges allowed their decisions to be influenced under Philip III as much as today in the colonies of Queen Christina; and *when a fault is the habit of a people* it survives political reforms and any number of turnings of the kaleidoscope." Typical of a thousand cases was that of Guzman de Alfarache, who was robbed of his baggage by a friend. The facts were clear; the thief was caught with Guzman's clothes on his back; but he had influential friends—he was acquitted. He prosecuted Guzman for a false accusation, got a judgment and ruined him.

But like even the most excoriating of Cuba's critics when they possess sensibilities worth a few grains of salt, Froude was entranced with the magnitude and fullness of the island's life. He had thought of Cuba as a decrepit state, bankrupt and on the edge of social dissolution, but he found "Havana at least a grand imposing city—a city which might compare for beauty with any in the world." Amidst Spanish faces, Spanish voices, and Spanish smells he lingered in the faded grandeur of palaces and plazas, of towers and colonnades, of monasteries and churches—and loved it.

"Churches here," he whimsically noted, "are as thick as public houses in a Welsh town." Church beyond church, palace beyond palace, the narrow streets where neighbors on either side might shake hands out of the upper stories, the private houses with the

windows grated towards the street with glimpses through the
street door into the court and garden within, with its cloisters, its
palm trees, and its fountains; the massiveness of the stone work,
the curious old-fashioned bookstalls, the dirt, the smell, the carriages, the swearing drivers, the black-robed priest gliding along
the footway—Havana was to him another Toledo or Valladolid.
He considered what the scene would have been if England had
been the colonizer instead of Spain, and he was thankful to give
the glory to Spain. "We English have built in the West Indies,"
he said, "as if we were but passing visitors, wanting only tene-
ments to be occupied for a time. The Spaniards built as they built
in Castile . . . as if by some Aladdin's lamp a Castilian city had
been taken up and set down again unaltered on the shore of the
Caribbean Sea."

He talked with the Americans at the hotel in which he was
staying and found them delightful individually and rather dreadful *en masse*. He put together what his historical researches had
taught him and what he gathered first hand. "The Americans,"
he wrote, "looked at the island which lay so temptingly near
them, but they were wise in their generation. They reflected that
to introduce into an Anglo-Saxon republic so insoluble an element
as a million Spanish Roman Catholics alien in blood and creed,
with half a million blacks to swell the dusky flood which runs too
full among them already, would be to invite an indigestion of
serious consequence." The hills of solid iron and virgin copper
which he learned about, he knew the Americans would one day
develop—and at the Cubans' invitation. But he knew the Americans would not come during the present administration, for
the profits would have been swallowed up in taxation. He
doubted if America would *ever* find it to her interest to *annex*
Cuba, although he felt she would most probably be "the supreme
arbiter" of the island's fate.

At length, to escape the persistent buzz of the American-tourist-
voices in the city hotel, Froude went to a small country inn—"on

the sea seven miles from Havana to a place called Vedado."
There he luxuriated in the "beautiful wild country," in the "delicious rooms," where the sea washed coral rocks under the windows. He loafed down at the village with its picturesque harbor
and fishing boats and nets hung to dry, where people were kindly
but never bothered him with questions, and where the salty
jargon of swarthy boatmen did not grate his ears.

While entertained at some country estates, he looked into the
aftermath of slavery, which had been finally abolished not two
years before (1886), Cuba being the last of all civilized countries
to say, "Now there are no slaves." Those who had been slaves,
Froude found, continued to work at the same locations, receiving wages instead of food and maintenance and were well content with the change. "This remarkable revolution had been carried out with an ease and completeness which found no parallel
in any other slave-owning country."

Returning to Havana again to take steamer in pursuing his
odyssey, Froude recalled that the city's charm was unfortunately
somewhat corroded by its evil smells—"odors worse than those
Coleridge found at Cologne and cursed in rhyme." The drains
of Havana, he discovered, like orange blossoms, gave off their
most fragrant vapors in the dark hours. As the rowboat put out
to carry him to the steamer lying in the bay, the smell of three
centuries' pollution rose overpoweringly when the oars stirred
the water. And the phosphorescent light shivering with a sickly,
sulphur-like brilliance made him fancy he was in Charon's boat,
crossing Acheron in Hades. Taking a last backward glance at
Cuba's shore, as his ship steamed into the ocean, the Britisher
summed up his impressions: "Perhaps they will yet succeed in
achieving freedom; but Spanish, at any rate, they are to the bone
and marrow, and Spanish they will continue."

Six years after Froude had made copious objective notes of
what was spread before him in Cuba, Henry Adams, accompanied by Clarence King, drifted into the precipitous little town
of Santiago on a day in January 1894. Adams looked up into

azure space; into himself; into the odd pretty life about him, as multi-colored as stained glass at Chartres; into himself again. With impeccable taste, plucking only a perfect plum or two to enrich his education, he arranged a few choice phrases in his note-book. "The picturesque Cuban society, which King knew well," he wrote, "was more amusing than any other that one had yet discovered in the whole broad world, but made no profession of teaching anything unless it were Cuban Spanish or the *danza;* and neither on his own nor on King's account did the visitor ask any loftier study than that of the buzzards floating on the trade-wind down the valley to Dos Bocas, or the colors of sea and shore at sunrise from the height of the Gran Piedra; but, as though they were still twenty years old and revolution were as young as they, the decaying fabric, which had never been solid, fell on their heads and drew them with it into an ocean of mischief."

If only Henry Adams had given us the details of that Cuban society which he found more amusing than any in the whole broad world, or had taken us with him on some secret excursion where he himself waded even ankle-deep in a tiny pond of mis-chief! Instead he censored his personal recollections sharply and paused to speculate on revolution. "In the half-century between 1850 and 1900," he wrote, "empires were always falling on one's head, and, of all lessons, these constant political convulsions taught least. Since the time of Rameses, revolutions have raised more doubts than they solved." For yet another year, however, he lingered on "these outskirts of the vortex, among the pic-turesque primitive types of a world which had never fairly been involved in the general motion and were more amusing for their torpor." The sojourn lasted long enough to convince him that whatever the American people thought or said about it, sooner or later they would have to police the West Indies, "not against Europe, but for Europe and America too."

And within four years Adams's country was to be drawn into the vortex, and those buzzards he was pleased to watch floating innocently on the trade-wind were soon to be pecking at the eyes of American youths dead on the seared and devastated hills of El Caney.

8

THE REVOLT OF '95

The Cuban insurrection of 1895 was made in the United States. It began precisely when it did, not because of any freshly resented oppressive act of Spain nor specifically because of the world depression of 1893 with the consequent economic distress to Cuba following the drop in the price of sugar, but because a Cuban living in New York named José Julián Martí decided the time was ripe. Martí was a remarkable little man, internationally known, and on the whole internationally admired. Anyone who knew anything of Cuba knew of Martí—he had lived in Europe, up and down South America, all about the Caribbean, in the United States. He wrote for foreign journals in countries his feet had not penetrated. When a half-grown boy he had dedicated his life to the cause of Cuban liberty, astounding his mother by the maturity of his words, "To many generations of slaves must succeed one generation of martyrs." Like the youthful poet Herédia, he was an exile; and more, he had the authority of the martyr to back him. For in the first year of the Ten Years' War, Martí, a frail fifteen-year-old youngster, was arrested in Havana for composing seditious poetry. His sentence was six years' hard labor in the quarries, to work shackled with chain and ball. Influence got the sentence lightened, and in 1871 he was deported to Spain, where he was permitted to study at the University of Madrid. He made a name for himself pleading the cause of Cuba in speech and writing. He did not return to Cuba until after the Pact of Zanjón. Nor was he allowed then to remain long. Captain-

General Blanco regarded him as a crazy man, but a highly dangerous one, and sent him once again a prisoner to Spain in September 1879. Martí did not see his native soil for sixteen years. Shortly at liberty, he lived in South America for a space of years, served Uruguay and the Argentine as consul in the United States, and then for many years made his headquarters in New York, continuing zealously to agitate sympathy for his country's struggle for freedom. His quiet magnetism and sincerity commanded attention and confidence. Everywhere he was hospitably received and honored. From 1891 to 1895 he labored superhumanly "forging the Cuban colonies into a single effective instrument for revolution." He reorganized the dubious Cuban junta in New York with Estrada Palma as its president and bound it together in a remarkably efficient unanimity. He collected money and gifts of ammunition.

Martí had something of the power of a great evangelist. The Cuban cigar-makers in Tampa and Key West worshiped him. He was called The Master, and as if Jesus had spoken, saying, "Sell all thou hast and give," Martí's words stirred them to sacrifice for the cause everything but the barest necessities of life. Men gave up smoking and turned their watches into cash; women proffered their gold baubles and feast-day mantillas. Even wedding rings went on the altar. Such was the gentle persuasion of The Master.

By the end of 1894 all was in readiness for active revolt, when the three ships outfitted by the junta were seized by the American government in observation of neutrality laws. Disappointed, but not shaken in resolve, Martí went on with fresh plans and operations. On February twenty-fourth, 1895, in the village of Baire near Santiago, the new cry of freedom, the *Grito de Baire,* was launched. On April first, the fighting mulatto, Antonio Maceo, bearing the scars of twenty-five wounds received in the Ten Years' War, arrived from exile. Ten days later, on a black tempestuous night, Martí himself touched his native soil for the first time in sixteen years, when his little boat was tossed onto the

Playitas beach. Accompanying him was seventy-two-year-old General Máximo Gómez, the Santo Domingan commander-in-chief of the last war. Together the two foremost heroes of the Cuban people dropped to their knees on the sands in sacramental resolution. Martí, having proceeded from New York to Santo Domingo, had called at the cottage of Gómez in Monte Cristo and tendered him command of the army. Abandoning his family, "in whose company he was living calmly and happily," the old veteran set off with the poet-liberator and four followers, declaring, "We will conquer and be free, cost what it may, or happen what will, and though we have to raise a hospital in each corner and a tomb in each home."

Martí had never been a soldier; and because of the greater service he could render in foreign countries, it was not intended that he should remain in Cuba. But he knew that a taste of fire would prevent enemies from calling him "rice powder patriot." Within six weeks of his landing, Martí was dead—shot from his white horse on May nineteenth, after having been betrayed by a guide.

The Spanish glee knew no bounds. The Queen Regent cabled ecstatic congratulations to the captain-general in Cuba. "The soul of the revolution" being dead, the Spanish looked upon the war as finished. They had not taken it seriously even at first. One Spanish officer had expressed excessive boredom at the prospect of having to "chase mountain goats." "Mere bandits already in flight," some dispatches characterized the new conflict. Tories called it "a war of Negroes against whites." As far back as 1823 Spain had expressed herself as feeling peculiarly secure about her "Pearl," because "the fear the Cubans have of Negroes is the best weapon Spain has to guarantee its domination in that island." And now being rid of Martí and his fantastic power for stirring men's hearts, Spain exulted in the belief that the white Cubans would straightway recall their loyalty to the Crown.

Spain's triumphant transports at Martí's demise quickly sobered, however. For the death of the "soul of the revolution" proved as effective in rousing the Cubans as some miraculous transfiguration. Recruits flocked around the standards of aged Gómez and prime Maceo with fanatical spirit. Spain became so alarmed at new slashing victories of the rebels that she dispatched Martínez Campos—"her greatest general," who had settled the Ten Years' War—to resolve the present one with celerity. But the three years' struggle from 1895 to 1898 was destined to be more devastating and more bloody than the prolonged decade of warfare had been.

From the first the rebels fought against monstrous odds. They were outnumbered five to one. They had no uniforms and small rations. Their equipment was haphazard and casual since ammunition and war gear were most uncertain of delivery from filibustering ships. Rifles, shotguns and pistols of quaint and antique models served as firearms for many. For swords, sabers, bayonets, wire-nippers, trail-cutters, they used the ubiquitous machete. The machete is a large heavy-backed, keen-edged knife about two feet long with a short thick wooden handle and a curving blade slightly convex. Designed as the perfect implement for cutting sugar cane, the machete is the king of weapons to the Cuban, as the scimitar was to the Saracen, as the kriss is to the Malayan, the revolver to the Yankee, and the razor to the Southern Negro. So companionable in cane-cutting, soil-cultivation, meat-chopping, and a hundred household uses, the machetes can be diabolically mortal in angry fight. All Cubans of every station and degree possessed them and they used them with infallible and lusty skill.

Spain's military strategy "being largely based on principles of defensive warfare rather than attack, which the circumstances called for," proved embarrassingly inefficacious. Her troops were almost entirely infantry; when considering the terrain, the climate, and the here-and-gone movements of the guerrillas, cavalry was what was needed. As his most effective *coup,* Campos expended great labor and money in constructing across the island *trochas,* or trenches, with a line of blockhouses and barbed wire entanglements to obstruct the Cuban advance. But whenever the notion struck them, Gómez and Maceo jumped their men back and forth over Campos's *trochas* with more easy audacity than they would have at a chessboard.

Surrounded by the armies and navies of Spain, outnumbered fantastically, the untrained Cubans proved unconquerable. The peculiar power of the rebels lay in their horses and machetes: for they had spent their lives on horseback; and the Spaniard justly had a disintegrating horror of the cane knives. As General Boza said, speaking of that most ghastly item of the revolution, a machete charge, "What a horrible thing it is. We are changed by it from men into beasts, lashed on to a hunger for blood and butchery." The sight of the yelling rebels (mostly blacks), waving deadly naked blades and dashing down upon them on excited steeds, threw rank after rank of otherwise courageous Spaniards into panic. The blinding bafflement of spurting blood and the physical agony of steel cleaving through bone and sinew transcended human endurance. No such terrifying fighting had been known in the civilized world since the introduction of gunpowder into Europe.

Gómez, the wily commander-in-chief, exhibited superlative military shrewdness in organization and execution; but it was the mulatto Antonio Maceo who caught the imagination of the whole world by the daring and ferocity of his machete attacks. They called Maceo The Centaur, because he and his horse seemed fabulously one, and The Lion, because he was magnificent in destruction. The negro in him scorned the white man's unromantic trigger-pulling and cried out for a cutting edge. With a bloody death-dealing machete in his dusky hand, Maceo attained the fearsomeness and grandeur of god-head. He was a handsome, stalwart buck of heroic mold, weighing some two hundred and ten pounds. He wore a little beard much like George V's and as elegant as any to be seen on Paris boulevards. His odd passion for frequent bathing and his penchant for perfume and clean linen, which amused his brother, General José Maceo, were

quaintly inconsistent with the fury of his onslaughts and his ultimate reputation as the greatest military commander ever produced by the Negro race.

A noteworthy consideration of the war's history was the significant part blacks and colored played in it. Although completely trustworthy figures of exact numbers cannot be obtained,
it is the opinion of several prominent Havana lawyers who have
made considerable study of the subject that not more than one-
third of the rebels in arms were white. And the majority of historians agree that the colored population formed "the backbone
of the rebel army." So it can be safely surmised that certainly not
less than half were black or colored. As a result of which—Lind-
say has pointed out this fact—the colored race has secured a
standing and influence in Cuba which it does not enjoy in any
other country where the Caucasian is dominant.

The Ten Years' War having failed largely because it never
penetrated the western half of the island, Gómez resolved to carry
the revolution, with the help of Maceo, to the tip of the west.
The old general had set his heart to win his war even if it involved the destruction of Cuba; or as he proclaimed in a manifesto of November sixth, 1895, he was determined to "furl triumphantly, even over ashes and ruins, the flag of the Republic
of Cuba." If the Spaniards would not have the grace to leave
where they were unwelcome, he would make the island useless
to them by destroying every possible source of revenue. First, he
ordered all the sugar plantations to stop their labors on pain of
severe penalties. Then more drastically, he ordered the plantations totally destroyed, their cane and outbuildings burned. (This
proclamation applied to all plantations except certain ones upon
which he levied a ransom "tax," the price of being spared destruction. By this taxation he added materially to the insurgents'
thin financial resources.) Soon the torch became a terrifying
weapon. Conflagration and confusion spread over the land. With
the policy of terrorism Gómez proposed to stop the economic life
of the island, and by adding to the prevailing want and unem-

ployment, to drive men into the rebel ranks. As a consequence of conditions created by Gómez-measures, many peace-at-any-price men among them were forced into the war—and Cubans, despite all contrary opinions, are instinctively a peace-loving people.

As the "invasion" swept westward it carried flame and misery, pillage and plunder with it. (Calixto García, a veteran of the past war, was left in charge in the east, to continue unrelenting disturbance there.) Captain-General Campos with a hundred thousand troops at his command seemed powerless to halt the destruction. "His columns were impotent to check the fluid forces of the insurrection." Gómez and Maceo had made guerrilla warfare a military science. To the machete and the torch they soon added dynamite as a potent weapon. Bridges were dynamited; railway lines were totally destroyed. Around Christmas, Gómez audaciously swept up to Mariano, a suburb of Havana, terrorizing and burning, a wily maneuver to attract attention, while Maceo was cutting a havoc-making swath through the westernmost province of Pinar del Rio. On January twenty-second Maceo had reached Mantua, winning recruits and heroic fame all along the way. In all technical movements, the insurgents had had the better of it. Campos, broken in reputation and having lost favor in Havana, was recalled. General Valeriano Weyler, the somber Marquis of Teneriffe, known in Cuba as "The Butcher" since the Ten Years' War, was selected as the man most capable of squashing the "colossal brigandage" with finality and expedition.

Three days after Maceo rode triumphantly into Mantua, Weyler —ceremoniously blessed by the Bishop of Barcelona, and his vast army placed under the holy guardianship of the Mother of Christ —sailed from Spain to clean up the mess in Cuba. On February tenth he arrived to begin his Augean task.

That chaos about which Tacón had howled in derision, yet found highly stimulating to his formidable abilities, was a child's playground to the maelstrom upon which Weyler looked. The entire country was split asunder with distraction and division of

mind, as well as by rebel dynamiting and incendiarism and loyal-
ist reprisals.

Although there was much disloyalty in the capital when
Campos departed, Havana was far from being united in heart
with the revolutionaries, who they knew would unhesitatingly
have ravaged their golden city, smeared it with gore, burned it
black. Had they not beheld the sickish pink glow in the sky that
proclaimed the awesome burning of estates at their very gates?
So when new detachments of "dusky boys of Spain arrived, the
bayonets twinkling over them," many citizens of Havana oddly
regarded them in the light of rescuers and made festival. Roses
were dropped from balconies and "birds adorned with ribbons
were flung by fair hands from windows into the ranks." At night
excited children danced to the music of Andalusian bands in the
streets strung with red and yellow flags. And certain prominent
folk not only grasped the cool, finely-shaped hand of the new
governor, but bent to kiss it fervently. At Weyler's arrival the
clergy, merchants, tobacco- and sugar-planters, members of the
professional class and many of the old conservative families were
not in favor of independence—though the younger sons of the
latter were, and had joined with the rebels. On the whole the
insurrection was being carried on by idealists, upper-class youths,
would-be politicians, bewildered country people, brigands, and
Negroes. But by the time Weyler left, due to the severity of his
methods, virtually the entire population was in sympathy with
the revolution.

Weyler saw only one way to bring order to the island. He
introduced the policy later known as "reconcentration." All Cubans in the country districts were ordered into garrisoned towns
or into guarded encampments surrounded by trenches or stock-
ades, out of which they could not move on penalty of death
and forfeiture of property. Enemies of Weyler cried out that the
policy contravened the principles of civilized warfare in important particulars, for it involved making prisoners of noncom-
batants, and neglected "to afford them the treatment which the

least humane nation concedes to military captives." But the insurgents themselves had hardly been making civilized warfare, and in their own ruthless destruction they had taken small care of the comfort of their victims. Weyler's scheme was uncompromising, brutal. As a military measure, however, it was not altogether unjustifiable, as thinking Cubans today admit. In a sense he had taken the idea from the insurgents themselves, for Gómez had previously ordered Spanish sympathizers to garrisoned towns and had moved Cuban women and children to the hills. Weyler did order provisions made for rations and housing, and he set aside certain nearby areas for the cultivation of food crops. In the general callousness of war, however, he failed to see that his orders were carried out, and his deputies grafted unconscionably. But famine stalked the land anyhow. Long before Weyler's coming Gómez had strictly forbidden the carrying into the towns of food products from the country. And the rebels themselves now attempted to starve their own people by destroying the cultivated zones of the *reconcentrados*. Cases were reported proving that the patriots slipped through the guarded barriers into the zones where food crops for the Cubans were being raised and uprooted the young plants. Gómez's tactics brought on about as much misery as Weyler's. The net result created a potent publicity in the United States.

There was no denying the horrors of *reconcentrado*, as exaggerated sometimes as the United States press pictured them. In the crowded towns the hungry multitudes were forced to seek employment where there were no jobs and to beg charity from hungry people. Disease vied with starvation in carrying the standards of death. Tales to make devils weep could be told with authenticity, and the pencils of American journal artists had small need to draw from nightmare models. Wretches by the thousands dropped in their tracks and died. In the province of Havana alone half a hundred thousand perished. President McKinley in his message of December 1897 referred to Weyler's policy of reconcentration as "extermination." "The only peace it could beget was that of the wilderness and the grave." In the name of humanity Weyler was besought through the American and European press to relinquish his cruel policy. Interviewers called in person to learn what manner of man the brute could be.

The Marquis of Teneriffe was a general of unsoldierly bearing, diminutive, rather shriveled, but extraordinarily dynamic. He was very dark, with that quality of murky complexion that often proclaims the ill-functioning of intestines. His clothes were black (it was his custom to wear alpaca); his hair, black; his beard, a blacker black. His dark eyes were alert, acute, penetrating, fearless. They were not black, but the color of "sherry with ice in it" according to an American lady visitor; and on occasions they "twinkled naughtily." His speech had the authority of a tragic actor of the old school, ranging from the peremptory, harsh, menacing, to the gallant and gracious. There was a subtle magnetism in his voice and in his cool hand-clasp. Weyler was a man who gave himself completely up to whatever job was set for him, as his firm long chin, protruding with indomitable perseverance, revealed; but he loved life itself no more joyously than long-lived Thomas Hardy, yet was he destined to retain breath in his unenthusiastic body for ninety years and to die "only yesterday."

Weyler's chief delight in Havana was his bathroom—such an apartment as would have warmed the cockles of Maceo's mulatto heart. (It is an odd parallel that these two great opposing personalities, the Spanish marquis and the Negro rebel whose brains were devoted to human destruction possessed bodies continually drawn to a bath.) With pride Weyler would show visitors this large room with walls of pale blue marble. Turkish towels were kept stacked in "beautiful profusion" and there was a cane couch with pillows where the marquis could relax and take his siesta. The bath was his sanctuary from the agitations, criticisms, vituperations, horrors of the outside world. Where Lincoln read *The Tempest* to calm his mind, Weyler took a bath.

With an old-world courtesy sometimes intense, sometimes cold, sometimes weary, Weyler listened to his visitors, and quietly agreed that war was cruel, that all wars were cruel in their very essence and definition. His duty, he explained, was to end the suffering of the present one as quickly as possible by whatever strong means were necessary.

The truth was that the Spanish commander had met the insurgent commander more than halfway in the processes of starvation —in not scrupling, if expedient, "to raise a tomb in each home." The entire Cuban people were being ground to death between two indomitable engines of war, controlled by the stubborn wills of Weyler and Gómez, who were each implacably resolved on victory, and seemingly as callous to the cost of blood and tears as two monster automatons. The Spanish Prime Minister, backing Weyler's policy, declared, "Cuba shall remain Spanish though it takes the last man and the last *peseta*." In Spain they could not train troops fast enough. Besides the militia and Tory volunteers, as many as 200,000 regulars were in Cuba at one time, many of them mere boys.

The suffering of the Spanish troops is another painful story. Though their bravery and courage were applauded by their enemies, the privates had little interest in the fighting. They fought under compulsion, often so near exhaustion from malnutrition that death was eagerly welcomed. Disease undermined the ranks. Thousands succumbed to yellow fever. Typhoid drew the pith irrevocably from the fighting arms of score upon score. Dysentery and malaria incapacitated whole regiments. An epidemic of smallpox laid hundreds low; and young troopers, unattended, scratched the handsomeness out of their faces and died miserably from neglect. The suns of tropical summers played havoc with the foreign soldiers' headpieces and sent some of them chattering idiotically to lose themselves forever in the devouring jungles. Gómez shrewdly counted June, July, and August as his "three important allies." Another great ally was Spanish greed: the privates were rankly treated by the officers, who grafted inhumanly on their underlings' supplies and rations, forcing them to subsist on the most meager allotment of food possible, and pocketing the price of their discomfort. The odor of the scandal drifted to Spain, where members of the Cortes rose accusingly to cry that the troops were allowed to starve, while the higher officers were bringing back so much gold that they actually "caused a drop in the gold quotations."

As for the Cuban in arms, his is a phenomenal tale of prodigious endurance, inured even as he was to hardship. Whereas the Spanish soldier was often eight months in arrears in pay, the Cuban patriot fought throughout the war with no pay at all. Ammunition for him was sporadic. Quinine to relieve his malaria was most uncertain of delivery. During the third year of fighting he fared on as bitter a broth as brew from the witches' caldron in *Macbeth*. The destruction of food crops by both Cubans and Spaniards made lizards and snakes seasonable to insurgent stewpots. Occasionally soldiers would be lucky enough to bring down a buzzard, and would feast gratefully on vulture flesh that had been fattened on their dead comrades. A gorge-heaving vegetable soup concocted of weeds and grass was sometimes their diet for days on end. In many districts, however, even the grass had been burnt, and the horses themselves nuzzled desperately at stubble cinders, gnawed unnourished at tree bark, and perished, leaving to their masters a painful heritage of long foot-weariness, but temporary relief to their bellies. However, "neither the starvation of the aged and of women in the reconcentration camps," says Horatio Rubens, American counsel for the Cuban junta, "nor his own physical suffering and periodic starvation could swerve the Cuban soldier from the liberty he sought."

For eight months Maceo had miraculously withstood the concentrated efforts of troops Weyler sent against him. But on December seventh the revolution received an almost mortal wound: Maceo was killed from ambush near Punta Brava, less than a score of miles from Havana. Gómez, smitten with grief and distress, declared that Cuba had lost "the most glorious of her sons; the army, the first of her generals." The Marquis of Teneriffe paid tribute to the dead mulatto as a "valiant man, a fighter, indefatigable, tenacious." He believed success would come swiftly now. Gómez he discounted as "sick and old." He was wrong in his calculations. There was plenty of craft and fight in the old warrior yet.

Having spread the rebellion clean across the island, General Gómez avoided all direct contact with Spanish forces, and moved fox-like through the forests, dashing out from time to time to harass the enemy and to destroy or burn anything within reach. The Spanish chased the rebels futilely, got hopelessly lost, were literally bitten to death by mosquitoes, died from exposure and fevers. Then Weyler adopted Gómez's tactics with a vengeance, fought fire with fire. He gave orders to destroy everything the rebels missed, including particularly the sugar estates from which Gómez drew a ransom "tax." By July of 1897 when Cuba was wont to be at its moist loveliest, with tuberoses thick among the green corn, the entire countryside was as black and cheerless as widow-weeds.

PART III

The Spanish-American War and Leonard Wood

THE JINGO PRESS

IN October 1897, just as Weyler was convinced that victory was within his grasp, he was recalled—his friend, the Spanish Prime Minister, had been assassinated, and a new party, desirous of placating the United States, had taken control. General Blanco was returned as his successor. On November twenty-fifth the Queen Regent signed the decrees granting autonomist government to Cuba; on New Year's Day 1898, Cuban autonomy was declared established. It was what Campos had urged on his retirement as the only just and workable solution. It was what the United States had demanded for Cuba. But conciliation had come too late. The insurgents would have none of it. Gómez declared anyone who subscribed to autonomy a traitor to the patriot cause. The reconcentration policy had by now lost Spain the great mass of the middle class who had wavered in uncertainty. And the proletariat was so benumbed with misery that it was willing to endure a little more to gain a prize in which at first it had small faith.

Meanwhile, such a violent prejudice against Spain had risen in the United States that Spanish retention of the island was as unacceptable to the American public as to the Cubans. The Cuban junta in New York, under the leadership of Tomás Estrada Palma, former principal of the Central Valley School for Boys, had become increasingly powerful. In disseminating propaganda, the mild-mannered schoolmaster, undoubtedly the only worthy successor to the mantle of the martyred Martí, represented the cause of the Cuban patriots in a most admirable manner. His sincerity, his integrity, his complete unselfishness, and his inspiring devotion to the cause of Cuban liberty won the sympathy and support of the American public as no other living Cuban could have done. Practical Gómez had written to idealistic Palma significantly: "You are at the mouth of a gold mine; work it!" And Americans had responded liberally with financial assistance.

At America's insistence the reconcentration system had been virtually abandoned with the coming of Blanco, and now hundreds of thousands of perishing people were turned loose to wander aimlessly about a countryside desolate of sustenance. The situation was as bad as it was before, if not worse. The American Red Cross began to rush relief supplies to revive the dying multitudes. The insurgents, instead of being grateful, resented the intrusion. Starvation was one of Gómez's most potent weapons. Its horrors made better publicity against Spain than the faked atrocities.

The American newspapers had already given the affairs in Cuba a publicity beyond Gómez's wildest expectations. Flagrant fabrications, garbled rumors, and dreadful insinuations were passed unabashed by editors' desks and on to front pages. These newspapers had made the most of incidents growing out of filibustering, and had persistently urged the United States to recognize Cuban belligerency. Following the lead of the *World,* they had exploited Spanish "atrocities" on the island; and the New York *Journal,* under the stimulation of young Mr. Hearst's new ownership, had resorted to an aggressive policy in "uncovering" several episodes that stirred the country like Gothic romances.

But now since the framework of autonomy had been set up, and material charity flowing into Cuba began to alleviate the misery, the newspapers were reluctantly obliged to dose the hysteria of their typography with some common-sense sedatives. By the second week of January, Cuba was actually relegated in many dailies to the second page.

Then, on January twelfth, one of those fateful little incidents that lead indirectly to destiny's cataclysms took place in Havana. A group of Spanish army officers attacked some newspaper offices in revenge for printing articles which reflected on the army's conduct. It was over in an hour or so. Many witnesses declared the officers were unarmed. There was no demonstration against Americans. But Consul-General Fitzhugh Lee, portly veteran of the Confederacy, chose to see cause for grave alarm. In ambiguous cables throbbing with bugaboo innuendoes, he hinted that ships should be sent to Cuba to safeguard American life and property. After twelve days' departmental dilly-dallying, the armored cruiser *Maine* was ordered to proceed from Key West to Havana on a "courtesy" call. She entered the harbor the morning of January twenty-fifth. There was no demonstration whatsoever. The Spanish acting-captain-general paid the correct visit and sent a case of the finest old sherry as a gift to the American officers. Lee, who had been dispatching one cable after another all day reporting "No demonstration so far," dictated one final message before going to bed: "Peace and quiet reign." Even he seemed convinced now that his funk was bogus. But his perturbations and maneuvers had not been in vain; at least they had brought him the gratification of focusing a sharp shaft of limelight on his post. And incidentally they brought on a war.

For on the night of February fifteenth, 1898, the *Maine* mysteriously blew up. Two hundred and fifty-two American sailors were torn to bits by the explosion. The catastrophe occurred less than a week after a sudden uproar over the printing of a stolen private communication of the Spanish Minister, Dupuy de Lôme, in which he had contemptuously called President McKinley "a would-be politician who tries to leave a door open behind him while keeping on good terms with the jingoes of his party."

When news of the disaster was brought to Governor-General Blanco in his weathered gray palace on the Plaza de Armas, he smote his desk sorrowfully. "This," he said with dark foreboding, "is the saddest day Spain ever saw!" Tears were streaming from his eyes when he came into the reception room to meet Fitzhugh Lee, who had dashed up in a cab on his way to the waterfront.

Captain Sigsbee, commander of the *Maine,* prudently cabled, "Public opinion should be suspended until further report." Little effect his just caution had. Public hysteria engulfed the United States. The newspapers went mad in pyrotechnics of phraseology and type. Howls for vengeance on Spain reverberated throughout the nation, while Havana put on deep mourning and closed its theaters and shops. "Remember the *Maine!*" became a war-cry that called for a declaration of war.

Spain pleaded for joint investigation and arbitration in the *Maine* affair. But America, instructed by the newspapers, had immediately made up her mind to Spain's guilt, and would not consider her pleas. The majority of those who not unreasonably thought the accident might have been due to some inefficiency on the navy's part kept their mouths shut.

The *Maine* disaster crystallized American sentiment in favor of war. Since nothing can make newspapers sell like a war, publishers and editors took up the crusade with a righteous zeal that seemed to transcend holy ecstasies—one which scarcely anything but the elixir of gold could have induced. Mr. Pulitzer had originally called the tunes in exploiting the Cuban rebellion, only to be out-shouted by Mr. Hearst and beaten at his own dance. While word was sent out from the White House that there were no grounds for suspecting a plot and that the explosion must have been accidental, Mr. Hearst's inventive geniuses discovered that the Spaniards had blown up the ship; and further, the *Journal* was preparing drawings to show just how the torpedo had been placed and set off. A bold caption proclaiming "The War Ship *Maine* was Split in Two by an Enemy's Secret Infernal Machine" took up almost half a front page. When Long, Secretary of the Navy, was quoted as saying after a cabinet meeting, that the "elements of Spanish official responsibility for the *Maine* explosion might be considered eliminated," the Hearst paper charged the Secretary and Mark Hanna with having betrayed the nation to "Wall Street." (Wall Street all along had strongly opposed war.)

On March tenth the *Journal* announced that the actual declaration of war with Spain seemed to be only a few days away. However, when the naval court of inquiry finally completed its hearings after a month of investigation and deliberation, the official report was as follows: "In the opinion of the court the *Maine* was destroyed by the explosion of a submarine mine, which caused the partial explosion of two or more of the forward magazines." *The court could not fix responsibility.* The *Journal* straightway confided to the public that "suppressed testimony shows Spain is guilty of blowing up the *Maine*." (In the thirty-six years since the disaster there has not been unearthed one item of positive proof that a mine existed. The mystery is still unsolved. Certainly no Spaniard who possessed the skill to have laid such a mine would have been guilty of a deed so foolishly and patently ruinous to Spain. On the other hand, Cuban insurgents at about the end of their strength had the best reason in the world for desiring just such a sensational event to swing America into direct action against their enemy. If they would pull up growing plants, thereby starving *reconcentrados,* why should they have scrupled to destroy an alien ship for their own desperate ends? But experts seem to doubt whether they would have had the technical ability and the opportunity to lay and set off the mine, and others doubt whether they could afterwards have concealed all facts connected with the crime. Mr. Millis believes the *Maine* destroyed herself, perhaps through spontaneous explosions from unexplained causes within the ship.)

On April fourth, the *Journal* announced that its circulation had passed the 1,000,000 mark. Blood-red print had been employed as an additional sensation. The first three pages of every issue of the New York *World* from the day of the explosion on were devoted to Cuban news, principally accounts telling of plans for war. On April second, 1898, the *World* stated that there would be "from three to five days more of polite exchange of formal notes between the United States and Spain—and then war." On April seventh, it proclaimed that the President and Congress were united for war, adding that Spain had been given five days of grace "before an ultimatum will be sent by the United States," after which hostilities would begin if she did not agree to give up Cuba. Before the war was over, the *World* was to reach the phenomenally gratifying figure of 1,300,000 copies sold in a single day.

Looking backward thirty-five years to the days when he was business manager of the *World,* Mr. Seitz, in the February 1933 issue of the *Bookman,* confesses succinctly: "Between the *World* and the *Journal* we barked President McKinley into a war that was none of our business." But Mr. Pulitzer lived to repent, for "in the end the war was far from satisfying the owner of the *World.* He never wanted another one."

The fight with Spain has too often been referred to as Hearst's War, but Dana's *Sun* and Bennett's *Herald,* as well as Pulitzer's *World* and hundreds of lesser publications from coast to coast, played up the martial spirit in their most stirring trumpetings. The pulse of the people—as distinguished from their business and political leaders—responded in eager pounding.

Mr. McKinley, "bedeviled and bullied on all sides," grew haggard as he passed diplomatic notes back and forth with Spain, hoping against hope to avoid war. "The mob was yelling at his heels," writes Mr. Millis; "the Lodges and Roosevelts were plotting their international piracies." Despite Roosevelt's sneers at the President's "weakness and vacillation," McKinley would not have lacked powerful support if he had held out for peace. He was backed by Wall Street, as well as the honest opposers of imperialistic aggression, and the undeluded and cool-brained among the masses. The Vice-President, Speaker Reed from Maine, the Republican Senate Leader Hale, Senators Allison, Aldrich, Fairbanks, Platt, Mark Hanna, and practically all of the Cabinet were stout advocates of peace. While belligerent Mr. Roosevelt impatiently howled for action and pushed forward "his own private plans for a war" with seething vigor, Mr. Atkins, the sugar planter, who knew Cubans and Cuba's condition better than anyone else, endeavored vigorously to swing the "better elements" in Congress to peace. "Mark my words," he kept repeating, "the Cubans are not capable of maintaining a stable government."

McKinley in his great bewilderment might well have taken a leaf from his predecessor's book. Despite pressure, despite politics, Grover Cleveland as President had stood incorruptibly on his own feet and faced the situation with the clearest-sighted eyes. "Gentlemen, there shall never be a war with Spain over Cuba while I am President," he had said conclusively to a committee of senators who came to anounce that they had about decided to go to war. When the *Journal* pressed the ex-President for some public expression over the *Maine* disaster, he telegraphed with icy contempt, "I decline to allow my sorrow for those who died on the *Maine* to be perverted into an advertising scheme for the New York *Journal*." When the war was finally declared, Cleveland, sick at heart over his country's behavior, wrote with remarkable clarity and foresight: "McKinley is not a victim of ignorance, but of amiable weakness, not unmixed with political ambition. . . . The senate will not hesitate to leave him in the lurch, and Lee will strut and swagger, I suppose. . . . Roosevelt too will have his share of strut and sensation. . . . We shall find Spain so weak and inefficient that the war will be short and the result may be not much worse than a depreciation of national standing before the world abroad, and, at home, demoralization of our peoples' character, much demagogy and humbug, great additions to our public burdens and the exposure of scandalous operations."

While Wall Street and the leading business men were sending a flood of cautioning telegrams urging moderation, the unwarlike, gentle-hearted Senator Thurston of Nebraska, whose wife had died "pitying Cuba" while on an inspection tour sponsored by the *Journal,* presented this singularly materialistic slant on the situation: "War with Spain would increase the business and earnings of every American factory; it would stimulate every branch of industry and domestic commerce; it would greatly increase the demand for American labor; and in the end every certificate that represented a share in an American business enterprise would be worth more money than it is today."

The full story of American diplomacy preceding the Spanish-American War and the chronicle of the war itself cannot be elaborated in a book of this scope. The details of the two years are brilliantly set off by Walter Millis in *The Martial Spirit*. It is doubtful if a country has ever been more superbly written down as "ass" by one of her own sons than by Mr. Millis in his satirical history of 427 pages. With Voltairean detachment Mr. Millis culled facts from faked chaff and presented them with Voltairean malice. "Seldom can history have recorded a plainer case of military aggression," he writes; "yet seldom has a war been started in so profound a conviction of its righteousness."

Throughout the end of March and the early part of April Spain carried her overtures for peace to the point of utter humility. She reminded the United States again and again that almost all of her grievances had already been met. The American Ambassador Mr. Woodford begged McKinley in a personal telegram not to humiliate Spain since she was going and "loyally ready to go as fast and as far" as she could.

On April tenth, the day before McKinley was to deliver his message stating that the captain-general had been authorized to declare a suspension of hostilities, new amicable proposals came from Spain declaring a willingness to "grant Cuba the same sort of self-government that Canada enjoyed."

On April eleventh, weak-kneed with righteous doubts, McKinley, after hours of praying for divine guidance, presented his message to Congress, asking for authority to intervene in Cuba. In a tacked-on anticlimactic paragraph to his noble peroration, he barely mentioned the fact that less than twenty-four hours previously Spain had virtually made an humble capitulation to every demand.

The Senate adopted Foraker's Resolution which recognized the Government of Cuba as the true government of the island. On April thirteenth the House resolution passed by a vote of 324 to 19. It confined itself largely to authorizing the President to intervene and was strangely silent on the fate of Cuba!

Horatio Rubens, a young American attorney, a member of the Cuban junta, hurried to Washington to confer with Senator Teller of Colorado, an ardent friend of Cuba. "I tell you, Senator, the administration intends to steal the Island of Cuba," he cried. "If you intend to give Cubans liberty, why can you not say so?" Taking a pad and pencil, Teller straightway drafted the famous significant lines known as the Teller Amendment. The last clause reads:

> "That the United States hereby disclaims any disposition to exercise sovereignty, jurisdiction or control over said Island except for the pacification thereof and asserts its determination when that is accomplished to leave the government and control of the Island to its people."

Just before the vote on the Joint Resolution of Congress was taken on April twentieth, Teller presented his amendment. "In the excitement it was adopted without a vote." It turned out to be the instrument whereby annexation was prevented and the honor of the United States preserved.

Diplomatic relations with Spain were severed on April twenty-first. On April twenty-fourth was passed the actual bill declaring war. The jingo newspapers had won the victory they had stooped for.

The populace outdid themselves in hollow glee, and those without good jobs rushed to the nearest headquarters to volunteer. In the basses and tenors with which they had inspired church choirs back home in preëlection days, congressmen bawled lustily, "Hang General Weyler to a Sour Apple Tree," some of them unaware that the sardonic Marquis of Teneriffe had for several months been ironically surveying the world from the secure towers of his castle in Spain.

2

THE AMERICANS COME

That the Spanish War was by no means a necessary conflict is attested to by numerous writers on international law in whose opinion the United States' action was "irregular, precipitate and unjust to Spain." Secretary of the Navy Long believed that if the President had been allowed to handle matters in his own way without duress, independence would have come "without a drop of bloodshed, as naturally as an apple falls from a tree." On April fifteenth he had sent a letter to the editor of the Boston *Herald* stating that the President had obtained from Spain a concession on every ground except independence. Yet before a week had passed, he issued orders to Admiral Sampson at Key West to blockade Havana.

In the dawn of April twenty-second, the American fleet sailed from Key West, and by three o'clock that afternoon officers and newspaper correspondents on the flying bridge of the flagship *New York* beheld the much-photographed profile of Morro Castle. The blockade was on. "Life on board," wrote Richard Harding Davis, "was like cruising the summer seas on a yacht."

The navy's principal objective was to intercept a Spanish fleet, commanded by Admiral Cervera, which was expected to be coming shortly to help the Spaniards in Cuba. The squadron was known to be in the Cape Verde Islands, where it had halted on its way to the West Indies to take stock of its ill-condition and its needs. The fleet was comprised of four armored cruisers, flagship

Infanta María Terésa, the *Cristóbal Colón,* the *Viscaya,* and the *Almirante Oquendo.* There were six torpedo boat destroyers, only two of which were any good. Not one of the cruisers was in prime condition; the best one, the *Colón,* lacked her main battery. Supplies and ammunition were grossly insufficient. Cervera knew too well that his squadron would be annihilated if he met the American fleet in open battle. In fact, he was convinced of the hopelessness of any move he might make. Yet the politicians in Madrid insisted that there be some naval fighting for the honor of the government. Spain at home and at sea and in Cuba had not the faintest hope of actually winning the war. She began the struggle paralyzed by a conviction of defeat. Her rôle was merely to make the best dying gesture possible under the circumstances. For this gesture, which would do credit to the noble politicians, were to be sacrificed those pawns of state, the soldiers and sailors. Despite Cervera's protests at the inevitable disaster, he was ordered to Cuba vaguely "to protect the island." The admiral, disclaiming all responsibility, sailed on April twenty-ninth with his lame-duck squadron to offer his ships and his unfortunate men upon the sacrificial altar of fruitless honor.

Sampson, who had been waiting at Havana for a week, received the news of Cervera's departure with tight-lipped content. He saw glory swiftly coming to him.

On May Day, many thousand miles from Cuba, Admiral Dewey ruined a Spanish fleet in Manila Bay. At the news of the victory, pandemonium really broke loose in the United States. And in Havana there was no less exuberance. The despatches from Madrid proclaimed that Dewey's sick ships had been blown to smithereens. It was implied that the American sailors were all drunk at the time of the engagements, and that now their liquor-sogged, swine-like bodies were floating idiotically in Manila Bay. The Spaniards in Havana made jokes. "It is a pity all that American pork is being wasted in Manila Bay when meat is so dear and scarce here," they said to each other. They went to the sea's edge and hurled fist-shaking insults at the gray blockading battleships half-mooned about Morro promontory. Those hated ships had cut off supplies from a hungry land, and Havanese epicures had been reduced to eating such stuff as cod-fish salad, without coffee to wash it down. At night when the Prado and all the streets were devoid of light because of a military order, every inch of floor space in the cafés was jammed with Spaniards listening to table-top speeches advocating crucifixion and other exquisite tortures for all the Americans they captured.

While the people of Havana were exulting in the false Madrid despatches, "On to Havana!" became the lusty, impatient battle-cry of the frenzied private citizenry in the United States. In the midst of the patriotic drunk, it was discovered that Spain had about 100,000 trained fighting men in Cuba, while America's standing army of 28,000 men had become somewhat rusty through disuse since the Civil War. Yet McKinley, now swept away on the tide of nation-wide hysteria, determined with his councilors that the first Havana expedition should sail within a fortnight, notwithstanding the fact that just a week before he had proclaimed that no press clamor could induce him to rush raw troops into the sickly Cuban rainy-season.

In the meantime wild rumors concerning the destination of Cervera's fleet filled the front pages. The whole Atlantic seaboard from Maine to Key West was riveted with excitement at bulletin boards, wondering at what defenseless coastal town the Spaniards might strike. For a fortnight there was no authentic news of Cervera's fleet. The squadron took on the mystery of ominous phantom ships. Then on May thirteenth came a reliable communication that the fleet had been seen off Martinique, headed west. Commodore Schley in command of the Flying Squadron, which had been held uncertainly at Hampton Roads, was despatched south to trap and destroy the oncoming armada. Sampson was urged to hasten his return from a false-scented chase to Puerto Rico to the defense of the Havana blockade.

Schley darted here and there about the Caribbean, apparently as full of whim as the will-o'-the-wisp he was after. At last on

May twenty-eighth, after repeated insistence from headquarters, the commodore took a second peep at Santiago harbor, and, sure enough, he saw the Spanish fleet snugly at anchor. Cervera with his entire squadron had slipped quietly and unmolested into Santiago nine days before. The navy had sadly burked the business of intercepting and destroying the enemy fleet, which had sailed across the Atlantic in a crippled condition, had stopped at Martinique and Curaçao and made port at Santiago without having been glimpsed by Sampson or Schley. On June first, Sampson, on the flagship *New York,* followed by his squadron, sailed around Cape Maysi and arrived to reënforce Schley and to take command of the Santiago blockade. With the Spanish fleet bottled up, the possibility of the enemy's getting supplies or fresh troops from the continent was nil. The end of the war was already in sight. Without losing a life America could have waited until the Spaniards sued for peace, when starvation faced them.

To make it conclusively impossible for the Spanish ships to take to sea, Lieutenant Richmond Pearson Hobson volunteered, with a crew of seven helpers, to ground the bow of the collier *Merrimac* in the narrow channel entrance. In the blackness of early morning on June third the *Merrimac* steamed under the shore batteries of Morro into the gut between the bluffs. The enemy guns opened fire. The tiller ropes were shot away. The collier became unmanageable and got too far up into the harbor before Hobson could succeed in sinking her. When she finally settled, she was in deep water, and little impediment to a passing ship. The gunfire ceased. The Spaniards who went to investigate found Hobson and his seven companions clinging to a life raft uninjured. The Americans were made prisoners of war and the Spanish officers extolled their bravery in glowing sentiments. That Hobson's deed was profitless in no way detracted from the glory of his courage in facing almost certain death.

(In the end it proved most fortunate for Americans that the feat was a failure, for if the entrance had been successfully blocked, Cervera could not have attempted his famous sortie exactly one month later, on July third, which resulted in the demolishment of the Spanish fleet and led up to the swift finish of the war.)

The papers now had one glorious authentic act of heroism to chant about. Never was a courageous deed more handsomely praised and never was praise more richly deserved. The press of Europe, including that of the Spanish enemy, paid tribute to the young Alabamian. Joseph Conrad wrote to Stephen Crane's wife warm congratulations on the exploit of Hobson. "That was worth all the Manila battle," he said in unaccustomed exclamations. "Magnificent!"

While the martial American public continued to yelp for action, blood, and an assault upon Havana, the purely administrative problems of the mobilization had plunged headquarters in an urgent situation that seemed beyond its depth. Washington was tangled in red tape. The training camps were seething with confusion. Ludicrous chaos reigned at Tampa, where the major divisions of the regular army were concentrated for embarkation. "The struggle for place among the ambitious gentlemen who desired to serve their country in high-salaried and high-titled positions, and the jealousies and mutual criticisms of army and navy officers were most wearing on Mr. McKinley," wrote Mr. Cortelyou, the President's private secretary, in his journal.

Theodore Roosevelt, the warlike Assistant Secretary of the Navy, who had bullied President McKinley in galling, contemptuous terms, resigned from the navy to be made a lieutenant-colonel of the volunteer army. With infectious gusto, he recruited a picturesque contingent of young millionaire clubmen, publicized college athletes, Wild West cowboys, and actors, and thereby provided the papers with a highly dramatic cavalry outfit for copy. "Teddy's Terrors" and "Rocky Mountain Rustlers" were the catch nicknames that subsequently gave way to the immortal "Roosevelt's Rough Riders," a title which the Colonel himself had happily hit upon. While Dr. Leonard Wood, an army surgeon, upon whom Mr. Roosevelt had "modestly bestowed the colonelcy," went through the processes of training his cavalrymen, Mr. Roosevelt remained in Washington until he had pulled every wire possible to get preference in everything for his outfit. "The idea of riding into battle at the head of a command of cowboy cavalry had long been a dream of Mr. Roosevelt's own more martial mind," says Mr. Millis. "Mr. Roosevelt's command, however, was destined to figure so very largely that at times it almost seemed to be the war, and one might have supposed that the whole scheme had been primarily designed to display Mr. Roosevelt's remarkable qualities before an admiring nation. Perhaps it was."

On June third (the day of Hobson's feat in Santiago harbor) with the "railway system in wildest confusion," Roosevelt and his Rough Riders arrived in the thick of the country-fair agitations of Tampa. The whole place, from the gaudy Planters' Hotel to the end of the single pier, vibrated with the dynamic arrival. The thousand veranda rocking chairs of the officers and their farewell-bidding families jerked alertly in the enervating heat. War correspondents sharpened pencils briskly and made notes at lightning speed, while nervous telegraph operators wilted over the new, long, vibrant messages, public and private.

For over six weeks the Regular Army had been milling about in Tampa under the command of ponderous, three-hundred-pound Shafter, waiting news of Cervera's whereabouts before venturing on the seas. But despite headquarters' messages arriving daily urging immediate departure, for a fortnight after the bottling of Cervera's fleet Shafter's army was still not in condition to sail.

That the war was mismanaged and bungled in every possible way is a well-known commentary. It can only be recorded as a glaring example of inefficiency, criminal unpreparedness, and contingent graft. At first it was taken as a lark, a little good fun. Climatic conditions and tropical diseases were disregarded with customary American heedlessness. The uniforms were of thick wool, dyed a fickle blue that changed to an odd batiked motley in

Cuban sun and rain. (Most of the supply of khaki was to come after the war was over.) Some regiments had no blankets and tents, some no socks and underwear, others no arms. Except for Roosevelt's men there were no modern smokeless powder rifles for the volunteer troops. The food was not all that might be desired: packers palmed off the worst sort of embalmed beef at top prices. There was a distressing lack of horses, mules and wagons. When the train loads of supplies arrived, nothing was labeled; no one could tell whether they contained harness, siege guns, dog tents, or tinned food until the boxes were broken open. Colonel Wood summed up the situation in a letter to his wife on June ninth: "Confusion, confusion, confusion."

On June fourteenth after repeated postponements, countermanded orders, and individualistic disorganization, the first detachments of troops under General Shafter sailed from Tampa for the region of Santiago, Colonel Roosevelt seizing one of the best boats assigned to some other troops for his Rough Riders.

The reason for sending the army to Santiago instead of Havana was not only that it was decidedly a softer spot strategically, but that the navy uniquely called upon the army to help her capture the Spanish fleet trapped in the harbor. The American fleet was afraid to approach the Spanish ships because of the forts and mines. So the army was asked to capture the forts from the rear and to cut the wires connecting with the harbor mines, in order that the American ships might sweep in smoothly to easy victory.

On June twentieth the army transports arrived in sight of Guantánamo where a landing of marines had already been effected. Admiral Sampson boarded the *Seguranca* to confer with General Shafter. They disagreed on plans of attack, and together in a navy gig they sought the coastal headquarters of General Calixto García, who commanded the undefeated tatterdemalion insurgent army in Oriente Province. The grave problem of getting General Shafter's three-hundred-pound bulk up the precipitous heights to García's camp caused dismay, and gained immortality for the "small white mule" which had "the stout heart" to achieve the hoisting feat. Daiquirí and Siboney were the only two possible landing places in the vicinity and the former was García's choice. (Historic Daiquirí has been honored by having named for it the finest of Cuban cocktails—a delectable mixture of Ron Bacardi, the juice of green limes, sugar, and shaved ice.)

The landing was to take place in the early morning of June twenty-second. The night preceding was brilliant with stars. Even to the hardest realists among the soldiers the heavenly luminaries seemed infinitely nearer and far more numerous than in northern latitudes. And as the Southern Cross arose to bless the exotic night with especial inspiration, the loud-mouthed became quiet-voiced and the heavy-footed trod the decks softly. On the morrow they would all touch the soil of that romantic foreign island about which they had heard such varied tales and held such varied imaginings. And according to their natures they felt vainglorious or troubled by the mystery of beauty and presentiment.

In the early morning the landing began. One of the first boats bearing troops from the transport *Yucatan* carried the flag of the Rough Riders, which had been made in Phoenix, Arizona. The flag was hoisted over an abandoned Spanish blockhouse on the hill to the right, as a signal that the first landing had been successfully achieved. An officer on shipboard, watching the proceeding through a fieldglass, threw his hat on the deck, jumped to the top of the bulwark, and yelled: "Howl, ye Arizona men—it's our flag up there!" The Arizona cowboys howled as only Arizona cowboys could; and the mascot dog howled with them in confused terror. Someone grabbed the whistle cord and tied it down. Every man who possessed a revolver shot recklessly into sky or water. The band struck up "A Hot Time in the Old Town To-night." As if touched by one electric current, all the whistles of the fifty transports and odd craft turned loose their shrieking sirens. A chorus of maniacal cheers from thousands of male throats reverberated, and the guns of the warships let off a stout salute to the flag. Colonel Roosevelt bared his executive teeth in his broadest grin and with a Yankee Doodle gesture tied a blue polka dot handkerchief about his sombrero. The Americans had come.

With the outfit had come eighty-nine war correspondents, a greater number than there were surgeons. But America had figured it was to be that kind of a war. Because there was no cavalry escort to guide them, many of the boats ran aground on a shoal. Threadbare Cuban patriots, who had come to greet their allies, waded into the sea up to their waists and carried the Yankees ashore on their shoulders. Though there was little ceremony and pomp in the conquerors' landing, there was plenty of raucous glee and holiday spirit.

On shore in a long line of salute, white and black Cubans stood to welcome their brothers-in-arms. They offered them water of the green coconut to refresh them and insisted that they ride on their tottering half-starved nags, while they themselves walked.

But the insurgent leaders were less enthusiastic over the Americans' arrival than the ragtag-and-bobtail followers. Gómez had not wanted American troops landed in Cuba. He desired ammunition and supplies only. He wanted to win his own war. From now on he was ignored—and his attitude to his allies became increasingly cool.

On the tenth of June, twelve days previous to the Daiquirí landing, six hundred marines had landed on the east shore of the Bay of Guantánamo. Among them was Stephen Crane in the capacity of war correspondent for the New York *World*. As the famous author stepped ashore, the red glow from a burning village edged with palm trees turned "the coronal of leaves into enormous crimson feathers." Tense and excited, Crane moved restlessly here and there, while some men dug trenches and others tried to catch up on their sleep. These latter, he noted, spent most of the night slapping at the stinking mauve-colored land-crabs that rustled across their faces and frames as if they had been mere hillocks of sand. Crane, however, made no attempt to rest, but talked away all his first night in camp with an army physician about consumption—the disease his Cuban sojourn was to bring on swiftly and fatally.

By checking up on reality, white-faced, eager Crane, who had savored the grimness of war only in his mind's eye when he wrote *The Red Badge of Courage,* was to prove to himself the uncanny and phenomenal integrity of the artist's imagination. His conceived picture turned out to be the thing itself. With his dark eyes swirling with somber lightnings, he ironically contemplated "all this manure," the barbarous inefficiency, the lack of a decent water supply, "the crime on men rendered defenseless by discipline." Fascinated by the cruel tragi-comic workings of humanity, he kept himself in the thick of the fights with fatalistic disregard of danger. And so appalled was he by actualities that the newspapers found the truth he wrote too ugly to tell in print. As a war correspondent, the most authentic American talent of his day was considered a failure by his newspaper, and contemptuously fired on his return. It was not for the purpose of truth-telling that patriotic publishers had sponsored war.

3

THE VALIANT AT EL CANEY

Disintegrating rivalry sprang up between the officers and the men of the several divisions for the honor of striking the first blow. General Shafter was quite nonplused by the "individualism" of his army. Before half the supplies were landed, General "Fighting Joe" Wheeler, bantam-weight veteran of the Confederate Army, sniffing at battle like an old war-horse, decided to plunge straight into action without waiting for instructions from the commander. He ordered an attack on Las Guásimas, a meeting place of two trails joining at the apex of a V three miles from Siboney. At five o'clock on the morning of June twenty-fourth the First Regiment of the U. S. Volunteer Cavalry (the Rough Riders), under Colonel Wood and Lieutenant-Colonel Roosevelt, and the Tenth Cavalry were roused in the early mist and sent forward. They moved with the zest of game-hunters, thrilled to get to practice with their spanking new Krag-Jorgensen rifles. At seven-thirty as the sunshine cleared the mists and illuminated the tropical foliage with golden-green splendor, the regulars confronted half a mile ahead of them stone breastworks staunchly set on a hill. The troops fell into a skirmish line and waited with uncertainty. General Wheeler ordered a questioning shot fired at the breastworks. In a flash, bullets from Spanish Mauser rifles were cutting the leaves about the Americans like hailstones. A man fell at the astonished Fighting Joe's side. Soon men saw their comrades on all sides grabbing at wounds with pain and dismay. And then, recovering from their gasp of surprise that Spaniards could really shoot, the Americans began to fire back. Sergeant Hamilton Fish, promising scion of New York's crème de la crème, was shot through the heart in the beginning of the fight and died instantly. It was ironic that perhaps the first man killed in the engagement should have been the grandson and namesake of that distinguished Hamilton Fish who, as Secretary of State under Grant, had labored successfully to prevent America's involvement in a Cuban war two and a half decades previously.

The Americans could hardly believe that the lark was over and that stinging realities of war had gripped them. After hours of fighting in staggering heat, when it looked as if his whole force might be slaughtered, Wheeler reluctantly agreed to send to General Lawton at Siboney for help, thereby dimming the luster of his premature maneuver. Lawton, extremely irritated at Wheeler's and Roosevelt's rashness, rushed an infantry regiment to the rescue. But just a few minutes before it arrived, the Spaniards withdrew from their entrenchments (as they had planned to do even before the fight began) and retreated towards Santiago.

General Wheeler, in the excitement of the moment, whooped victoriously, "We've got the damned Yankees on the run!" The regulars and the Rough Riders swept up the hill and arrived in possession of the insignificant little breastworks simultaneously.

The bloodshed the American populace had sentimentally howled for had been offered up. The newspapers could now carry their tallest headlines, and they did not pass up their opportunity. Richard Harding Davis, who had been right at Roosevelt's heels throughout the skirmish almost in the manner of a personal publicity agent, played up the Colonel with the infectious fervency of hero-worship.

From the crest of the Las Guásimas hill a wide jungle-covered basin extended towards Santiago, barred a few miles southwest by a series of ridges known collectively as San Juan Hill. Just at the foot of San Juan Hill lay a meadow about a third of a mile wide, thick with tall grass and occasional small trees. The meadow was strewn with complicated barbed wire entanglements, and was within deadly range of rifle-pits and trenches on the numerous nearby slopes.

Before the meadow could be reached the American troops had to traverse dense forest country crossed by swift little streams swollen beyond their banks by summer deluges. The muddy roads were so ill-conditioned as to make it impossible for the heavy siege guns to be transported to the seat of action. The trail the men were to take followed the somewhat labyrinthine meanderings of the overflown San Juan River. It was so narrow in spots that four men could hardly march abreast, and two wagons could not pass each other. The slushy road became jammed with supply wagons which often seemed irretrievably sunk in mud holes. The tropical afternoon rains were violently regular.

In the milling confusion the Americans bivouacked uncomfortably wherever they could find a cleared space—the divisions necessarily separated. The damp nights chilled the marrow of the troopers who had nonchalantly thrown away their blankets, which the half-naked Cuban soldiers had avidly assumed and now snuggled contentedly under in hills too distant for recovery. The blanketless soldiers suffered not only from dampness but hunger, for the pack trains could not always get to them conveniently. And from the wetness all about, millions of plaguing mosquitoes were generated to pepper the wretched fellows with stings and fever germs.

On the morning of June thirtieth General Shafter, suffering cruelly from the morning heat and chafed by his woolen uniform, rode three miles along the Santiago road "as far as it was safe and secured" to have a look-see. Returning, he called his divisional commanders to his tent, told them it "looked all right" and gave orders to attack early the next morning. General Lawton with his infantry was assigned to capture the village of El Caney with its stone blockhouse (about two miles off the main road to Santiago). The cavalry regiments would lead down the road and deploy to the left. Together these latter would storm San Juan Hill, reënforced by General Lawton, following his quick capture of El Caney. After giving these commands, the enormous bulk of General Shafter sunk to its cot, prostrated with the heat.

Despite the confusion, the hastiness and sketchiness of plans, Shafter was right in his general desire to capture Santiago as quickly as possible to prevent the escape of General Linares with his 13,000 troops or to prevent the arrival of General Pando with 8,000 Spanish reënforcements. Moreover Shafter knew the ways of yellow fever. He had had the disease himself. He knew that within three, four, or five weeks his army would most likely be helplessly in the throes of black vomiting.

Neither Shafter nor any of the subordinates had been guiltless of undervaluing the enemy. With characteristic American cocksureness they had discounted both the courage of Spaniards and the fury of their firing. Two hours at most was all that had been allowed for General Lawton's capturing of El Caney. In this confident expectation, they met with an astounding rebuff.

About four o'clock on the morning of July first, just before sunrise, Lawton roused his men, who had been marched through the night and allowed to sleep only since midnight. He gave them a hasty brig-fare breakfast of hardtack and water and hustled them to their positions from which they were to make the attack, "every line of which approach was commanded by Spanish earthworks." By the early light—the day was Friday, the soldiers noted—the defenses of El Caney looked surprisingly formidable. The name El Caney meant *sepulcher*—" for the Spaniards" the Americans told each other cheeringly. Because the battery had not been provided with modern smokeless powder, the clouds of billowing smoke became the target for the concealed Spanish artillery and it soon ceased to function. Instead of being over in a couple of hours, the battle lengthened through noon and approached mid-afternoon. Although the Americans, enormously out-numbering the Spaniards, had practically surrounded the place by four o'clock, the fight would seemingly have gone on for a day or two if the latter had not exhausted their supply of ammunition. Just before he was shot down, General Vera del Rey told all his men who could to escape. When at length the Americans rushed the fort they found only five men left alive. In their valorous stubborn resistance the small band of Spaniards had killed or wounded 375 Americans, a number almost equal to their entire force. The Americans, touched with admiration for the courage of the valiant Spanish commander, paid his remains every military honor. And as the setting sun spread a phantasmagoria of vari-colored tropical beauty across the west, Lawton's tired heroic men, who had fought all day on a meager snack of hardtack after a scant four hours' sleep, began to search out and gather up their dead comrades to bury them against nightfall.

4
BUZZARDS' PRANKS

In the meantime San Juan Hill had been won about four o'clock in the afternoon. It had not been intended to attack San Juan until the next day (Saturday, July second). But surprised at the sound of continued firing at El Caney, and alarmed that the Spanish might reënforce the place, Colonel McClernand, acting as the ailing Shafter's representative, gave orders for Kent's infantry and the dismounted cavalry to advance. This command, which produced a devastating confusion and an unnecessary holocaust, also led to the courageous, unscientific capture of San Juan.

The unknown country in which the Americans had to fight had been scouted only in the most perfunctory manner. The approach to San Juan, as has been stated, was by a trail through tangled woods which opened on the savannah beneath the hills, and upon the entrance of which the Spaniards undoubtedly had their guns trained. General Chaffee pointed out the grave danger to Shafter and urged the cutting of a new trail. "If our men leave cover and reach the plain from those trails alone," he had desperately declared, "they will be piled so high that they will block the road." But Shafter would not delay. The men were ordered forward down the marked trail, "driven as cattle to slaughter into the chutes of Chicago's cattle pens." To make matters infinitely worse, Colonel Derby of the Engineers in a scouting balloon hung suspended between air and earth like a false heavenly herald directly over the trail, so that the Spaniards could not have failed to pick out the line of march even if their previously plotted calculations had been mislaid. Like a magnet he was to draw hours of enemy shrapnel, not on his balloon, but on the miserable warriors stewing helplessly in the narrow ribbon of roadway beneath him.

Ten thousand blue-shirted men with their tooth brushes stuck jauntily into the bands of their dirty slouch hats surged into the muddy trail. On both sides the jungle crowded in so greedily that there was just room enough for four men to march abreast. The traffic congestion was increasing. And adding to the confusion General Kent's infantry was halted and pressed against the prickly jungle to allow Roosevelt's Rough Riders to pass, "presumably to give them the first chance at the Spaniards . . . Richard Harding Davis in full khaki regalia was with them." (The vibrant Roosevelt was now in command, for Colonel Wood had been advanced to brigade commander.)

As the July sun rose to noontime directness, the heat waxed terrific, and the tension of congestion at the last ford became insufferably nerve-harrowing. Men were pushed out into the meadow edges and stood choked in the thick tall grass not knowing what to do next. All at once some of them pitched forward on their faces, shot dead by Spanish sharpshooters concealed in trees and undistinguishable because of their smokeless powder. From the enemy rifle pits in front, the Mausers poured forth a stream of murdering bullets. Tearing shrapnel splattered the trail under the tell-tale balloon far behind the advance troopers. The falling dead jammed the road. Columns ceased to advance. Every single yard of ground for a mile behind the first troops was inside the zone of Spanish fire. In the midst of the destruction, General Sumner (now in command of cavalry since the heat had worsted plucky little Fighting Joe as well as the obese Shafter) halted his men to await orders, as General Shafter had directed. To avoid the red hot hiss of bullets that tried to singe their hair, the men spread themselves flat against the grass and held itching fingers just off the triggers. For fifty minutes they waited, caught in a slaughtering fusillade, swearing rebelliously in their inactivity and worked up to the point of panic. Trapped by the barbed wire defenses before them (and having mislaid their wire-snippers) they could hardly advance, nor could they retreat because of the jammed road. Nobody knew what to do or what had gone wrong. They only knew that both ways were blocked and they were being hit now with ghastly rapidity. They had orders not to return the fire, but to lie still and wait for further commands. The situation grew maddening, beyond human endurance. At last the strategy of common sense came to the rescue. After a quick consultation with Kent, Sumner waited no longer, but deployed his division of men to the right where they had the protection of a stream bed and foliage. The Ninth Cavalry, a colored regiment, was in the lead, followed by the Sixth and Third and then Roosevelt's First.

Kent hurried his infantry along a newly discovered trail to the left which seemed to promise access to the meadow before the hill. The volunteer Seventy-first New York, "the pride of the state troopers," was in the lead here, followed swiftly by the Sixth and Sixteenth regular infantry. As they plunged down the unknown trail, criminally equipped with revealing black-powder rifles, under painful fire from an enemy they could not see, they suddenly decided (like the adventurous old planter with de Soto in Florida) that they were fed up with the war, and determined to go back to base. Kent's staff officers "practically formed a cordon behind the panic-stricken men and urged them to again go forward." But when they adamantly refused to be cajoled or bullied, General Kent begged them to lie down in the thicket, which many of them did, gratefully if a little shamefacedly, to the everlasting embarrassment of their papas back in New York. Kent advised the officers of the oncoming second brigade to tell their men to pay no attention to the irregularity of the Seventy-first's taking siestas at such a crisis.

The regular infantry regiment passed them on the run, compelled to move in a single file because the feet of the reclining Seventy-first were sticking obstructingly towards the middle of the road. Discretion bred of forgivable panic had routed valor and blackened reputations, but it had temporarily saved lives. After a breathing spell most of the Seventy-first regained their morale, and entering the fray enthusiastically to make up for their funk, unfortunately let out a rousing cheer when Lieutenant Parker arrived with a battery of Gatlin guns. This ill-advised shout of joy swiftly drew enemy fire and silenced forever some of the unlucky guardsmen, thereby saving them from the sneers of the folks at home who knew the acrid odor of war's actualities only through sniffing printer's ink.

Just as Lieutenant Parker daringly got his guns into place, the general troops decided that the heights must be taken, and pluckily began the hazardous advance. To those in sheltered positions it looked as if the blue line was creeping into unshunnable death. Parker opened fire on the trenches. The effect was magical. The Spaniards scampered out and dashed over the hill. The sweating, bleeding men in the long hot grass made a run across the meadow for the ridge, and started up the slope under cover of the hillside. They were nearing the top, when the American artillery, which could not see much of what was going on from its position on El Pozo Hill, untimely decided to lend assistance, and fired so near the heads of the soldiers that the blue line had to creep back down, and halt perilously on the hillside until the artillery could be shut off. When the guns were finally silenced, the infantry rushed the top. A Cuban with fantastic bravery dashed ahead to cut the last barbed wire obstructions. As he finished his job he fell dead, shot to pieces. The Americans poured by him, jumped down into the abandoned trenches, and began firing at the backs of the Spaniards.

While the infantry was making its direct rush, Colonel Roosevelt, on the north side of Kettle Hill—a position between his cavalry and the main ridge—waved his sombrero and started forward at the head of the Rough Riders and some Negro cavalrymen. Achieving Kettle Hill, he saw the depression with a shallow pond separating him from the crest of San Juan. Again he waved his hat with the streaming polka dot handkerchief, and went down the hill, his Rough Riders and the others hot behind him. It was the supreme moment of which he had dreamed. Galloping across the marshy space, he rode triumphantly to the main height. On the crest he found that the Negroes of the Tenth Cavalry had already arrived there. Noticing the infantry engaged away to the left, Roosevelt poured in a fire upon the flank of the retreating enemy. "As the newspaper despatches went off describing the heroism of the Rough Riders and their lieutenant-colonel," says Mr. Millis, "another military genius had been given to the American people."

The Spaniards disappeared from view. Beyond on a hill three miles away, behind its stout fortifications, stood the multicolored city of Santiago, serene, secure. The exhausted American troopers looked at each other. "Well, hell, here we are!" one of them said.

There they were and what of it? The sweating lines clinging to the crest were very thin and ragged. They were weak from their heroic exertion, nervous, half perished for food and water, and some of them fainting from loss of blood. Their position was "painfully suggestive of Humpty-Dumpty on the wall." In one day Shafter had lost one-tenth of his entire force in actual casualties. 1,475 killed and wounded had been sacrificed for a dubious and precarious advantage.

As night closed in, Wheeler, having risen from his sickbed and resumed his seniority as divisional commander present, wrote to Shafter: "A number of officers have appealed to me to have the line withdrawn and take up a strong position farther back . . . I have positively discountenanced this, as it would cost us much prestige. The lines are now very thin, as so many men have gone to the rear with wounded, and so many are exhausted, but I hope these men can be got up tonight . . . Tomorrow . . . will be a severe day." Wheeler's stout spirit saved the hour.

The message arrived along with the bloody hordes of wounded, who suffered unspeakable agonies as the rough-floored oxcarts jostled over the torturing roads. The hospitals quickly filled beyond capacity. Subsequent arrivals had to be accommodated on blankets on the sand, and still later arrivals were stretched out on the sand without blankets. The surgeons worked fiendishly all night. They were handicapped not only by lack of medical supplies (a quantity of chests had still not been unloaded from the transports) but by lack of lamps. Luckily there was a bright moon. Many tedious operations had to be performed by the moonlight and candlelight. The suffering men groaned as little as possible. Only now and then some supersensitive soldier, dazed by the awful thing that had happened to him, burst the restraining bonds of manhood and cried out sharply against his luckless fate or died singing lustily to keep from whimpering.

Dozens of the wounded were not discovered for two or three days after the fight. Frank Norris saw a man shot through the throat who had lain without water or food under chilling night and baking sun for forty-eight hours. Scouting parties coming upon dead bodies were horrified to find the faces of their comrades mutilated, with eyes gouged out, noses and lips ripped off. "By God, the filthy Spaniards," they cried, "desecrating the dead!" The revolting rumor passed rapidly from mouth to ear until the entire soldiery was gritting its teeth in indignation. Then a group came upon two dead men lying not far apart who had a different story to tell. The cold stiffened fingers of each corpse clutched a lifeless buzzard in deadly grip. The greedy vultures had attacked their wounded prey before the final breath had left the bodies, and the soldiers with their last ebbing strength had victoriously strangled their assailants.

Shafter, feverish and anxious as the casualty accounts rolled in, was compelled to keep to his cot, fully conscious that his forces were in gravest danger, and that a frontal assault on Santiago would be ten-fold more hazardous than the capture of San Juan. Santiago was defended by numerous forts, to say nothing of trenches, barbed wire entanglements, and 13,000 fighting men.

The next morning Stephen Crane, sitting in a sheltered position on San Juan Hill, watched the arrival of Lawton's tired men trotting up under fire. There was not a high heroic face among them, he noted. They were simply the faces of men intent on business. That was all. But there was something sublime in the "simple, majestic commonplace." As they pegged up the hill one man behind another, Crane regarded the flat and obvious way in which they did their duty, and to him it was pageantry, "the pageantry of the accomplishment of naked duty."

The weary Americans were not allowed much rest, for the Spaniards kept up an annoying sporadic fire all day. In the midst of the firing Crane, moving about with stark unconcern for his personal safety, turned again and again to look at a red-headed Spanish corpse lying outside one of the enemy's trenches. Because the game of life and death was still being played too hotly to bother with ceremonies of burial, the corpse lay unburied, staring like a sardonic spectator. The troopers all saw him—the lively red hair glistening hot with sunshine and defiantly crowning the cold, awkward body. The red-headed Spaniard fascinated Crane. At odd intervals, returning from this errand or that inspection, he would look to see if his red head had been buried. But there he reclined, "his strong simple countenance a malignant sneer at the system which was forever killing the credulous peasants in a sort of black night of politics where the peasants merely followed whatever somebody had told them was lofty and good." Continuing to regard the Spaniard so irrevocably dead despite his glowing hair, Crane pondered, "To what purpose dead? The honor of Spain? Surely the honor of Spain could have existed without the violent death of this poor red-headed peasant."

As the day wore on to Cuban dusk, the heavy firing ceased, the red-headed soldier got covered over with trench dirt, and the Americans reckoned their casualties which had mounted alarmingly. In desperation Shafter called on Admiral Sampson to force entrance into Santiago Bay "to avoid future losses among my men." "You can now operate with less loss of life than I can," he maintained. Sampson, with a fleet tremendously superior to the Spanish fleet, did not seem to fear losing men, but he was not going to risk losing even one of his costly battleships. He insisted that Shafter get on with it, capture the forts and cut the wires connecting the mines. Notes were sent back and forth between the rival-colleagues repeatedly, while the American troops "were hanging to the crest of San Juan Hill by their teeth and finger-nails."

At length the generals, becoming desperate, agreed that Shafter must show himself at the front or be relieved of his command. They did not care which one of them was in command so long as someone was. A council was held at El Pozo. Shafter, too weak to sit up, was borne on a door unhinged from a peasant's hut. The generals gathered about his recumbent form and argued in low tones. They considered the possibility of retreating from the hills. Nothing was decided, and Shafter retained command. The situation on the morning of July third was gloomy in the extreme. Colonel Roosevelt, his feathers suddenly drooping, appealed to Cabot in a private letter, "Tell the President for Heaven's sake to send us every regiment and above all every battery possible. . . . We are within measurable distance of a terrible military disaster; we *must* have help."

After a miserable night, Shafter gathered himself together in the early morning to send a cable to Washington.

> "The defenses [of Santiago] are so strong it will be impossible to carry it by storm with my present force and I am seriously considering withdrawing about five miles and taking up a new position."

An hour after this disconcerting despatch had been sent, Colonel McClernand approached the commander's cot and said quietly, "General, let us make a demand on the Spaniards to surrender—or otherwise we will shell the city." After a long pause Shafter said, "Well, try it."

Simultaneously the dismayed dignitaries in Washington perused the proposal to retreat, and General Toral, the Spanish Commander in Santiago, read Shafter's bold ultimatum demanding surrender. Shortly after these amazing despatches had been sent, Admiral Sampson's flagship the *New York* was seen approaching Siboney across a glass-blue sea drenched in Sunday-morning sunshine. He had condescended to come for a conference with the sorely-pressed commander who lay prostrate not only with fever but abject despair.

5

DEMOLISHMENT OF THE SPANISH FLEET

At that very moment America was saved and the war lost to Spain through a foolish order from perplexed Captain-General Blanco in Havana. Never did the unaccountable whimsies of destiny favor one nation and put its curse on another in more thoroughly Olympic decisiveness than on this bright morning of July third. For several days previous to the San Juan assault, Admiral Cervera had been pressed by the remote politicians in Madrid to attempt escape with his squadron from Santiago Bay. He had insisted that such a move would be suicide for his ships and the greater part of their crews. The harbor entrance was doggedly guarded by a semi-circular arrangement of American battleships in a radius of about five miles, every nose pointing directly at the gut. In an official reply, he said, "I, who am a man without ambitions, without mad passions . . . state most emphatically that I shall never be the one to decree the horrible and useless hecatomb which will be the only possible result of the sortie from here by main force."

On June twenty-eighth he was told to spare his pessimistic comments and to get out at any cost when Santiago's fall seemed imminent. So when San Juan was taken on July first—with the Spaniards' ammunition in Santiago running short, and no food left but a small quantity of rice—the order for the fleet to attempt a sortie was considered mandatory. Cervera made one last appeal to Havana. But Blanco, nervously pacing the marble galleries of his palace, said unequivocally, "Get out!"

A final council of officers was held. Resolutely Cervera decided that his flagship *Infanta María Terésa* should engage and ram the swift cruiser *Brooklyn* commanded by Commodore Schley, while the other three Spanish battleships and two destroyers attempted escape westward towards Cienfuegos. The unhopeful crews cheered their courageous admiral; the boilers got up steam; anchors were weighed; the red and yellow battleflags gallantly strung. At about nine o'clock, the hour of the American Divine Sunday Service, those sailors not at worship were astounded to see the Spanish flagship, followed by her consorts, sail under full steam straight past Morro Castle into the open sea and the jaw of the American fleet. The great but unexpected moment had come. And Schley was in command. His chief was eight miles away to the east about to confer with Shafter.

At half-past nine Captain Concas of the *Infanta María Terésa* received Cervera's permission to open fire. The bugles reverberated the order. As their silvery tones pierced the tense atmosphere, the death knell of Spain's four centuries of greatness was proclaimed. "My bugles," Concas said, "were the last echo of those which were sounded in the taking of Granada." And those first significant clarion notes Christopher Columbus, god-father of Spain's glory, had heard with his own ears when he stood inconsequentially in the celebrating throng, clothed in obscurity but transfigured with vision. "Poor Spain!" murmured Concas to his beloved admiral, as the second gun from the deck battery fired the first shot. Cervera, however, was so full of emotion that he could no more make audible reply than could the ancient ghost of Cuba's discoverer had it been hovering near.

(The astonished Sampson at Siboney heard the shooting and put a consternated eye to the glass. The Spanish ships had come out. He could see their profiles. He saw, too, the American vessels closing in to do battle. This was the climactic hour of the war and he was not there! Stonily suppressing his disappointment, the admiral gave urgent orders. The *New York* swung around. But Sampson arrived only to witness the destruction which had been administered by his fleet under Commodore Schley's command. It was perhaps the neatest little irony of the war.)

Shortly the enclosed area of sea was blazing with cannon fire from both sides. In the dense smoke the American ships got dangerously into each other's range, and in the confusion it looked as if the fleeter Spanish ships would get away. But the fatal flaw in the construction of the enemy vessels proved their ruination: their decks were of wood. These quickly caught fire. The flames fanned by the ship's motion scorched the gunners painfully and turned them from their batteries to desperate but futile fire-fighting. With the whole interior of the *Infanta María Terésa* a roaring furnace, Cervera ordered her beached and abandoned. The wounded and blistered men hurtled over the side into the water. The admiral himself was forced to swim for shore stripped to his undershirt and trousers.

The decks and cabins of the *Oquendo* were also soon in a blaze. The gallant red and gold pennants turned to brief serpentine tongues of flame, then to barren white ashes that drifted into nothingness. Sailors struggled courageously to get their wounded off in the two life boats that had not been destroyed. In the midst of his heroic agitations, the captain died of heart-failure. The Americans began to send out boats to save the drowning.

The two Spanish destroyers were next ruined. The *Plutón* blew up. The *Furor,* shot to pieces and on fire, hoisted a white flag. From the shambles, the Americans rescued the few remaining alive, just before the burning ship was rent with explosions, which sent it rapidly to the bottom of the sea.

The *Iowa* stopped to rescue the crew from the burning *Viscaya.* As the wounded Captain Eulate, who was hauled up in a chair over the side, saluted his unhappy ship, calling out "Adios, *Viscaya!*" the forward magazine exploded.

The *Cristóbal Colón,* namesake of the great Admiral, was the only enemy ship left undestroyed. By noon she had got forty miles west of Santiago out of range of the pursuing Americans. But her supply of good fuel gave out, and with the poorer grade of coal speed slackened perceptibly. At one o'clock the oncoming *Oregon* found her within range. The *Cristóbal Colón* turned in to shore and ran aground in the same territory where Columbus had made his farewells to Cuba and had been lectured on retribution by the old Indian councilor.

Except for the grounded namesake of Columbus, the Spanish squadron was a complete loss. The casualty list of killed and wounded totaled 400. The American casualties consisted of one dead seaman, who was beheaded by a shell passing over the deck of the *Brooklyn*.

The gloomy prognostications of Cervera had come infernally to pass. He and his men had gone to their foredoomed failure with heavy heart, but undaunted courage. The stiff-necked state officials, with the same heedless callousness that had cost Spain her colonies one by one, had disregarded his intelligent requests and sent the ill-starred squadron into destruction with as little feeling as irresponsible boys shoving cardboard ships about a duck-pond.

6

SHAFTER'S BLOODLESS DÉNOUEMENT

Official Washington, sweltering throughout a Sunday hotter than that in the tropics and spiritually sunk at the pessimistic prospect of Shafter's withdrawing from his newly gained advantage, was struck dumb with wonder again and again that night as sequent hazy telegrams from the general arrived unfolding the naval engagement.

In the first hour of July fourth, the destruction of the Spanish fleet was confirmed beyond doubt, and Shafter proclaimed reassuringly, "I shall hold my present position!" At two o'clock, city folk were being roused from their beds by newsboys screaming the headlines of annihilation and victory. The nation's Fourth of July celebration took on the ecstasy of an evangelical revival. The war was considered finished.

As the news was signaled about the globe, Cuba became the center of the world's attention. In the British Isles particularly were the wires hot with details that Fourth of July; for imperialistic England was vitally concerned about the balance of power in the East and she reveled in Spain's drubbing. The mild-tempered Henry Adams, luxuriating in the charms of a fine old country house in Kent, had listened with an unwonted enthusiasm to the flashing messages for the past week. "Never since the battle of Hastings could the little telegraph office of the Kentish village have done such work," he commented. And that sultry Sunday afternoon, sitting reposefully under ancient shade trees in an English garden, he received the news of the destruction of the Spanish Armada, "as it might have come to Queen Elizabeth in 1588."

Scarcely pausing in his ruminations, the ultra-conservative Mr. Adams began to dispose of the Spanish colonies, philosophically and materially, just as the rest of the more impulsive world was doing.

"Puerto Rico," he reflected—doubtless swayed by the pervading English predilection for regenerating a backward world—"must be annexed." But he would gladly have escaped the Philippines. "One felt no call to shoulder the load of archipelagoes in the antipodes," he wearily considered, "when one was trying painfully to pluck up courage to face the labor of shouldering archipelagoes at home."

But the disposition of the alien colonies was, however, a trifle premature. For as yet stony Santiago was far from conquered. And in the late afternoon of Sunday four thousand Spanish reenforcements from Manzanillo marched without molestation into the city.

In the days following, Shafter, much recovered from his prostration, began to conduct a remarkable series of negotiations to induce General Toral to capitulate. White flags of truce bobbed up and down the rolling landscape between the thin American lines and the Spaniards stoutly entrenched behind forts and protected by a magnificent network of villainous barbed wire. "Where another man might have risked a bloody assault, General Shafter achieved the result by correspondence," Mr. Millis observes shrewdly. And, not without certain admiration, he adds, "Unlike Colonel Roosevelt, Shafter regarded it as his business not to achieve personal glory by fighting successful battles, but to secure the larger purposes of warfare with the greatest economy of life."

Although the Spanish fleet lay charred and drowned, Admiral Sampson was still strongly disinclined to risk an American ship to help Shafter take the city. And Shafter refused to have his men slaughtered in the labyrinth of barbed wire entanglements. So for a fortnight after the naval victory, Shafter temporized and bluffed.

On July sixth, Lieutenant Hobson, who had been held prisoner and whose "mysterious" death had been frequently rumored, was exchanged for Spanish prisoners, along with his seven comrades in heroism. Hobson was provided with a horse to ride into the welcoming arms of the American troops, and the blue jackets rode in an army wagon. The little procession followed a trail between high banks with tall palms making a triumphal arch. Silently they came forward, illuminated by the glory of the sun setting behind them. The tall, pale young officer in navy uniform rode in front and looked down at the lines of men with grave steady gaze. Every man took off his hat. Hobson stopped his horse and sat motionless. For some minutes the men stood looking up at him in unpremeditated absolute silence. It was the perfect tribute. And then a red-headed trooper broke the emotional tenseness by leaping forward and yelling, "Three cheers for Hobson!" The army descended on him in a mad scramble of ecstasy and welcome. "Few men have ever tasted such a triumph," said Richard

Harding Davis, an eye witness, "certainly very few young men." (Hobson was not quite twenty-eight.)

On Saturday July sixteenth under a giant silk-cotton tree—now famous to tourists as The Peace Tree—General Toral made his bloodless capitulation. Moved by Shafter's shrewdly generous offer to transport all military prisoners back to Spain at America's expense, Toral signed the surrender not only of 11,500 Spanish soldiers in the city but of 12,000 additional armed men within a radius of fifty-five miles. The bluffing, note-sending Shafter admitted afterwards that he was "simply thunderstruck." "I had no earthly chance," he confessed, "of getting those 12,000 men who were absolutely beyond my reach." Thus the much condemned Shafter, who had blundered egregiously through the day of the San Juan Hill victory, mitigated his mistakes by a clever, if unorthodox, bargaining, which cost not a single life. It makes one wish that all battles could be so painlessly won and lost—by suave pen flourishes of commanders, instead of bayonet and bullet prickings by defenseless men transformed into beasts.

The next day at noon over the Casa Consistorial in Santiago, which had been the site of Spanish headquarters since the governance of Diego Velasquez in 1514, the Stars and Stripes were run up. Just before that historic minute, the most distressingly *opéra bouffe* incident of the whole war took place. While the Ninth Infantry was drawn up at attention in the Plaza, and the cathedral clock was at the point of striking the hour of twelve—the signal for the hoisting of Old Glory—a correspondent named Sylvester Scovel earned himself an everlasting, if inglorious, place in the annals by jabbing a punch at Shafter's nose. (Scovel had resented Shafter's order to throw him off the palace roof where he was defiantly trying to get himself prominently photographed for his newspaper, the *World*.) Luckily the monumental general ducked and thereby saved himself the ignominy of a black-and-blue memento of the supreme moment of his career. Ordered arrested and held incommunicado, Scovel—because there was no time to hunt up a jail—was set upon a pedestal and guarded by two soldiers at the points of bayonets. He made such a funny statue that gaping citizens turned their gaze on him and missed the most significant exchange of bunting in the four centuries of Cuba's chronicles.

Just as the ceremonies were concluded the navy representatives arrived out of breath. (General Shafter had ingeniously delayed sending the invitation to Admiral Sampson.) The delegation was much amazed to see the damp Mr. Scovel drooping on his pedestal in the blazing midday sun. But they were more enraged than amazed at not being permitted to affix the navy's signature to the document of capitulation. With courteous aloofness Shafter pointed out that he did not consider that the navy had played a significant part in capturing the city. And when they were not allowed to take charge of certain Spanish merchantmen lying at the docks, which they claimed for prize money, the naval officers were positively staggered with indignation. Rushing to seize the ships despite Shafter, they were greeted by soldiers with fixed bayonets already in possession. The navy representatives stood about baffled, impotent, and furious, much like Diego Velasquez when he watched from the same shore Hernando Cortés sail for Mexico and audaciously turn a stone-deaf ear to his commands to stop. The fruits of victory Shafter demonstrated, as forcibly as the wily Cortés did, belonged to himself and to his army. He was not sharing glory with anyone else—not even with Calixto García, commander of the rebel troops in Oriente Province. García, who had more or less since 1868 been waging battle for the overthrow of Spanish domination in Cuba, was not present at the surrender ceremonies. He had been invited in such cool phrases that he stayed away. And when it was made clear to him that he would be allowed no part in governing the city, he disappeared into the interior smoldering with resentment, presumably to join forces with Commander-in-Chief Gómez.

FEVER GERMS

Surrender had come in the nick of time, for the dreaded yellow fever entered the American ranks on July ninth. And the cloudburst of July eleventh seemed to have loosed battalions of malignant malarial germs. The Fifth Army Corps staggered in their muddy tracks and dropped down helpless with fevers and dysentery. Within ten days after the surrender, 4,122 of the Americans were prostrate. There were scarcely enough fit soldiers to guard the Spanish prisoners—although the latter were being sent home as rapidly as possible. The morale of the sick American troops sank depressingly near zero, as they took time to recapture the recent past and, reliving the war in their minds, to formulate personal definitions of its essence and values.

Among the casualties of that brief Cuban campaign, which carried off two thousand Americans, the two finest literary talents in the United States were sacrificed. Stephen Crane and Frank Norris did not die in Cuba, but there they breathed in feverous germs which mortally undermined their constitutions. Crane was temperamentally more prepared for the ugly shocks than Norris, who, coming as a novice to the field of battle, was nauseously disillusioned—the whole business seemed to the young author of *The Octopus* "a hideous blur of mud and blood." "There is precious little glory in war if the Santiago campaign is a sample," he wrote, "and where you try to recall the campaign, it's only the horrors and the hardships and nothing on the finer side."

One night Norris made a roof for himself to sleep under. The next morning he found that he had used boards that were one glaze of dried blood. At El Caney he was the first to discover in an abandoned house the body of a little girl who had been raped and then knifed to death just before the beginning of the battle. When the fight was over he helped the American Relief feed the famished multitudes—6,000 refugees from Santiago who streamed into El Caney during the second day's truce. Dressed in dirty white they wound down one hill and up another like frantic victims on some penanced pilgrimage. As they surged, stretching out in supplication 6,000 empty pans, pots, pails, tin cans, they wailed with pinched and agonized voices, "Comida! Co-*mee*-dah!" Food! Food!

Watching the great pots of mush boil to readiness, the crowd fought and whined in desperate impatience. The relief workers had to drive them back into their corners brutally and by main force. "But even as I pushed and thrust," wrote Norris, "a little hand—ever so little a hand—took hold of my wrist. It was that of a tiny girl, almost too weak to stand, but she held a pitiful empty sardine can toward me, and whispered confidentially, with a great attempt at cheerfulness, 'Comida, eh? Comida por me?' and put her hand, not to her lips, but to her stomach. We came to know this gesture afterward. So long as they pointed to their mouths we could allow the applicants to wait their turn, but when they pointed to their stomachs we knew that we must be quick and that it was almost time for the restoratives."

Exhausted from their labors, the pots scraped empty, the Americans went supperless to bed in the village church. For better security they brought their horses through the back door and led them through the chapel out upon the terrace. They off-saddled in the chapel itself and used the communion rail for a saddle rack. But the holy aspect of the church had been thoroughly desecrated previously. It was strewn with Mauser ammunition, bayonet scabbards, Red Cross sacks of meal and sugar, and three half-empty goods boxes that had been full of calicoes and ginghams from Waltham, Massachusetts. The very altar itself was littered with bullets and rifled Spanish haversacks. And that night the torn altar cloth flapping in a draft frightened a broncho pony from California into such rearings and cavortings that for a moment the thousand housed refugees were thrown into a panic. At last when quiet was resumed, Norris, fatigued to irresponsibility, lay down to rest at the foot of the altar, unknowingly flanked by two yellow fever cases on one side of him and an amputated arm half buried in the dirt close to his blanket on the other. The light from the commissary candles shone dimly—and from the altar, the Mother of God in painted plaster looked down with benediction on all in her profaned church, and in her gentle smile there was forgiveness even for the cowpuncher's pony which had reared up at the flapping altar cloth "woven by fingers that were dust two hundred years ago."

To forget what the Spanish-American War signified for him, Norris went to "wallow and grovel in the longest grass of California on the cliffs overlooking the ocean, and absorb ozone and smell smells that *don't* come from rotting and scorched vegetation, dead horses, and bad water." But the disturbing memories remained to haunt him and the treacherous malarial fever "which got a twist on him somewhere between Daiquirí and San Juan" clung to his system like Cuban marsh leeches until it finished him off.

The ever violently active Crane crumpled up about the time of the surrender. He had allowed himself the extreme minimum of rest, and during the fighting, he had run, exposed to fire, all over the battlefield helping wounded men to shelter. (In the midst of imminent death, he had taken time to note that men shot in the chest continued to run forward before falling, while men shot in the abdomen dropped on the spot.) After the San Juan Hill fight, he had stood in a feverish daze watching a surgeon operate on wounded Spanish prisoners on the altar table pulled close to the sunlit doorway of the church at El Caney. When his nervous force began to drain away and "his limbs became like dough and his spinal column burned like a red hot wire," he kept on his feet with whiskey and quinine. But soon he became irresponsibly ill and shortly delirious. He managed to recover enough to get fired for incompetency by the New York

World, and to get back to England where his wife waited for him. Before he expired, he set down his ironic impressions of the pain and waste and grim humor of the war in the little masterpiece called *Wounds in the Rain.*

On August eighth the first transports began moving the weakened troops north, as fresh regiments—largely from the Southern States—arrived to take their places. In one of the first boats to get away were the Rough Riders. With them went Colonel Roosevelt, his appetite whetted for the political plums the Republicans were eager to spoon-feed to him.

In the midst of all the hullabaloo of the conquering hero's return it was the incorruptible Stephen Crane who gave Roosevelt the one bit of praise that has the ring of impartial authenticity. While the reporters were whooping up Roosevelt as a dashing cavalry hero, Crane, blankly silent on the Colonel as a military commander, wrote of him thus: "Say, this fellow worked for his troopers like a cider press. He tried to feed them. He helped build latrines. He cursed the quartermasters and the—"dogs"—on the transports to get quinine and grub for them. Let him be a politician if he likes. He was a gentleman, down there."

In Paris on the first day of October five commissioners from Spain met with five commissioners from the United States to draw up a definite treaty. The work carried over well into December. One tough controversy was over Spain's "relinquishment" of Cuba. Spain favored annexation to the United States, because such a disposal would guarantee better the security of the lives and property of Spaniards who resided or had estates in Cuba. But despite the Spanish concern over Cuban instability and Mr. Atkins' warnings, the United States seemed to have no apprehension over Cuba's independence—and besides she knew the entire world was watching her. However, the United States did agree for the time being to act as a trustee of the island, while it was in its raw and topsy-turvy condition, and to be responsible for the protection of life and property. The disposition of Puerto Rico, all the other Spanish islands in the West Indies, Guam, and the Philippines, was at length arranged with diplomatic facility. But Spain argued vehemently about the Cuban debt. Spain wanted Cuba to assume at least the non-military portion of her debt, but the United States refused to recognize any of Cuba's past obligations. The entire debt estimated at $400,000,000 the American commissioners decided Spain must swallow, regardless of the violent internal nausea it would certainly produce. "My dear friend, it is cruel, most cruel," Señor Castillo, Spanish Ambassador to France said to his life-time personal friend, Commissioner Reid. "Pray God that you may never be likewise vanquished." To sugar the bitter dose, the United States offered to pay $20,000,000 for the Philippine Archipelago. It was but infinitesimal consolation. The Spanish commissioners set down their signatures much as if they were signing their own death warrants.

As the fading splendor of Spain's glorious old flambeaux sickened to snuff-colored twilight, the incandescence of America's brand-new imperialism burst forth in gaudy little flashes here and there under the eastern and western suns. The seasoned British Empire smiled condescendingly at the new illumination from her cousin's callow piracy. But the Cuban patriots, who had not been invited to the peace conference to have a voice in the solution of their own future, marked sullen time in the dusk, full of misgivings and wondering darkly what sort of light would be vouchsafed them.

8

LEONARD WOOD AT SANTIAGO

Leonard Wood did not return with the Rough Riders to triumphal processions and politics. He remained as military governor of Oriente Province. No choice of an administrator could

have been more happily inspired. At the time he took over a post
that had succeeded from Diego Velasquez and Hernando de Soto,
Wood was in the prime vigor of his thirty-eighth year. A leonine
man with broad shoulders, an iron will and the handgrip of a
Beowulf, Wood was a human dynamo blessed with an absolute
self-command. His attractive, shining "Herculean" countenance
bespoke authority and good nature. Bold, confident and tireless,
he possessed a Greek love for athletic games and a benevolent
tyrant's autocracy and imagination.

From the very first, he felt a strong affection for the territory
of his guardianship. The ardors of his task, the mourning, suffering, suspicion, squalor and general demoralization heeling three
years' warfare, did not blind him to the natural glories of his domain. "God's own country—beautiful as a dream," he could write
frankly as a cosmopolite, not in the spirit of provincial sentimen-
tality. Gazing up at the "great mountains green to their tops,
filled with coconut and royal palms" and down at the "dear,
quaint little towns, hundreds of years old," he saw the beauty of
Oriente, while he remarked what needed to be done.

In its natural setting Santiago, the capital of the province, is the
most picturesque city west of Portugal and north of Rio de
Janeiro. Tumbling down a series of hills to the rich blue waters
of a bay so land-locked that it looks like a lake, the painted stone
houses suggest streaks and splotches on an artist's palette, with
salmon, old rose, yellow and mauve predominating. From an eminence, rectangular patches of fern-green patios seem dropped with
casual geometry into the faded terra cotta of wavy Spanish-tile
roofs. The white square of the central plaza is the only sizeable
flat space in the picture. Levels vary in a thousand manifestations,
as houses climb hills in sharp staccato accents and as the iron-
barred side-windows of one house look down upon the terraced
roof of the next one beside it. Occasionally, narrow streets mount
so steeply that they break into flights of stairs like their prototypes
in Naples, rising from an equally blue bay, and in Rome on her
seven hills.

Although Santiago has undergone earthquakes and hurricanes, the battering of incessant years has done the city's beauty no further harm than to spread an enhancing patina over the austerity of its masonry. The harmony of evergreen leaves accentuates the atmosphere of mellowed Spanish-Moorish antiquity. Latticed blinds and judas-windows and jutting casements with curving grills of wooden spindles hint that Arabian Nights' tales may be enacted in a modern New World.

To the north and to the west across the bay rise the enduring silver-green mountains, the Boniato Range and the Sierra Maestra —gently magnificent, sensuous, voluptuous in outline. On their crests, smoke-violet clouds drift as idly as in pre-Spanish days when the Indian savored life unmolested, when there were no thoughts to shake mankind and the mind marched little farther than the body. "Beautiful as a dream," said Wood, no idle dreamer.

But the enchantment he felt through the flattering mists of distance lessened upon a closer view and became flecked and flawed with man's sordid neglect. The corroding influence of war was only partially responsible for the disrepair. Santiago in 1898 was as isolated as it was nearly four hundred years before. Since there was no railroad connecting it with the more up-to-date Havana, there had been little intercourse between the two cities. For several decades, it had been touched only by the influence of Spanish officials, sea-farers, and scum seeping in from the West Indies. And the natural Spanish disregard of dirt and sanitation displayed by the Crown's servants, augmented by that languor and procrastination the tropics breed, had left Santiago in sorry plight. General Wood set ruthlessly to work to remove the ugly spots that fouled the heaven- and man-made beauty.

When he took charge, people were still dying from starvation or malnutrition, and shortly epidemics of smallpox and yellow fever broke out. Even while the American victory was being celebrated with music and wine in cafés and clubs, on side streets not three blocks off, breathing cadavers picked their way among

decomposing heaps of rubbish and dead curs and cats and don-
keys, carrying crusts to those too ill to do their own begging.
Children without home or parents fought like little wild animals
over garbage. The undernourished succumbed to fevers they
could ordinarily have thrown off. The very atmosphere was laden
with death. And those buzzards the fastidious Henry Adams had
watched with idle delight not five years ago dirtied the azure
sky with black-winged scrawls as they meandered capriciously
from feast to feast. The death rate went as high as two hundred a
day. The able-bodied were too badly needed for cleaning the
filthy streets to spare time for grave digging, so the collected
corpses were piled in great heaps on grills made of railroad iron,
drenched with "thousands of gallons of kerosene," and burned
to ashes.

Under Wood, the streets, equaling those of Turkey in dirtiness
and bad odors, were given the first thorough cleaning in their history. Drinking-water cisterns, which were found in the most revolting condition, were cleansed and dosed with purifying chemi-
cals. Every private home was inspected, and those persons persistently unsanitary were threatened with public whipping. Lines
of sewer pipes were laid to supplant foul black open wells that
filled the air with malarial poison and stench.

Allowing for no shilly-shallying, Wood conducted his campaign of cleaning, burning, disinfecting, under martial law. Clara
Barton and her Red Cross workers helped with the nursing and
the feeding. Soon every person in Santiago had either work or
free food.

Besides routing the specters of disease and famine that stalked
the place, Wood had to combat another grave threat to the town's
health and sanity. The Cuban riff-raff had looked to the surrender
as a signal to make a holiday of looting. Terrified Spanish merchants, property owners and those professional men who had opposed the revolution threw themselves on the protection of the
American soldiers. Wood sharply checked thieving and vandal-
ism. The rabble, thwarted in the glutting of their ire, were galled

to the point of mutiny. But Wood permitted the devil no opportunity to hatch villainies in idle brains. To eat, every well person had to work. When the labor of cleaning was over, Wood set them to work on public improvements, paving streets, building roads.

The *guajiros,* the country people, he sent back to their farms with a supply of food and seed and some farming gear. The farmers, victims of *reconcentrado,* were glad to be away from the miserable crowded city. Cheerfully they helped each other set up palm-thatched *bohios.* They planted crops—first, quick vegetable crops, then the longer maturing sugar cane and corn. Sometimes there was only one plow to serve several farms, and when there was neither horse nor ox, men let themselves be harnessed to the plow and took turns plowing with each other.

The task before Wood in 1898 was more difficult and complex than any Spanish administrator had ever faced. Not only was he called upon to set on their feet a crushed people suffering from a heritage of dishonesty, ignorance and oppression, but he was to help them to erect a governmental structure from the bottom upward. His mission, as he himself expressed it, was "the building up of a republic by Anglo-Saxons, in a Latin country where approximately seventy per cent of the people were illiterate." Moreover, about half the population of Oriente was black or colored, and there were strains of Negro blood in many middle-class families. Not always had immigrants from Spain brought their women with them, and many of those who had not had mixed with Negroes. A few mulattoes who had gained wealth had wedged into society by buying in Spain titles which gave them entrée to official functions, although they were never received by Cuban aristocrats. The black-and-white problem was more significant in Santiago than in Havana or the more blue-blooded Camagüey and Trinidad.

As the Americans came into shoulder-rubbing contact with their allies in the streets of Santiago, strangely there developed an odd attachment to their Spanish enemies. Without attempting to penetrate the differences of Cubans and Cubans, General Young and several others came to the blanket opinion that the patriots were "a lot of degenerates, absolutely devoid of humor or gratitude." The idealist Martí had foreseen the confusion of values which would inevitably arise when Spain's yoke was thrown off. "Remember," he had written warningly to his own people, "that, during war, the thief, the robber, the bandit, even the murderer who fought for liberty, was at once the lily white patriot. Now many will turn again to be what they were, before being inspired by patriotism. Rascals will struggle to infest politics here, as they do politics the world over."

However, by the time the commissioners began the formulation of a peace treaty in Paris, the Santiago district was not only orderly and peaceful but self-sustaining. The issue of rations in Oriente Province came to an end in October, but the lush valleys of Oriente, traversed by innumerable streams, brought crops to maturity as if by magic. Shortly scarlet-sashed muleteers were driving strings of bell-adorned *mulos* laden with paniers of vegetables through Santiago's resounding narrow streets past the Cathedral to the public market. It was a phenomenal recovery. "When it is remembered," General Wood wrote, "that this country has been in a constant condition of more or less continuous warfare for the past four years, and also that the long and serious wars which have recently taken place were of a most brutal and demoralizing character, it is remarkable to see how little brigandage exists and how quickly the people have returned to peaceful occupations." The glory belongs mostly to Wood's skill in dealing with the Cuban temperament, but the result is a valuable commentary on the Cuban's good qualities when properly brought to light and governed.

Gradually as the bloom came back to Oriente and as the renovated city settled into Spanish-American routine with unpolluted air in its lungs and wholesome food in its stomachs, the gayety of that society Henry Adams had found the most quaint and delightful in the whole wide world returned. Many Americans made friends with amiable Cubans who spoke English. When one came to be tolerant of the traditions, social customs, and codes of the other and to smile at respective foibles as seen through alien eyes, real friendship and affection were born. They admired each other for the very qualities they themselves lacked—the energy and efficiency of the one, the sensuous design for living of the other. The Americans were welcomed at all Cuban social clubs. Balls, dinings, musicals were given in the great houses and at the legations, and entertainments of various kinds on American and foreign ships. Some sophisticates were advanced enough to give mixed swimming parties, when married ladies and gentlemen would go by boat to beaches three miles down the bay near the spot where Hobson sank the *Merrimac.* Here the men and women would separate. Half a mile away from where the men swam, the ladies, guarded scrupulously from masculine eyes, would assay the water sportively, swathed in high-necked outing-flannel gowns with long sleeves and black stockings.

Cocking mains again assumed focal points in social intercourse, and on Sundays from early dawn a stream of rustics, black and white, trudged into the city with their roosters under their arms. All day birds fought, bled, died, crowed in triumph; while men yelled, cursed, kissed the victor's bloody head, lost their last pennies, won small fortunes. Through the nights the savage, insidious music of the rumba throbbed, as mulattoes danced themselves into orgiastic exhaustion.

American soldiers with intentions gayly dishonorable beguiled the time in amorous dallyings with dark-eyed houris, and bought or won Latin loves as freely and simply as young satyrs. They learned to emulate the Cuban trick of boasting of goat-like prowess, while drinking infinite small glasses of Bacardi, the world's nonpareil in rum, which was manufactured at the foot of the city. They bought high Spanish combs for girls back home and snake-skin belts made from the gigantic native boa for themselves and their young brothers. They bought banana fritters from an old black woman who had squatted for forty years over her charcoal burner and temporarily shifted her stand only when the military cleaning brigade swooped down upon her. They learned to distinguish between mangoes, to know that the golden-fleshed *biscochuelos* were the most delectable of them all. And some of them caught the Latin disease of "sweet-to-do-nothing" of which they could never be cured in the States, but had to go back to Cuba to spend the rest of their days doing occasional odd hours of business, but mostly sitting on the veranda of Casa Granda— where they still sit in 1934 "catching the shade and breeze" and resettling the affairs of the world anew each evening.

To those soldiers and officers who were not fortunate enough to penetrate into the exclusiveness of Cuban family life but saw it only through grilled windows, Santiago was a huge painted prison of many thousand compartments, with the prisoners virtually all women. Only on Saturday and Sunday late afternoons did the women emerge en masse to stroll about the central plaza to band music and to absorb admiration from a masculine world.

It was easier for the Southern officers to understand the complexity and subtleties that go with sun-ripened Spanish characteristics than for the more literal Northerners. By inheritance, Southerners and Cubans—borrowing an idea from Stark Young—had much the same family sense, the same proud taste for a friendly, semi-formal, complaisant living. The ideal of both their societies was a social existence rather than mass production, competition and barter. They could share the same sense of freedom and life and joy that the sun breeds. They knew the value of leisure, and the value to themselves of putting their highborn women on pedestals. But the Cuban idea of keeping their ladies harem-like behind bars was too Moorish even for the Southerners. Yet the beauties behind the bars appeared happy enough, and seemed delighted to let the passing world catch glimpses of their unveiled loveliness, as they bent over embroidery frames or played snatches of gay waltzes on small Viennese pianos. At night the narrow sidewalks were streaked with the shadows of young men, who stood outside the barred windows, courting young ladies who sat within, or, as a special mark of favor, leaned against the bars, clasping the cool black rods with warm fingers. The conversations were low-toned, punctuated by almost interminable pauses. For always within sight or earshot was the mother or chaperon, rocking in a mahogany rocker, fanning herself vaguely, often pretending to doze. Fortunate young men, having been admitted to the family circle of some houses after long window-service and favorable introductions, would sit playing Lotto in a parlor forest-thick with chairs and tables littered with bric-a-brac. Loitering in other doorways buttressed from the moonlight that flooded the street, disconsolate youths, whose window-courtships were not sanctioned, surreptitiously gazed heavy-eyed and sighed vain overtures of love to night air. The very atmosphere of the streets was charged with desire, as well as with the perfume of star-jasmine and heliotrope.

Though the American merely smiled with amused superiority at the hardships of Cuban wooing, there were some items in the alien social attitudes to give him pause. The soldier who loved his liquor too well was surprised to learn that Cubans considered it a disgrace for a man to get drunk, but that a married man might respectably have four or five mistresses or "according to what he could do." One Cuban of distinguished family related to some officers the story of his uncle, a wealthy plantation owner, who had seven mistresses and twenty natural children. Every morning when the milk was brought into the city from the farms, his wife, a "fine, splendid woman," would have her husband's little bastards file by her, give them each a quart of milk and ten cents, and ask solicitously, "And how is your mother today?" She accepted her husband's peccadillos as a matter of course, without resentment or jealousy. She was his wife, and asked for nothing more than the security and distinction such a position gave her; for all honors went to her, and never under any circumstances did he humiliate her or recognize his mistresses in public. As with all high-bred Latin American women, security was to be desired above everything else in life. The privilege of sitting in a cool, high-ceiling room all day and in a star-canopied patio at evening gossiping with the women of their household, or prattling with their children, secure in the knowledge that a husband would return sometime in the night, was sufficient for the happiness of Cuban women in 1898.

The arabesques of courtship, the quaintness of Cuban moral codes, Wood made no effort to constrain. Although a New Englander, he was neither a Puritan nor an instinctive moral reformer. But because of the smallpox and yellow fever epidemics he made some drastic changes in funeral customs. It had long been the Santiagoan custom for the coffined dead to be borne on the shoulders of friends to the cemetery. If the deceased was wealthy, the body was carried to several different churches for service and blessing and halted at street corners where Te Deums were sung by orphanage children, the cortège winding round and round, up and down the Santiago hills before arriving at the cemetery. This long-drawn-out procedure was inspired by wily priests, for each stop put money into their purses. Not to spite the Church, but because of the supposed contagion from fevers, Wood made a law which prohibited the coffin's being carried on shoulders except to get it from house to hearse, and which made it imperative for the procession to go the shortest route to the graveyard. Formerly Santiago's deceased often lay over-long in odorous state, taper-lit, while hired mourners wailed professionally with relatives, friends and servants. By Wood's law, the body had to be buried within twenty-four hours. Though a damper was thus put on ostentatious grief, widows of the twentieth century continued to mourn behind closed doors for two years, and for five years to wear only deep black of the plainest cotton cloth.

In one decree only did Wood show a spot of blue in his New England nose. To give a tone of well-being and self-respect to the appearance of the general public, he ordered that men should not go out on the principal streets or lounge in the ornamental parks without their blouses. So the masses donned jackets of cotton crash or denim, and for a while washed their faces and brushed their hair on week days. But in hot countries even jackets of linen may become burdensome, and though the law has not been changed to this day, the Cubans interpret "blouse" as any outer upper garment that hangs below the belt behind, and now proletarian shirt tails are edged with tape so that a shirt serves also as a coat. Or by a more whimsical evasion, shirt tails are merely pulled out to hang down behind, the front ends being tied in a rakish knot about the midriff.

When Wood had revived and set the city in order, he crowned his solid achievements by constructing a military road to the top of Boniato Hill about ten miles north of Santiago. Here he established a military camp in the healthiest spot of all Cuba, with abundant drinking water crystal-pure. The place was a regular garden of Hesperides, spilling over with fruits and flowers, and ever vocal with bird song. Because of its engineering difficulties and the fact that today it is used only by tourists and the few travelers to the north, Cubans have designated the road Wood's Folly. But it has stood for thirty-five years a tribute to its builder's skill and imagination. The anacahuita trees, with medicinal properties soothing to the lungs, which he planted on either side of the road, now shade it prodigally in full-foliaged maturity.

Looking to the south from the crest of Boniato—where at midsummer noon it is as cool as North Carolina mountain tops, while Santiago lazes below in an amphitheater of humid heat—undulating hills fold one on the other, in greens and lavenders and coppery colors. Here and there can be seen a gray *bohío* perched on a hillock half-hidden in a patch of mango, banana, and coffee trees. On small plateaus are Chinese vegetable gardens, their patterned green rows proclaiming the harmony between Oriental design and industry and the fruitfulness of dark, opulent Cuban earth.

9

WOOD, MILITARY GOVERNOR OF CUBA

On January first, 1899, the Spanish Governor-General in Havana formally surrendered the government to General John R. Brooke. Jamming the waterfront to watch the raising of the Stars and Stripes over Morro Castle a weaving crowd gathered. Its varied complexion ranged from the opaque ivory of Castilians and the ruddy scrubbed freshness of American doughboys to the coffee-and-milk and African black of the rabble. As the American colors were run up, a livid wave of intense hatred swept over thousands of dark faces and a low growl of resentment reverberated threateningly. The mob believed the Americans would never take down their flag. But except for some desultory rioting, there was no overt outbreak that evening.

The Spanish officials had left the administration buildings in an indescribably filthy condition. What they could not salvage, they had destroyed, including light fixtures and plumbing. Chapman recounts that twelve hundred cubic yards of rubbish were removed from the custom-house alone. The records were either destroyed or removed; not an article of furniture was left. The American official taking charge had to appeal to the retiring Spaniard for a chair and a desk for himself. Johnson sums up the finale of Spanish rule: "There was nothing in all their record in Cuba more unbecoming than their manner of leaving it."

Like Santiago five months previously, the streets of Havana were crowded with wretches in every stage of misery, filth and starvation. The sidewalks were as thick with beggars as summer flies about a shambles. Under the marble arcades that edged the principal thoroughfares, mothers with three, five, seven children squatted on pavements without blanket or shawl, patiently awaiting the charity of God. They had been there for months; they were duplicated by thousands. The country districts were hardly any better off than the city. Sugarmills had been vandalized, expensive machinery rendered useless by sabotage, crops gone to weeds and ruin. Of the 1,260,000 cattle in 1898, all but 70,000 had been killed during the war.

Brooke's administration during the chaotic first year was entirely praiseworthy, as the Cubans themselves admitted. Although the United States had assumed full military control, about ninety per cent of the new officials were Cubans, who were thus straightway given training in responsibility. But Brooke's "conspicuous" honesty, generosity and fairness were not enough for them. Their gratitude for America's aid in freeing them from Spain was small indeed. The dubious Cuban Assembly was downright inimical. The handling of the Cuban force still under arms was both ticklish and annoying. Máximo Gómez, idol of the populace, piqued at his allies for snatching the victory of what he considered was his war, and deeply wounded at having been ignored by the Americans, moved from town to town, broadcasting his injured feelings. "The Americans have embittered the joy of the Cuban victors with their forcibly imposed tutelage," he proclaimed in acrimonious speeches. For a time, Atkins, the sugar planter, and many others who knew the temper of the insurgents, seriously feared an uprising against the "American benefactors." García in Oriente had threatened to fight Wood, and Wood had replied, "Why don't you try it? It might be the easiest way to settle it."

The armed Cubans were strongly disinclined to disband until they should be well paid for their war services. Gómez hinted that sixty million dollars in gold distributed among his officers and men would salve the army's feelings. This amount would have necessitated a much larger loan than Cuba's depleted resources warranted. It did not seem expedient to put such a debt on the country in order to benefit some 33,000 men—particularly when at least half of the "lily white patriots" were illiterate blacks, and some were undoubtedly those normal-time brigands and thieves Martí had cited.

After considerable haggling and diplomacy, Gómez finally compromised for three million dollars—a free gift from the United States out of the surplus remaining from the war appropriation. In a fury the Assembly deposed Gómez for taking the smaller bonus, and because of this disloyal act to the national hero, the Assembly lost popular favor. The soldiers turned in their arms, received cash, and slipped back into civil life according to their inclinations and opportunities, each with at least seventy-five dollars in his pockets—enough to start a small farm or a small shop, or to make an impressive stake at a rural cockfight.

When the Cuban army disbanded, Brooke proceeded more easily with his good works. Like Wood, he alleviated suffering, nursed the sick, did much cleaning and provided some sort of start for the country people. He began the reconstruction of governmental machinery, set the custom-house in working order, put new excise taxes on liquor, and laid the foundations for popular education. As far as it went, Brooke's work was entirely meritorious. An illuminating Cuban criticism of his abilities was that "he was even of a somewhat better stamp, perhaps, than was fitting for a man in such a high post in that difficult and exceptional situation."

In the last month of the last year of the century General Brooke was superseded by General Wood as Military Governor of Cuba. The two men had quarreled almost immediately after Brooke had been given the higher appointment. Wood was not temperamentally equipped to work under anyone, and he had won out in the controversy by using political influence. On the other hand his substantial accomplishments of seventeen months in Oriente had won him epithets of "model administrator" and "administrator from another planet." Of the two excellent men, Wood was the better choice for the job. Not only was he shrewder and more

far-seeing than Brooke, but he was more masterful and at the
same time more genial and magnetic. He was an out-and-out
autocrat, but his autocracy was tempered by a strong diplomatic
caution, and he had the felicitous ability of winning the admiration of enemies. In the combination of these qualities, he had
caught the Cubans' imagination.

On the morning of December twentieth, Wood's boat steamed
into Havana harbor, saluted by guns from Morro and bands playing American and Cuban National Anthems. Characteristically
Wood had arrived at sunrise. New Year's Day, 1900, found him
installed in the beautiful age-roughened palace of the governor-
generals, which had been completed in 1792. The new century
could not have dawned more auspiciously for the island.

Washington instructed Wood to groom Cuba speedily for an
independent republican government, to arrange an efficient system of justice, and to establish a public school system. With
vigor and thoroughness, the new governor saw to it that government employees did no loafing, took no three hours off for
luncheon and siesta, but put in a full day's work—an amazing
and disconcerting innovation to sinecure-holders.

Retaining all the Spanish laws that had been tested by time
and would hold water, Wood added liberal doses of the United
States Constitution. The treatment proved remarkably efficacious.
Where Brooke was criticized for letting his Cuban Secretaries
dominate him, Wood was criticized for making tools of his ap-
pointees. From the first, however, he strove to make the military
side of his régime as inconspicuous as possible. Instead of employing American soldiers in the interior provinces, he expanded
a system of rural mounted Cuban police which he had inaugurated in Oriente.

In reorganizing the department of justice, he decreed that
judges and other court officers should be put on salary and the
abusive system of fees abolished. He extended the net-work of
police courts to all parts of the island. He made drastic prison
reforms and released six hundred prisoners after a quick, pene-

trating investigation. He introduced the right of *habeas corpus*. He provided lawyers for the poor. He prepared a mercantile register. He organized municipal self-government. Scrapping much of Brooke's work in education, he inaugurated a public school system under the combined auspices of Alexis Frye and Lieutenant Matthew Hanna. (In the summer of 1900, 1,500 Cuban teachers accepted Harvard University's invitation to study there, with all expenses paid.) He reorganized the University, which had gone to seed. He sanctioned the separation of Church and State. (Brooke had already made civil marriages legal.) He repaired public buildings, and began more public works than had been undertaken in a quarter-century of Spanish rule. He built bridges and roads, developed telephone and telegraph services. Included in his sweeping campaign for sanitation and health was the efficient regulation of hospitals and charities. He issued a law prohibiting cruelty to animals, with due provision for the punishment of those violating it. He beautified the Prado and the Malecón, two of the most memory-haunting boulevards in the world.

The principal criticism of Wood's administration was that the economic conditions did not keep pace with the other improvements and innovations. An unfavorable sugar-situation, due to poor world market and the demoralization caused by years of warfare, added to Wood's difficulties. Although encouragement of foreign capital might have helped the island out of its economic depression, it was politically salutary to avoid the least charge of exploitation by American big business. So for this reason the United States Congress had passed the Foraker Law which prohibited the granting of franchises or concessions of any kind during the occupation. Despite the lack of stimulation from foreign financial aid, there was not one business failure during the intervention—a particularly noteworthy fact since the greater proportion of business was controlled by the hated Spaniards.

Twice General Wood sanctioned and abetted a circumvention of the Foraker Law. The first case was particularly far-sighted and commendable, for by the evasion, Sir William Van Horne, who had built the Canadian Pacific Railway, laid a railroad eastward from Santa Clara to Santiago. With the energy of another Wood, he completed the road by the first day of December 1902. Formerly the journey from Havana to Santiago had taken ten days. Now it could be accomplished in twice ten hours. It opened up the richest part of the island to productive development. Furthermore, Sir William used his best abilities to carry out his promise to develop the resources of Cuba "in all practicable ways." Besides bringing prosperity to thousands of Cubans, he endeavored to teach them, by example, to make the most of the beauty that lay at their doorsteps. With the help of Alcides Betancourt, he laid out the lovely courtyard garden of the Hotel Camagüey, which today flourishes as a memorial to Cuba's railroad-building benefactor.

The second evasion of the Foraker Law abetted by Wood gave a ten-year monopoly to a jai-alai company, which proposed to introduce the favorite game of the Basques to Cuba on a professional scale. Wood, who had become a proficient and ardent jai-alai player, believed the sport might supplant the Spanish love for the blood-stained excitement of the bull-fight, which had been discontinued, and for cockfighting, which was ubiquitous. But especially he hoped it would take the place of that more disintegrating gambling mania fostered by the lottery, which inhabitants seemed willing to become paupers to gratify.

Wood's services in bringing sweetness and light to Cuba were much like those of Las Casas a century before, except that their bounty was more profuse and far-reaching, for Wood worked with the demoniacal energy of a Tacón. However, surpassing in significance all the foregoing impressive list of achievements, the isolation of the *stegomyia* mosquito as the cause of yellow fever, and the subsequent world victory over the disease, remain the chief glory of Wood's régime.

YELLOW FEVER CONQUERED

Romantic Havana had long been feared as a death trap; in summer months foreign travelers avoided it as they would a lepers' colony. Just where yellow fever came from no one is sure. Some contend it was brought from Africa with the first Negro slave ships, but better scientists have presented clearer proof that it existed in America before the discovery of Columbus. From the Isthmus of Panama and Mexico it seems to have spread over the West Indies, thence to Spain, and as far north as Wales. The disease had definitely appeared in Cuba as early as 1647. In its most virulent form it was brought to Havana in the autumn of 1761 by an East Indian ship which had touched at Mexican ports. It played havoc not only with the inhabitants, but more especially with the English and American invaders under Pocock and Albemarle, who captured the city the next year. After that date, although Cuba was never free from yellow fever deaths, the natives themselves came to suffer little from its ravages. Doubtless the majority of them had the disease as babies, and most of those who had not died in infancy were *immune*.

It was new arrivals who suffered. Cubans looked with certain affection on *fiebre amarillo* and called it the Great Patriot, because it was an enemy of aliens and took its annual toll of Spaniards. It was not necessary, however, for Americans to visit Cuba to know the horrors of yellow fever. Cargo ships coming from Havana loosed the disease in American seaport towns: New Orleans, Mobile, Charleston, Baltimore, New York. In the summer of 1898, it terrified the whole Mississippi Valley.

The worst epidemic in Philadelphia occurred in 1793, when

one-tenth of the population perished. Those who did not get
the disease were driven to frenzied hysteria trying new theories
of preventives. Among other things, it was believed that the
air should be purified; and staid Philadelphia was shocked continually through the summer hours by the booming of cannons
and the flaring of gigantic bonfires. Dignified citizens would not
stir out-of-doors without camphor-soaked sponges at their mouths,
or smelling bottles of vinegar at their noses. Gentlemen paying
court to ladies were permitted to puff clouds of cigar smoke in
fair faces, while the bewildered gentlewomen munched garlic
buds as if nibbling sweetmeats. Even those who wore talismans
of tarred rope about their necks, like a garland or a hangman's
noose, feared to go to their own relatives' funerals and let them
be buried hugger-mugger by a lone Negro attendant who drove
the death cart. Had frost not come early that year—no scientist
connected the coming of frost with the passing of mosquitoes—
prim Philadelphia would likely have become a gibbering mad-
house.

In Cuba, by 1900, preventives had ceased to be fantastic.
Local inhabitants had come to shrug and leave matters to fate:
there were no preventives, as there were no specific remedies
or treatment. A man got the disease or he did not. If he got
it, he died or he got well. If he recovered, he would never have
the disease again. That was all there was to it. A few aged Negro
women still clung to orange-leaf tea as a cure. But people now
paid no more attention to them than to Dr. Carlos Finlay, who
had been proclaiming for nineteen years—ever since he gave an
address on August fourteenth, 1881, before the Academy of Sci-
ences in Havana—that the guilty agent of yellow fever was the
stegomyia mosquito. Dr. Finlay, born in Camagüey in 1833 of a
Scotch physician father and a French Creole mother from the Island of Trinidad, had studied medicine in Philadelphia and returned to Cuba to practice. From 1872 he had dedicated his life to
the discovery of the cause of yellow fever, and after nine years of
experiments he had convinced himself of a theory. He had hit

upon the greatest medical discovery of the modern age, but he could not prove it. Scientists smiled condescendingly—"Theorizing old crank with mutton-chop whiskers, poor Finlay!" they said. For nineteen long years Finlay tragically begged the world to believe him. And all the while, he went on experimenting, breeding batches of mosquitoes, conserving dry eggs, and yearning for a chance to prove his thesis before he died. He was approaching seventy when Wood became military governor.

It was generally believed that yellow fever was a filth disease. Major William Crawford Gorgas, an Alabamian, who was shortly to be assured a high place with the Immortals for his great work in Panama, had for many months conducted a cleaning campaign as Chief Sanitation Officer under General Brooke. But in 1900, the first year of Wood's military governorship, the scourge broke out just when Havana was extraordinarily more sanitary than it had ever been. Because Wood had checked an epidemic in Oriente by cleaning Santiago and segregating the victims, he ordered a further scouring by the sanitation expert. This time Gorgas raided cisterns and cesspools and cleaned "hidden recesses of which the natives themselves were unaware." Plumbing was installed wholesale, new drainage put in, stables furnished everywhere with concrete floors. Chlorinated lime lay over the tropical city like a freak fall of snow.

Soon Gorgas had Havana the cleanest city in the entire world. The Americans gloried in their achievement. The Cubans were indifferent or even resentful, for they had no passion for cleanliness. Dr. Finlay had watched the procedure with interest, applauding the sanitation, but reiterating in a monotone like a speech-impedimented prophet, "The mosquito is the cause of yellow fever." Scientists continued to smile tolerantly at the pathetic old crank. Even Gorgas, a warm friend of Finlay, discounted the theory absolutely and pointed with humble modesty to the absence of yellow fever now as well as dysentery and typhoid. The triumph was short-lived. Havana was plunged in a fresh epidemic. And strangely enough the cleanest parts of the city suffered most. The Cubans were amused and delighted. Apparently sanitation had stimulated yellow fever.

Gorgas and his co-workers soon discovered why Havana had suffered little from yellow fever from 1898 to 1900. There had been no immigration during those two years. In 1900 twenty-five thousand immigrants, mostly from Spain, had entered Havana. Their non-immunity answered half the question of the latest epidemic. But what was the other half? Wood was convinced that the accepted views of filth as the origin of yellow fever were wrong. He appointed a commission, headed by Major Walter Reed, an army physician from Virginia, to get at the root of the matter. For want of anything better, Reed suggested making a searching test of Finlay's theory. Wood thought there might be something in it. It was fortunate for both Cuba and the United States that Wood was a man of medical training and experience. (He held a medical degree from Harvard.) In consequence, Finlay's technical presentation of his experiments and observation appealed to the military governor as it would have failed to do had he been merely a politician or a soldier. Wood furnished Reed with every facility necessary for the work, including money to buy human beings for experimentation.

The other members of the Board consisted of the Cuban yellow fever specialist, Dr. Aristides Agramonte, and two Americans, Dr. Jesse W. Lazear, a European-trained micro-biologist, and Dr. James Carroll, a dauntless, bald-headed, bespectacled ex-lumberjack. In conference, Dr. Finlay expounded his ingenious theory, showed records of experiments, and proffered some tiny, black, cigar-shaped mosquito eggs—infinitesimal objects which possessed properties as deadly as Spanish cannon and Mauser rifles. Lazear hatched the eggs in a warm place. The commissioners watched them metamorphose into wrigglers, and then into delicately handsome mosquitoes with legs alternately striped black and white and with silvery half-moons ornamenting their backs. The stegomyia is the aristocrat of mosquitoes and has the reputation of surpassing all seven hundred varieties in physical appearance. The scientists let the mosquitoes suck the blood of yellow fever patients. Then Carroll and Lazear—both of them were married and had young children—offered themselves as human guinea pigs, fully aware that if they developed the disease, death was a one-to-four shot. They made their beautiful gesture to give countenance to further tests in which men would have to play a dangerous game. The mosquitoes who had fed on contamination now fed at blood streams that nourished two super-valuable scientific brains. For a whole day they bit to their hearts' content at the doctors' underwrists, temples and ankles—favorite spots of the stegomyia. With some apprehension the Board waited watchfully. The doctors came through without the slightest injury, and more or less disgusted. The first experiments were "disappointing," because they ignored Dr. Carter's one-year-old discovery of "extrinsic incubation"—a period of ten days to two weeks having to intervene between one case of yellow fever and another apparently derived from it. They had used mosquitoes too fresh from a yellow fever feed. Somewhat discouraged by the results, Carroll and Lazear became careless with their mosquitoes. On September sixteenth Carroll felt chilly and indisposed. Shortly he was in the throes of the worst form of yellow fever. He came so near to death that he escaped by little more than a single heart-beat. While he was at ebb-tide, Dr. Lazear went down with the disease. Before he lost consciousness, he confessed that during some experimenting with soldiers he had failed to brush a mosquito from the back of his hand. In the early evening of September twenty-fifth, Lazear died, a martyr to science, an irreplaceable loss to humanity.

Though death had taken Lazear, and Carroll had barely escaped, their sacrifices had not made the experiments scientifically complete. At Quemados, near Havana, Reed built a camp with two houses and seven tents, and offered $200 to each man willing to gamble with death. When volunteers were called for, Private Kissinger and John J. Moran of the office force were the first to offer themselves. They did so on one condition: that they receive no compensation. "We volunteer," they said, "in the interest of science and for the cause of humanity." Though by a special gracious destiny both came out of their agony alive, these gallant fellows who deliberately marched to the valley of death for their brothers' sake were worthy of elegies composed by a Shelley. But beyond presenting the men with gold watches, no honors were accorded them. A peculiarly pitiful interest attaches to Kissinger, for the reason that not long after his sacrificial ordeal he completely lost his health and became a paralytic. His wife, performing the dual rôle of nurse and bread-winner, supported him by taking in washing. On March second, 1907, in recognition of his services to his country and humanity, the United States Government granted him a pension of $12 a month. The paralyzed Kissinger was permitted to live in stark poverty until December 16, 1922, when Congress increased the pension to a monthly $100—twenty-one years after his heroic act.

For three months the Board experimented. (At first Spanish immigrants were willing to take the sickly chance for the cash offer. However, after the first three became potently ill, even penniless peasants decided that $200 hardly compensated for the discomfort, to say nothing of the risk of death. In the end, the Board had to rely on soldiers and hospital attendants for their human guinea pigs.) Two identical rooms side by side were prepared: in one were stegomyia mosquitoes, who had bitten yellow fever patients; in the other, revolting paraphernalia from yellow fever victims' rooms. With a stove-fire burning briskly in the latter to keep the atmosphere above ninety, with a minimum of ventilation, three plucky men—they were named Cook, Folk and Jernegen—slept on mattresses on which people had died, between sheets disgusting with the stench of patients' discharges, and in pajamas stained and reeking with dried black vomit.

In this stinking atmosphere they sweated miserably for twenty days, being allowed the one luxury of feeding on delicacies fit for an emperor's table. At the termination of their hideous incarceration they came out of the ordeal hale and hearty. The men in the scrupulously clean, well-ventilated house next door, with nothing to molest their ease but a few soft-singing aristocratic stegomyias, contracted yellow fever.

The results of the Board's experiments revealed that ten out of thirteen contracted the disease in the sanitary mosquito-infested building; none, in the foul clothing-infected building. Reed had proved irrefutably the innocuousness of the patient and the harmlessness of his belongings. Still further ingenious tests were conducted. At length the Board was able to announce authoritatively that yellow fever is transmitted by the female stegomyia mosquito, that in order to become infected the mosquito must suck the blood of a yellow fever patient within the first three days of illness, that twelve to twenty days must elapse before she is able to convey the infection, that the person bitten does not show symptoms of the disease until three to six days have passed. Furthermore, it was determined that the disease was caused by a parasite, and that the parasite was submicroscopic, so small and yet so powerful that it retained its deadly qualities even when infected blood was filtered through porcelain.

Reed and his Board had proved the truth that Finlay had hit upon with an amazing medical clairvoyance. But their discovery brought little joy to the citizens at large. A new terror was added to daily existence. People had lived on intimate, if annoyed, terms with the pests all their lives. And now they came to regard the little mosquitoes zooming about them as if they were so many flying rattlesnakes. Billions upon billions of mosquitoes sported in every nook and cranny of Havana. They dwelt in prison dungeons and palace galleries. They perched on babies' cradles and ladies' nosegays. They made continuous carnival by night and by day. Worst of all, there could now be no surcease of anxiety even at noontime, for the deadly stegomyia (often called "the day mosquito") bit by day as well as night, whereas the species that carried malarial germs did its mischief only after sundown.

The American Board had presented Cuba with a hideous doom. No non-immune visitor would ever joy in Cuba again.

Though the great discovery had been made, Reed himself was alarmed and gravely perplexed over the problem of remedy. To rid a country of mosquitoes seemed a task greater than any the gods had set for Hercules. Reed called for Gorgas, who still thought that yellow fever might be caused in other ways—for was not typhoid transmitted by agencies other than the house fly? Gorgas, with his mild, unruffled assurance, said, "If it *is* the mosquito, I will rid Havana of mosquitoes." Reed doubted gloomily if it could be done.

General Wood gave the sanitation expert carte blanche, all the money he needed, and hearty coöperation. Working on the principle that the system of destroying mosquito larvæ is the essential in yellow fever control and that everything else is secondary to it, Gorgas set about to destroy the evil at its source. The war on mosquitoes began in March 1901. In his one-room office on the harbor front, Gorgas soon had cardboard records of every house in Havana and each of the city's three hundred thousand citizens, their cisterns, rain barrels, and every receptacle that might contain water, including jugs, vases, soap dishes, broken saucers and tin can tops set under table legs defensively against ants. At first housewives indignantly resented white-coated sanitation inspectors poking into every secret cupboard of their homes. It was a high tribute to Gorgas's tact and persuasive amiability that the doubting citizens turned in and gave him splendid coöperation.

In their larvæ destroying, the inspectors found out many interesting facts about the stegomyia which differentiates the species from the rest of its kind. It was known, of course, that the several hundred varieties of mosquitoes have common traits in their diet —they all feed on various vegetable juices and it is necessary for the female to suck blood before she can lay eggs. (The male is not bloodthirsty, and physically does not possess the apparatus with which to bite.) But the stegomyia is a domesticated, urbane mosquito. It scorns woods and marshes, residing only in or near human habitations. The female is fastidious to a degree. She will not lay her eggs in stagnant pools or in mud puddles like plebeian mosquitoes. She prefers fresh rain water in a stone or earthenware container, or a flower vase or a goblet of drinking water set aside and forgotten. And if she cannot find a place for accouchement that accords with her sensibilities, she will not perform her natural function, preferring to let her aristocratic progeny perish unborn. Naturally the tribe of stegomyias had regarded Gorgas's first general cleanings with enthusiastic appreciation. Ecstatic at finding such an overwhelming number of choice birthplaces for their young, the females had almost driven their mates mad with the excess of their sweet singing and had outdone themselves with the profusion of their egg-laying. On the other hand, hordes of harmless common mosquitoes, being deprived of mud puddles, clogged drains, and such accustomed laying-in spots, and not knowing the intimacies of homes or nunneries as did the stegomyia, or feeling self-conscious in flower bowls, birdcage baths, nuns' washstand jugs or communion chalices, had gone barren with confusion. In consequence, mosquito society had never been so dominantly aristocratic in history; and silvery half-moons, badges of noble breeding, were seen on mosquito backs everywhere. If they had been miraculously blessed like their scorned human victims with the intelligence to acknowledge a patron saint, Gorgas would beyond question have been the stegomyia's choice. But it is well they were not, for this same man who had so favored them turned diabolical and poured oil on the clean waters; and they saw their wriggling babies—forced by nature like the whale to come to the water's surface for occasional draughts of air—choked to death by the murderous slime.

Gorgas worked at his problem from the other end too. He kept yellow fever victims out of reach of mosquitoes. Since the first three days of the disease were the only dangerous ones for spreading infection, all cases were reported immediately at the first symptom manifested. The patients were taken in screened ambulances to screened wards in Las Animas Hospital, or if they elected to stay in their own homes, carpenters would come to screen the apartment. In the manner of an up-to-date fire department, squads of carpenters with wagons loaded with lumber, wire netting and tools were kept ready for duty day and night, alert to a telephone bell, so that within an hour after notice a stricken victim was either at the screened hospital or was being screened in at his own home.

Besides destroying larvæ, war was made on the live mosquitoes by stifling them within doors with the fumes from tobacco stems, the waste in cigar manufacture. Periodically massacres by suffocation were decreed in every household. The dead insects were swept into piles, the sizes of the hecatombs being carefully noted before the corpses were burned. The piles became smaller and smaller, until finally a live mosquito in Havana was a *rara avis*.

Ninety days after Gorgas began his devastating war, in which untold billions of mosquitoes perished and countless unborn generations were snuffed back into limbo, there was not a single case of yellow fever. In Gorgas, Death had met such an intrepid adversary that he was forced to take a holiday. For the first time in a hundred and forty years Havana was free of yellow fever. Malaria too was on its way to speedy obliteration. A comparison of figures for deaths from disease in the American army at the end of the United States occupation in Cuba will show the results of Gorgas's work: 20.26 per cent died in the Pacific Islands; 4.83 per cent in the United States; 1.67 per cent in Cuba.

The resultant good of the discoveries by Reed's Board, based on Finlay's hypothesis, and the routing of yellow fever from the earth's surface by Gorgas's methods, may be said, in one sense, to justify the Spanish-American War. Of course, it is an accidental justification. The United States did not enter the war—which was hardly her business and which cost her $861,000 a day while in progress—to save the world from yellow fever. But that was an indisputable good which came out of it. Those families who lost loved ones through battle or disease in the fretful summer of 1898, may console themselves that their men did not die in vain. The obliteration of yellow fever may stand as an ever-lasting memorial to those youths sacrificed to the spirit of military aggression, political ambition, or sentimental hysteria. After all it is something; while those who lost husbands, fathers, brothers, lovers in the last great war have little enough, God knows, to cling to by way of consolation.

Excepting the recent Walter Reed Hospital in Washington, where are the American monuments of marble and bronze to those other scientists, who rendered a service worth a hundred wars? To Gorgas, Finlay, Lazear, Carroll—and to Kissinger and the unnamed soldiers who risked death for the sake of humanity and posterity? In November 1902, two years after his achievement, Walter Reed, having received no other reward than the consciousness that he had conferred an inestimable benefit to mankind, died, murmuring that he was leaving "so little, so little" to his wife, who was no longer young. In August 1904, *The Nation* was pleading for contribution for some sort of a memorial to him, urging philanthropy, patriotism, and commerce to unite to honor him. Reed had helped to save the United States billions of dollars—to say nothing of human lives—and perhaps in peculiar consideration of that fact, twenty-one years after his death, on March third, 1923, Congress allotted to his widow a pension of $125 a month—a sum about equal to that which scores of adventurous Spanish-American War officers, who got no nearer Cuba than the coast of Florida, receive today.

The niggardliness with which the United States rewards her public benefactors is shameful, when compared with the palpable gratitude of other nations. The British Government granted Jenner, the discoverer of vaccination, £30,000 and a public subscription taken in India gave him £7,383. When Gorgas died in England (shortly after having been knighted by King George, who personally came to visit him in the hospital) he was given a magnificent state funeral in St. Paul's Cathedral, and all England recognized him as the greatest living American. When his remains were laid to rest in Arlington, the Gorgas family out of their slender means had to scrape up the money to buy a modest slab. In Gorgas's own state of Alabama there is no monument to honor the man who made possible the building of the Panama Canal. Nor in neighboring Louisiana, where one year of yellow fever was estimated to have cost that state alone 4,056 lives and $15,000,000. In many-statued Havana, which he made the healthiest city in the world and helped to make rich, there is no statue erected to Gorgas's memory. The grateful citizens did go so far as to change the name of Virtudes Street to Gorgas Street. However, everybody still calls it Virtudes, and it is somewhat notorious as a favorite haunt of girls who walk at night unaccompanied.

II

CUBA LIBRE!

To allay a growing Cuban suspicion that the United States would not fulfill her pledges, as early as April 1900, General Wood decreed a law of election. He called together an informal meeting of various important men to get their views prior to the enactment of his election law. The majority of the men favored a sweepingly democratic grant of suffrage, but Wood succeeded in limiting the rights more in accordance with the opinion of the minority and himself. As finally formulated, all native born Cuban males of twenty-one could vote, if they could read and write, or possessed $250 worth of property, or had served in the Cuban army during the war. The secret ballot and various well-known American features were provided for in the new election law on June sixteenth, 1900. It was tried out in the municipal elections, which were peaceful enough. The following month, General Wood issued an order for the election of delegates "to frame and adopt a Constitution for the people of Cuba, and, as a part thereof, to provide for and agree with the government of the United States upon the relations to exist between that government and the government of Cuba."

On September fifteenth, thirty-one delegates were elected, apportioned among the provinces according to population. On November fifth, when the Convention met in Havana, Wood reminded the body that after framing and adopting a constitution, they must formulate what in their opinion would be the relations between Cuba and the United States, "to the promotion of their common interests." He made no further attempt to intervene in the deliberations of the Convention, which went to work to prepare a constitution for Cuba.

Among the hundred and fifteen articles set forth, one of the most interesting was the abolishment of the Spanish system of a state-supported Church, and the granting of freedom to all religious sects. One of the worst decided upon—much against the will of the more cultivated—was universal manhood suffrage, except for insane persons and those civilly dead. This allowed an illiterate, degenerate, black beggar an equal voice in state affairs with a philosophic Varona. A chief cause of evil in Cuban life today, which has existed these thirty-two years, is that unlettered blacks and whites have helped to make fraud ubiquitous by selling votes to unscrupulous politicians. The delegates signed the Constitution on Friday twenty-first, 1901. Official Washington did not object to the document as it stood, except in that it ignored the matter of relations between Cuba and the United States. Washington required from the Cubans certain guarantees for the conduct of their government, and for the prevention of the island's falling into the hands of another nation. This was accomplished by including in the Cuban Constitution the provisions known as the Platt Amendment.

Briefly, by its more significant terms, Cuba bound herself not to incur debts inconsistent with her current revenues, to continue the sanitation administration installed by the military government, to lease to the United States lands necessary for establishing a naval base, and to grant the right of intervention. A violent and bitter struggle ensued before the Convention at length accepted the conditions of the amendment. Volumes have been written on the subject of the Platt Amendment pro and con by various Cubans and Americans. Certain American statesmen became vehemently abusive, shouting that the nation had broken faith with Cuba and made Cubans slaves. Some Cubans would have preferred to have its terms stronger.

The Convention at first would have none of it, particularly the intervention clause. Root reiterated that to insure fulfillment of The Treaty of Paris obligations, the United States must retain the right to intervene for the preservation of Cuban government, and the maintenance of a government for "the protection of life, property and individual liberty."

Strong letters, protesting and interrogatory, were sent the State Department. Root cabled that the Amendment was "not synonymous with intermeddling or interference with the affairs of the Cuban government." Not satisfied, a committee went from Cuba to Washington to learn the real intentions of the United States. Root handled the delegates with diplomatic suavity, and reassured them that the Amendment gave the United States no right not already possessed and exercised, that its chief purpose was to enable the United States better to protect Cuban sovereignty with reference to foreign nations. He emphasized that intervention should only be contemplated if Cuba should fall into anarchy or be menaced by a foreign power.

The commissioners returned with those assurances and with reciprocity promises from Root and the President, and also the subtle implication that the American army would not be withdrawn until the Platt Amendment was incorporated in the Cuban Constitution. After further hedging and debating and more diplomatic letters from Root and a notably firm settling of General Wood's jawbone, on June twelfth, 1901, by a grudging vote of sixteen to eleven (four members being absent) the Platt provisions were incorporated in the Cuban Constitution as an Appendix.

Undoubtedly the Platt Amendment was forced upon the body politic of Cuba. But it was welcomed by the conservatives, who felt strongly the need of some protecting safeguard from the potentialities of an ignorant rabble controlled by rascally politicians. The Spanish merchants, people of property, everyone who had resisted the revolution, still resisted the thought of Cubans running the island. As late as October sixteenth, 1901, Wood wrote, "There is an extremely strong sentiment for annexation." But Wood always told the annexationists themselves that they must talk annexation through their own government when it was formed. The belief was widespread that Cuba would eventually belong to the United States, that she would remain free until she was Americanized, which would not take long, and that then she would voluntarily apply for admission to the Union. Even such a severe critic as Albert G. Robinson wrote in *The Forum,* June 1902, "For Cuba to have found full independence as a state in the American Union would have been the richest legacy that could have fallen to her lot."

Allowing six months for the muttering to die down and to give the people sufficient time to ruminate on the wisest choice of administrators, General Wood called for the holding of a presidential election on the last day of the year 1901. The doughty Máximo Gómez, who had devoted his life to Cuba's freedom, was urged to stand for election. The people's idol would undoubtedly have been Cuba's first president had he consented. But making a new record in Hispanic American history, the Old Fox declined to run. Laconically he said, "Men of war, for war; and those of peace, for peace." With a whole-hearted gesture, he offered his overwhelming support to Tomás Estrada Palma, Cuba's chief representative in Washington, the mild-mannered schoolmaster, who had won the admiration and affection of the American people. Estrada Palma, "hand-picked" by Wood, was backed by the two strongest political parties in Cuba. His campaign papers were signed among others by José Miguel Gómez and Alfredo Zayas, who later turned against him and subsequently wangled the presidency for themselves, becoming respectively the second and fourth Presidents of the Republic.

Estrada Palma made no effort to campaign in his own behalf. He did not even return to Cuba until after his election. The sentiment was so overwhelmingly for him that Bartolomé Masó, the rival candidate, and his friends announced they would not go to the polls, on the grounds of dissatisfaction of the Central Board of Scrutiny, appointed by Wood. Estrada Palma's victory was as complete as that of George Washington at his first presidential election.

On his arrival from New York, Palma went quietly to his plantation home at Bayamo, Oriente. Visiting Santiago he laid a wreath on the tomb of the patriot de Céspedes, instigator of the Ten Years' War, saying memorably, "At last you have a country!" The defenseless, simple man's journey to Havana took on the aspect of a royal progress. The railroad not yet finished, the usual ten day trip was prolonged by an exuberance of receptions, dinners, balls showered upon him, to the accompaniment of exhausting rhetorical speeches and hurled flowers. As he traversed the island's uncomfortable roads to his inauguration, his small party grew into a dust-clouded cavalcade.

On May fifth, the first congress of the republic was called to give official approval to the newly elected candidates. During the next fortnight, since now the Cubans knew beyond any shadow of a doubt that the Americans were really going to turn their island over to them, society in Havana buzzed and took on a brilliancy it had not known since the gala days preceding the Ten Years' War. As if to leave a final fine impression of their lordly lavishness of hospitality, as well as their proverbial pride of race, the Cubans began "to throw the houses out the windows"

in the way of entertainment for the Americans, whose luggage
lay half packed.

The date set for the formal raising of the Lone Star Flag of
Cuba Libre was May twentieth, Ascension Day, the anniversary
of that miraculous day in which Our Lord rose straight from
earth to heaven. It was doubly significant in that it was also
the anniversary of a later day when the indomitable soul of
Cuba's discoverer, Cristóbal Colón, at length broke from the
moorings of its pain-racked body and drifted beyond the mor-
tality of temporal disappointments into Paradise—or, if it were
forbidden that opiate place, into some dream-created province of
its own, ineffably more glorious than Kubla Khan's fabulous
city, which the Admiral had missed, or that "most lovely land
ever human eyes beheld"—this Cuba, which he had seen and
smelt and heard and savored and set possessive feet upon. Now
for the first time in four centuries and a decade, since 1492, when
Columbus planted the banners of Aragon and Castile on Cuban
soil, the lovely land was free again. It was such a day as rarely
comes more than once in a country's chronicle, and the Cubans
were by nature equipped to make the most of it. For in the
phrase of Heine, Liberty is something the Latin loves as his
bride. "He burns for her; he is a flame; he casts himself at her
feet with the most extravagant protestations; he will fight for
her to the death; and he commits for her sake a thousand follies."

So overflowing with ecstasy at the realization of liberty, on
the night of Ascension Day Eve, the Cubans achieved the climax
of entertaining and celebration. All day citizens of Havana had
been larding their houses with flowers and hanging streamers
and bolts of bright-colored silks from windows and balconies.
Pastry cooks had drenched themselves in rivers of perspiration
to concoct masterpieces in sugar. Chefs had tasted their own
sauces until their palates were all but numb. The darkest, coolest
corners of wine cellars had been raided of their most precious
vintage wines. Stable boys had done their work a dozen times
over, sleeking newly imported horses and making new-bought

silver-studded harness dazzlingly resplendent. Barbers and hair-dressers had worked so continuously and feverishly that by late afternoon their razors and irons were dangerously like torture instruments, and they were squirting perfumes and slopping lo-tions with the prodigality of bathers pranking with seawater. Ladies' maids were in such states of excitement and fatigue that they kept themselves going only by sniffing their mistresses' smelling salts.

When darkness fell, festival sprang full-blown like Pallas Athene from the brow of Zeus. Joy smothered Havana in a de-lirious embrace. The purple-tongued leopards of Bacchus ranged unleashed through every street with hypnotic yellow eyes. Amer-ican soldiers got on their final drunk, and took prolonged fare-well of dusky-eyed señoritas, who this night were not purse-con-scious. The Cuban bourgeoisie, intoxicated with an idea rather than drink, made sudden jungle yells and kissed each other's cheeks resoundingly. Country families with strings of offspring gaped and gawked, marked time to the beating of Guinea drums and maraccas, and strolled throughout the night like troops of somnambulists. Fireworks in the most elaborate Latin manner were touched off continually. Cafés stayed open all night and Spanish proprietors grew love-sick from the sound of jingling sil-ver. Even the sandal-footed Chinamen, who rarely took notice of Cuban emotionalism, sat wakeful in their doorways, their shirt-tails out, talking chip-chop Chinese with unoriental animation. In illuminated palaces, beautiful ladies danced the soles out of their dainty ball-slippers and a haggard brilliance into their eyes, until at dawn their *duennas* bore them to their carriages nigh dead with the fatigue of fan fluttering and the repetition of dimpled smiling. With the sunrise, American soldiers bearing mementoes, photo-graphs or beads or Dresden statuettes, staggered weakly to their lodgings through the flowery streets. And in the palace of the governor-generals, where Tacón had played the whimsical caliph and Weyler had consoled himself in his blue bathroom, Wood's orderly buckled the last buckle on his departing general's luggage.

At noon, with the streets jammed thicker than blueberries between pie crust, a solemn ceremony took place. The Cuban flag was run up atop the Presidential Palace and on Morro Castle. Cheers, extravagantly more exciting than those of the American troops when they landed at Daiquirí, rent the May-serene air like a discordant chorus of a hundred thousand alleluiahs. The millennium had come to Cuba.

But here and there in the throng, the hearts of some men constricted when they saw the American flag come down and the Cuban flag go up. "We are not ready yet," their eyes said in revealing glances exchanged with other thoughtful ones, who understood so thoroughly their Spanish heritage, and who chilled watching the yelling, child-like, dark-streaked mob in that atmosphere oppressive with obvious greed of office-seekers. They recalled significant words of Martí: "The day will come when we shall place, on the strongest fort of our country, the flag of the single star. But then there remains a more patriotic and noble work to be done; to place on it another flag, on the white folds of which there shall appear this generous symbol of triumphant love, 'With all, and for the benefit of all.' "

In the midst of frenzy, Leonard Wood boarded an American ship and sailed out of the historic sapphire harbor. The last thing that caught his eye was the flag of Cuba Libre on Morro lighthouse. It floated joyously, confidently, in the sensuous sunlight of a Cuban May. With paternal pride and genuine affection, glancing back at the green-gold shore, Wood, telescopically, as in a dream's space, reviewed the intervention that was over. On the whole he was pleased. "The only difficulty," he repeated doubtfully, "lies in their own temperament. If only they will learn in civil affairs to act with deliberation, to control their emotions!"

PART **IV**

The Republic

ESTRADA PALMA—THE GREAT CHANCE

GENERAL WOOD had left the baby republic in the most capable pair of hands the island possessed. They were not young hands—they had weathered sixty-seven trying years —but they were steady, constructive, economical, well-bred, and absolutely incorruptible. To bring his country to a state of health and literacy was his first consideration. To make his people economically independent and teach them frugality were his secondary aims. Estrada Palma followed as closely as possible in Wood's footsteps. He pursued the ideals of the American sanitation department. One-fourth of the budget was devoted to education. It was his motto that the republic should have more teachers than soldiers.

Economy was the keynote of Estrada Palma's policy. By the unaffected simplicity of his own living, he set an example in thrift. According to Carlos Trelles, he governed with the phenomenally small budget of eighteen million dollars. Having found a surplus of less than a million in the treasury, within four years he managed to store up twenty-six millions, notwithstanding the fact that he constructed more kilometers of roads than had the Americans. Perhaps his greatest mistake lay in his economy. The politicians not in office itched to dig their fingers into the treasury.

In 1905, the year before the new elections, Cuba was thriving on honest government and general good times. The future seemed auspiciously rosy. The provinces had recovered from the war; Camagüey and Oriente were becoming world centers of colossal sugar enterprises. Real estate was leaping in value. The balance of trade was decidedly in Cuba's favor. Ordinary working people were affording luxuries.

But a fly lurked despicably in the ointment. As Chapman says, "The defects of Cuban character had not yet had time to cure themselves." The political "outs" wanted to get in. Like unsavory politicians the world over they were prepared to tear to pieces the fabric of government to line their coats. And it is true that among many of Estrada Palma's own officers there was graft and fraud. The old Spanish instinct for political plunder, like that disease of the heart for which Cortes told the Mexican chief the only specific cure was gold, was far from dead with the "ins," as well as the Liberal "outs." But at least a highly honorable man was at the head of the former, whereas the latter was dominated by men who have left no reputation for honesty.

When the time drew near for the presidential elections of 1905, the various political factions had resolved themselves into two main parties. The supporters of Estrada Palma, who included the better families, the professional and business men, were designated as the Moderates. The Liberals were made up of the political "outs," a few younger sons of the gentry and the rabble including the solid black electorate, which a man of Estrada Palma's type could not attract. Between the two parties there was only one matter of issue—jobs.

Estrada Palma hesitated to stand for reëlection. If he was really eager for the position, as enemies maintain, it was definitely not for personal glory and gain, but only because he believed he could be helpful to his country. The factor that finally determined him to run was his conviction that his rivals would waste the millions he had carefully accumulated for the public good. He was loath to see his successor unlock the treasury for himself and his partisans. Undoubtedly his surmise was correct, for each succeeding president has proved himself more selfish, wasteful, and corrupt than his predecessor. Estrada Palma had allied himself with no party; he had won the first presidency uncontested. But in February 1905 he definitely affiliated himself with the Moderates, a move which carried with it a certain admission to favor that party in the coming election.

That same month the Moderates persuaded him to appoint a new Cabinet that would be better adapted for campaigning purposes. The existing Cabinet resigned. On March sixth he appointed a new group of counselors made up of war veteran officers, soon called the "Fighting Cabinet." Among the number as Secretary of Government was General Fernando Freyre de Andrade. (He was the father of the three brothers who were murdered in cold blood on a September day in 1932 by President Machado's gunmen.) Freyre de Andrade was an intellectual and courageous man, but not cautious, and in no way diplomatic. He was resolved that Estrada Palma was the best man in Cuba and that he should control the next years' destinies of the country if he had to win the election by hook or crook. His strategical office gave him control of police and rural guards, supervision of municipalities, and the handling of the electoral machinery. Freyre de Andrade's blanket dismissal of government employees not obligated to the Moderate party caused much bitterness, particularly in the provinces where the *guajiros* projected their thoughts little beyond local affairs. Estrada Palma was led to believe that the removals had been effected because of incorrect administration on the part of incumbents.

On their side, the Liberals were on the verge of riot. They filled the public squares with fire-brand speeches. They openly talked of revolution, if the Liberals should be "robbed" of victory. (In Latin American countries "rob" in politics is synonymous with "defeat.") Liberal Congressmen threateningly reminded Estrada Palma, who had no concern in his heart but his people's welfare, that Charles I had lost his head. José Miguel Gómez, the rival presidential candidate (no relation of Máximo Gómez), hinted darkly at revolution. A government building in a Pinar del Rio village was burned by the Liberals as a warning. The hot-headed, determined Freyre de Andrade became more uncompromising.

As the time of election drew near, there were still no issues except the interest of parties ambitious for jobs. It was a fight to retain or get control of the millions in the treasury. The Liberals became noisy with "patriotism," that last refuge of scoundrels. In arraigning the United States, they made use of a sure-fire stimulant in Spanish American countries. As for program they had none worthy of the name. Estrada Palma proclaimed very simply, "What better or more eloquent platform can there be than deeds themselves? The past is guarantee and sure pledge of the future." The Liberals had no answer: the country was prosperous, and the financial achievements of Estrada Palma were indisputable. But the "outs" wanted "in." Estrada Palma, who like most scrupulously honest men think people better than they are, was not totally deceived by his Cubans. As late as September fourth, 1905, he uttered his famous remark, "In Cuba we have a republic, but there are no citizens."

The morning of September twenty-third, the date of the preliminary elections, dawned on an electrically charged Cuba. It was obvious that a Moderate victory had been provided for in advance and that force would be used if necessary. At noon the Liberals called followers from the polls. The Moderates had been so foolishly zealous as to make use of 150,000 fraudulent names. On December first, at the final elections, the Liberals ominously refused to vote. Moderate candidates walked away with the elections without opposition.

Plots to overthrow the Moderates were straightway fomented. Minor riots took place in Havana. Barracks were broken into, guards killed, horses stolen. Desultory bullets whizzed here and there invitingly. But the country as a whole did not rise yet. In the meantime Gómez, violent opponent of the Platt Amendment, went to the United States and virtually asked for intervention.

On May twentieth, 1906, Estrada Palma began his second term of office. The Liberals' hopes were now absolutely cut off for four years, unless they resorted to armed revolution. A formal revolutionary pact was drawn up and signed by various leaders, including Gómez and Zayas. The insurrectionists planned a coup d'état, in which they would kidnap the President and Vice-President and take possession of all Havana police stations within the same hour. The celerity of this move was now calculated to forestall American intervention. Both sides knew that revolution was imminent. Spies were full of leaking information. The details of the coup were known to the police. Gómez was shadowed. Only Estrada Palma seemed ignorant of the rumors. He was too absorbed in splendid plans for the next four years to listen. (To help him in his future work, he had the best Congress Cuba has ever possessed.) He could not be brought to believe that his people, ever extravagant in talk, would actually turn against him. Besides, if any such untoward event took place, surely the United States would protect him and his government. He had not created an army (such money went to schools), for he relied on good government and prosperity as safeguards, supplemented by the Platt Amendment.

On August sixteenth, General Faustino "Pino" Guerra, a Liberal representative who had walked out of the Congressional Halls in April muttering menacingly, "We must seek justice somewhere else," touched off the powder of the revolution in Pinar del Rio. A civil war was thus launched when Cuba Libre had been in existence four days less than four and one-quarter years. The leaders of the Liberals, including later-day Presidents Gómez and Zayas, had betrayed the future tranquillity of the country and the security of its nationality and institutions. Through consummate selfishness, they had offered to the multitude (which was more than half black) an object lesson packed with dynamite.

The government began to arrest Liberal leaders. Gómez was caught and imprisoned. Zayas, always a super-tricky one, escaped and remained in hiding. Other escaped leaders took the field at the head of armed forces. Mantanzas, Oriente, and Camagüey Provinces remained loyal; but in Santa Clara, Havana, and Pinar del Rio the revolution gained a momentum which surprised even the Liberal chiefs. The insurrectionists had a powerful weapon in their ability to destroy property of the conservative element, who consequently feared to support the government actively. The historian-critic Martinez Ortiz, who condemns the Moderate government, confesses that the bulk of revolutionists were "illiterates without landed property, desirous of adventure and novelty." In the pages of *El Figaro*, Enrique José Varona, the most admired intellectual in Cuba, flayed his countrymen for their hypocrisy. Shaking out newspaper sheets with excited fingers, Havana patriot-politicians read themselves reflected in a truth-telling mirror. In righteous wrath Varona wrote:

> "I have already said what is the attitude of the parties, which are joint authors of this dishonorable convulsion. They are concerned with nothing more than to make the best capital of the moment, at the cost of the country, destined beforehand to fill the rôle of a propitiatory victim. But what with greatest reason ought to cause us indignation is to see that they talk only of the good of the country, the honor of the country, the liberty of the country and those who speak in this manner are loosing upon the country that greatest calamity of the many that afflict the miserable human species, war."

The lovely land was on the verge of being once more soaked with blood and blackened by fire. Young General Mario Menocal, another subsequent president, suggested a compromise: all officials elected in 1905 except the president and vice-president should resign and new elections be held. At first Estrada Palma did not look unfavorably on the proposition. For four days he pondered, and then refused to discuss the matter until the insurrectionists laid down their arms. To compromise with this revolution, he said, would endanger the future, and destroy the moral dignity of the government. But Havana was at the mercy of the enemy. The government had no army with which to protect itself. There was nothing for Estrada Palma to do but invoke the aid of the United States. On September eighth, the acting United States Minister to Cuba, on behalf of Palma, cabled President Roosevelt to send two warships.

Roosevelt was unfeignedly loath to comply. But on September thirteenth, there came a message from the legation which he could not ignore. "President Palma, the Republic of Cuba, through me officially asks for American intervention, because he cannot prevent rebels from entering cities and burning property." Guzmán, a rebel leader, had declared, "If there is no satisfactory arrangement soon, I shall proceed to the destruction of railways and even of foreign properties." "To aid the Cubans in reaching a peaceful solution," Roosevelt despatched his Secretary of War, William Howard Taft, and the Assistant Secretary of State, Robert Bacon.

Cherubic and talkative, Taft arrived in Havana with his co-arbiter on September nineteenth. Straightway they paid a visit to Estrada Palma, who lucidly explained the situation. His digni-fied, earnest demeanor deeply impressed the emissaries, and they were touched by evidences of his sorrow at the lack of gratitude and patriotism on the part of the revolutionists. In their official report of this visit, they wrote, "He gave us a number of in-stances tending to show that the leaders of the insurrection were moved only by the basest of purposes—by pecuniary greed and de-sire for office." For two crowded days the commissioners con-ducted interviews with representatives of both sides. The fraudu-lence of the past elections being admitted on the testimony of Freyre himself, Taft and Bacon shortly came to the same conclu-sion as Menocal in his suggested compromise. The Moderates formally agreed to accept the arbitration of the American Com-missioners, provided the insurrectionists should first lay down their arms, thereby conserving the dignity of the government.

Zayas agreed to the Taft-Bacon suggestions, but would not consider the matter of "the Constitutionalist forces" laying down their arms prior to a solution. The deadlock seemed altogether too tough for Taft's flabby diplomacy.

Because of the election fraud, Taft at length decided that the government should waive the point of disarming. But Estrada Palma and the Moderates refused to treat with an armed force. Roosevelt impatiently cautioned Taft:

> "It is undoubtedly a very evil thing that the revolutionists should be encouraged and the dreadful example afforded the island of success in remedying wrongs by violence and treason to the Government. . . . I do not have much hope that with the example before them of such success in an insurrection the people who grow discontented with the new government will refrain from insurrection and disturbance some time in the future."

On September twenty-fourth, however, the commissioners publicly announced their suggestions for a compromise, minus the contingency of the insurrectionists disarming. That same day they met with Estrada Palma, who was dismayed at the attitude of the Americans. It looked to him as if Taft was afraid of the revolutionists, fearful that if any foreign property was destroyed his diplomacy would be discredited. Taft was demanding that he, the President of Cuba, should spinelessly accept a compromise offensive to his personal dignity and honor, a compromise promulgating a most dangerous precedent, merely because Taft desired to mollify an insurgent force which he himself characterized as "only an undisciplined horde of men under partisan leaders." This was too much for an idealist like Estrada Palma! The meeting took on a vehemence of manner to which both the perpetually-smiling Taft and the mild-tempered schoolmaster were unaccustomed. The fateful interview portended the failure of all Estrada Palma had hoped and striven for. He felt as if he had been betrayed into the enemy's hands by a big brother. In humiliation and despair he announced his irrevocable intention of sending his resignation to Congress.

Taft and Bacon urged him to reconsider. They did not know their Estrada Palma, in whose backbone there was not one wishy-washy vertebra. Roosevelt telegraphed begging him to propose another compromise if he would not accept the one offered. Neither Taft nor Roosevelt demanded that the rebels lay down their arms. If Roosevelt had taken such a firm stand, the rebels would very likely have complied. If Leonard Wood with his forceful persuasion had been on the spot, they *would* have laid down their arms.

The Moderates rejected the compromise on the twenty-fifth; the armed Liberals accepted it on the twenty-sixth. On the twenty-eighth Congress assembled, Estrada Palma tendered the resignation of his Secretaries, then his own. The Vice-President resigned. Cuba was without a government. Taft, who had played his cards with such astounding lack of skill, was left with an intervention on his hands, the one thing he had determined to avoid. In a proclamation to the Cuban people on September twenty-ninth, he had to sign himself, "Provisional Governor of Cuba."

The following day the clear-thinking, learned Varona published an ironical essay entitled, "The Heel of Achilles" which pertinently sums up Taft's egregious blundering.

> "There has occurred in Cuba . . . precisely the contrary of what it was reasonable to expect. The government of the United States, acting through the illustrious delegates of its distinguished President, after a very rapid investigation, has sanctioned the complaints of the insurrectionists of Cuba . . . and has proposed them as the basis for an agreement to the government *de jure* of this republic. *In a word, the government of the United States has exacted of the government of Cuba . . . that it abdicate before an armed insurrection.*"

The insurrectionists had discovered the Cuban "heel of Achilles" in their ability to destroy foreign property. The avoidance of any such contingency, Varona affirmed with justice, was the fundamental basis of the American Commissioners' decision. Capital wanted peace to protect its investments; it was little concerned in arguments about right and wrong.

Irene Wright, American journalist and historian, who made a many years' study of Cuban affairs, comments indignantly and not without contempt on the proceedings in September 1906.

> "Mr. Taft and Mr. Bacon trafficked with forces in open rebellion against their own country. It is a hard thing for Americans to accept, but the only explanation is that the Peace Commission was actually afraid of the horde of ragamuffins assembled at Havana's gates. Yet these unorganized hordes would have vanished at the Commission's mere mandate, or had they not, one charge of American cavalry would have dispersed them. It was precisely the effect of having to charge them which Mr. Taft, as head of that Commission, feared, for the time was close on the election in which he was to appear as candidate for the American presidency, and undoubtedly, necessary and wise as it might have been under the circumstances, had he had to use force to disband the Constitutional Army (as the rebels were called) it would not have made pleasant reading in opposition newspapers of the North. Therefore Mr. Taft temporized—and in so doing he gave tone to all the Provisional Administrations which followed."

It is patent that lack of confidence in all subsequent American meddling in Cuban activities had its roots in the deplorable diplomatic and administrative bungling in 1906-1909.

The day Varona's article was published, Estrada Palma and his family began to pack up their modest personal belongings. It did not take them long. The next day they were quite ready, the palace inventories in perfect order. The family purposed to go for a short visit to Mantanzas before proceeding to their old home at Bayamo in Oriente. Taft, really distressed, offered the former

President a battleship for his brief journey. Estrada Palma declined the courtesy in a gracious note. On October second, he and
his family quietly left the palace with their small luggage and
drove through the streets to the station unregarded. Hardly a
handful of people came to say good-by to the man whose inauguration had marked the climax of gala celebration in Cuba's
chronicle. Cubans forget to thank as quickly as they forget to
hate—so they say of themselves.

Estrada Palma boarded the train without one corroding drop
of bitterness in his heart. He did not murmur against his personal
fate. He was not touched with noble rage. But when the loco-
motive wheels began to revolve and the train passed beyond
the limits of the capital, he closed his eyes and contemplated the
overthrow of his four years' patient and glorious work. His soul
was overcome, as he himself said, with profound disenchantment.
Irrevocably he resolved to abandon public life, to seek "in the
bosom of his family certain refuge against so many deceptions."
Back on his farm in Bayamo, he lived for a year in uncomplain-
ing poverty. But in October of 1907 he did speak out of his heart
in a touching private letter. His family could afford no servants
(in a country where household help costs next to nothing), and
it was painful for him to see his aging wife obliged to rise early
to prepare the coffee for the family, to see his daughters washing
up floors. It hurt him to lack the means to give his young sons
any professional education, however modest it might be. The
hate of enemies hounded him in his retreat. Hostile politicians
encouraged squatters to settle upon his land, to despoil him of
what little he had left. "When I contemplate all this," he wrote,
"I ask myself: what sin have I committed in punishment of
which, despite having worked all my life, I find myself at the
end of it, when the weight of years is bending my body upon the
sepulcher, in such a precarious and difficult situation?"

The following fall Estrada Palma died in Santiago, heartbroken at the contemplation of what man will do to man. At
his funeral, as the clods of earth fell upon the humble coffin, the

governor of Oriente spoke feelingly of the great patriot who had died a pauper: "If he was a model in his private life, he was a model also in his honored public life; that is the mirror in which all Cubans ought to look, those that hear me and all the generations of those to come." Cuba has not seen Estrada Palma's like since. Nor is she likely to produce many Estrada Palmas in the centuries to come. Nor does she soon deserve such another. For the basest reasons, she repudiated one of her two noblest sons. (Martí was killed while comparatively young.) Dr. Chapman, who has made a special study of Cuba's first president and his work, sums him up in this wise: "In all his life one finds nothing that was mean or unlovely to detract from the beautiful and unselfish idealism of his character." Hundreds have said: Estrada Palma was too good for Cuba. No wonder Varona wrote in strong accusing ink, "Cubans themselves are the authors of their own misfortunes."

2

BLUNDERS OF TAFT AND MAGOON

When Taft found himself provisional governor, two thousand American marines and fifty-six hundred soldiers were presently swarming into Havana to give a background of confidence to his new job. Taft's first act was to release all political prisoners and declare an amnesty for crimes committed in connection with the revolt. He was deluged with claims of damages incurred in the revolution. He was swamped in petitions for jobs from Liberals who had made such a to-do about fighting for principles, not jobs. By the end of the first harassing week, the hearty-natured Secretary of War was eager to wash his hands of the whole mess. Fortunately for him, Republican Washington needed him at home—to groom him for the presidency.

When it became known that a new governor was to be chosen immediately, Cuba fervently hoped for a return of Wood. But Taft favored Charles E. Magoon, a mid-western politician, heavy of paunch, small of eye, as broadly smiling as Taft himself. Magoon formally took over the government on October thirteenth.

Taft stepped out of the breach a fortnight after he had stepped in. Never was a man more thankful for relief. Never was his smile more expansive than when he lifted his feet from Cuban soil. He was still smiling when he reached Washington. But when he faced Root, his smile faded. "Taft," Root said with rueful condemnation, "you've killed my baby!"

In Cuba Magoon sat ingloriously but good-humoredly in the seat of the mighty for more than two years. Laboring assiduously to offend no one, placating everybody in an effort to win good will, even lackeying underlings, Magoon granted a hundred petitions a day, entertained lavishly, and ironically achieved a contemptible reputation which very nearly wiped out the excellent impression of American administration created by Leonard Wood. Cuba's printed opinions, from top to bottom, discredit Magoon's government. Varona points to Magoon as the one "who began to write the annals of the dilapidations of the Cuban treasury." The grammar school text books today teach the young that Magoon "left a bad memory and a bad example in the country." Yet, as Chapman substantiates, not a single specific charge of dishonest action on the part of Magoon has ever been brought forward. He himself was personally honest. But to keep momentary peace he connived at the corrupting of administrative discipline by creating for the trouble-makers well-paying political jobs with nominal duties.

The Liberals, who had made such a howl about fighting for principles, not for offices, descended upon Magoon like a plague of locusts on plum trees in fruit. To keep them quiet, Magoon dished out soft jobs with amazing rapidity. The millions which Estrada Palma had amassed in Cuba's treasury by cautious economy were lavished as treats on his enemies. What Estrada Palma had feared from the Cubans had been brought to pass by the big brother Americans. Magoon calculated that this method was the easiest and surest way to keep peace. But it was a grave error full of vicious consequences. Many Cubans today unfairly excuse existing corruption on the ground that Magoon taught them to distribute *botellas*—nursing bottles full of rich milk for the political babies. Of course, sinecures had been distributed since the Spaniards first set up a government under Diego Velasquez in 1511. But Cuba, as Chapman points out, like other Spanish American countries, is prone to retain long and gloating memories over any past American administrative impropriety. However, in this case, the United States did fail miserably when she had such an excellent opportunity to give Cuba lessons in political restraint and integrity.

Magoon's main job was to see to it that "there was no Cuban problem to disturb Taft's race for the presidency in 1908." As provisional governor, Magoon took general orders from Taft and reflected his policies. He and Taft were continually in correspondence and met for four personal conferences. Taft could not have been ignorant of what was going on in Cuba, for the bad practices were violently denounced in the Cuban press and on street corners.

The work was by no means all roses and soft soap for Magoon. He worked under the handicap of a bad economic condition, for which he was in no wise responsible. In 1907 New York itself was trembling on the edge of panic. In Cuba cyclones and ruined crops added to the economic depression. Unemployment became menacing. To provide sustenance for the unemployed, Magoon started an extensive public works program. In two years he built 608 kilometers of roads, about as many as had been constructed in the preceding four centuries. (Many of the roads were poor, it may be true; but certainly Gómez, following an Hispanic American political device, was careful not to keep in repair his predecessor's roads.) In giving out contracts, Magoon was remarkably undiscriminating. Jenks says Cuba became a virtual paradise for contractors with or without experience. The politicians commercialized the favor with which the Magoon policy regarded them and profited handsomely by money received for considerations granted individuals and business firms. It seemed impossible for Magoon to say "no" to anybody. He was a "yes-man" extraordinary. Swayed by the least murmuring desire of importuning politicians, who may or may not have profited financially by the granted petitions, Magoon signed pardons by the wholesale. Over 1,100 pardons, the majority for common crimes, were granted during his régime—an average of forty-six a month, where Estrada Palma pardoned six.

As insurance against such another outbreak as occurred against Estrada Palma in 1906, Magoon in his third year provided for a permanent army. One of his last acts was ironic in the extreme: he appointed as commander-in-chief of the army "Pino" Guerra, the very man who had launched the revolution against Estrada Palma. Guerra was honored with free trips to the United States and France to survey army maneuvers and tactics that he might forestall the very kind of revolution which he had instigated. His visits were paid for out of Estrada Palma's economies. A Cuban army, of course, was created to be used only against Cubans. At great expense to the country's tax payers, the army has done little more service in this last quarter-century than to "control" elections, and to remain trump ace in the hands of whichever politician could hold and manipulate it. It has proved a potent weapon to keep tyrants in power, and it has kept itself well cared for and promptly paid through turn-coat threats.

On December twenty-fourth, 1906, an Advisory Law Commission was appointed to prepare five laws concerning the civil service, the judiciary provinces, municipalities, and elections. The commission, headed by Colonel Enoch Crowder, was composed of two other Americans and nine Cubans. The most important work of the commission was the preparation of an election law hopefully designed to obliterate various improper practices of former elections. It involved a careful registration of voters, which necessitated the taking of a census. The results of the census showed that the population had increased 30% since 1899—from 1,572,845 to 2,048,980. More than six hundred and forty thousand over ten years old were not able to sign their own names. A majority of this group, Chapman points out, went to make up the list of 466,745 voters. The foreign-born element was over-whelmingly Spanish, sixteen times as many as the Chinese, who ranked second with 11,000. The Americans came third with 6,713.

The concern of Cuban publicists for the economic, legislative and administrative reforms were paltry compared to their inter-est in political succession. Gómez and Zayas quarreled bitterly. The Liberal party was split in two factions, the Miguelistas and the Zayistas. This break was very distasteful to Taft and Magoon, who desired a Liberal victory to cover up Taft's original blunder. A Conservative party grew out of the old Moderate party, and gathered strength under the standard-bearing of General Mario Menocal, backed by the "better element." After much wrangling and rancor, the Liberals at length reunited with Gómez as candi-date for president and Zayas for vice-president. The campaign was exciting. The elections were fairly conducted. (Washington had warned Cuba that the elections must be conducted peacefully if the intervention were to end at all.) The fused Liberals won. Taft and Bacon were vindicated.

So besides stuffing complaining mouths with nursing bottles and calming strikes and panic, Magoon presided over an orderly election. When Taft's election for the presidency of the United States came off, Cuba was peaceful as an infant lulled with sooth-ing syrup. Roosevelt had determined that Magoon and the Amer-ican troops should clear out of Cuba when this happy event tran-spired. In the January after the Cuban and American elections, Magoon turned the government over to President-elect Gómez, prime conspirer for Estrada Palma's downfall and idol of the bulk of the Liberal party, which Henry Watterson characterized as "riff-raff, injin, nigger, beggarman, thief—both mongrel, puppy, whelp and hound, and cur of low degree."

Cuba had paid a big price materially and morally for her discontent with the estimable Estrada Palma. "All in all," Chapman says, "it is probable that Cuba paid at least ten million dollars to overthrow the Estrada Palma government, which would have retired some four months later than the intervention came to an end." Moreover, the deficit left in the Cuban treasury by Magoon was seven or eight million at the lowest estimate. Americans in Cuba were as indignant as Cubans at "the unrestrained profligacy in expenditures, the disgraceful prodigality in pardons, the demoralizing complacency in the distribution of unjustified positions."

On Martí's birthday, January twenty-eighth, the pliable agent of Taft, who had so servilely obeyed his master's voice, took his departure on a battleship, cheered by some bottle-holders. Behind him he left an ominous cloud of distrust, disillusion, contempt, and downright hatred for America's administrative officers. The cloud has never cleared to this day.

3

GÓMEZ RESTORES THE COCK-FIGHT

Magoon had not yet reached Washington when the Cuban Congress, meeting on the first day of February, revealed the turn of the tide back to traditional Spanish ways by introducing a bill for the restoration of cock-fighting, a barbarous practice which had been outlawed by Leonard Wood, vetoed by Estrada Palma, and frowned at by Magoon. Immediately afterwards, a sensational amnesty bill, a "political spoils act," and a national lottery law were brought up for discussion. After such a beginning,

Gómez's Congress showed itself interested in little more than political maneuvers and concerns which were of some material advantage to congressmen themselves.

The legitimatizing of cock-fighting was a strongly implied campaign pledge of the Liberal. Through a shrewdly calculated suggestion, the Liberals had adopted as their emblem "a cock on a plow." The device purported to symbolize "vigilance and industry," but to the *guajiros* and Negroes (the *ñañigos,* secret voodooistic sect, hold the cock sacred) it signified a promised return of cock-fighting. To the masses, both black and white, cock-fighting was by all odds the favorite sport, ranking with work, eating, and sexual indulgence as a major factor in the design of existence. The cock on the plow had done more than anything else to draw countrymen into the Liberal camp. The passing of the bill in Congress niched Gómez deeper in the popular heart.

As speedily as possible Gómez restored another old Spanish tradition: that government existed for the profit of office holders, who held jobs for the practical purpose of improving personal fortunes at state expense. Having entered the presidency a poor man with his farm heavily mortgaged, Gómez set the prime example for making hay while in office by retiring at the end of four years to a sparkling new marble palace on the Prado costing a quarter of a million dollars, and holding certificates for an estimated eight millions invested in mines and agricultural properties. At government expense he had stocked his farms with the finest foreign cattle, thereby realizing a youthful ambition to become the wealthiest cattleman in Cuba.

José Miguel Gómez, Cuba's second president, stands first today in the hearts of the populace. He was one of those buoyant, robust fellows exuding animal magnetism, with ever a ready smile, natural or simulated, on his lips, and an irresistible glint in his Latin eyes, which won friends at a glance. Cubans warmed heartily to his cattleman gusto, the jingle of his silver spurs, his rough clothes and vast panama, his affectionate man-of-the-people manner. They liked him; they loved him; they wished him great prosperity. Though fully aware that he was utilizing his high office in some measure to build up a private fortune, they merely shrugged and consoled themselves with the thought that "the measures involving graft had also some possibility in them of benefit to the public." If he grafted a little here and there, to be sure, why not? Was there any man in all the island they would rather have prosper? His gift for winning good will was so expansive that not only did everyone who came to deal with him find it difficult to resist him, but even fortune herself smiled bounteously on the *simpático* José Miguel and bestowed economic prosperity on Cuba during the full four years of his rule.

Besides the phenomenal good-humor that was native to his temperament—"All my life I have been jovial in spirit," he said—Gómez was endowed with an extraordinary perception with which to measure the intelligence and understanding of others—"I study men as others study books," he professed. He made it a practice to have his face light up with a smile whenever a visitor entered his office. His superhuman instinct for "meandering through the labyrinth of politicians without mistaking his way," his sound common sense, and his captivating personal attraction equipped him to be a great leader of crowds, despite his lack of education, or any formal training in statesmanship.

Gómez had had his political initiation in Santa Clara (his birthplace was the old ultra-Cuban town of Sancti Spiritus) where he had served in the two wars of his generation, emerging a major-general. After the surrender in 1898, he had rapidly become the political dictator of the province and his ten years' record there (he employed strong-arm gangs to win ballots) had gained him the epithet of "tyrant" in the 1908 presidential election. A more affectionate nickname which the people came later to use was *Tiburón,* the Shark.

In his program of government, Gómez shrewdly put economic interests above every other public question. Since crop and revenue conditions were generally good, and the people were for him, there was not apt to be any political disturbance. However, to make sure nobody would do to him what he had done to Estrada Palma, he used a considerable portion of the budget to strengthen the permanent army which Magoon had created. From commander-in-chief to private, the personnel was composed of Gómez-Liberals. The army provided pleasant posts for many of his intimate friends. For others with less martial inclinations, he expanded the diplomatic service unnecessarily.

Estrada Palma had striven to teach Cubans economy; Gómez, the good spender, knew his countrymen too well to tempt revolutionaries by storing up a surplus. The budget of the presidency in 1905 under Estrada Palma was less than $63,000. In 1910 under Gómez it exceeded $148,000. The item for "various" expenses increased from $600 to $15,000. New items which had not been mentioned in Estrada Palma's time were entered as "unforeseen" expenses $12,000, and "secret" expenses $25,000. Later, Gómez received $105,000 for "secret" expenses and spent the whole sum in a few months. In his lavishness with public funds, Gómez made Magoon look small, yet he himself was downright niggardly in expenditures compared with the three presidents to follow. The full catalogue of deals from which Gómez is said to have received the graft which laid the basis for his fortune would take up several pages of print. A few of the more notorious instances include the Speyer loan; railway construction; purchase of naval vessels; dredging projects; telephone company concessions, and countless other concessions; rental of buildings for public service; monopolization of lottery collectorship; road and bridge building; and, reminiscent of Governor O'Donnell and his frugal lady, sales of junk iron and sewerage contracts. In the matter of pardons, Gómez surpassed Magoon, granting some eighteen hundred. In all these improprieties the President was aided and abetted by the majority of politicians. Even a scrupulously honest man like Estrada Palma had been unable to control his own followers. The malady was bred in the bone.

Throughout Gómez's rule, those patriots who had fought for

an ideal without selfish thought were desperate and powerless. Any further sacrifice they could make for their country seemed futile. The American Provisional Government had betrayed them into soiled and thieving hands, which had proved even more callous and unscrupulous than they had feared. Since they considered the type of men raised to high offices (with America's help) an insult to their intelligence and culture, they refused to have anything to do with them socially or politically. Like Estrada Palma they renounced the fine services they might have rendered, and retired to the consolation of the family circle, shutting their doors and windows on the world, as if to avoid defilement. Remaining within doors, the spiritual offspring of Martí contemplated sorrowfully the light that might have been, and stayed away from the corruption of the polls.

As the time drew near for the 1912 elections, it became patent that Gómez, who had protested rather too much against reëlections, was determined to cling to his seat. Although by the 1909 party agreement the next presidential candidacy had been tacitly promised Zayas, Gómez at the ninth hour patriotically professed to see "dissolution, ruin and rout" facing his beloved country under a Zayas administration. Nobly he offered himself again to his people. Sometime before, as a prologue to this resolution, he had grown fearful of the loyalty of his army; for "Pino" Guerra, its head, was strongly committed to Zayas, although personally friendly to Gómez. To get Guerra removed from dangerous influences, he offered him various lucrative missions in Europe. When Guerra adamantly declined, Gómez invited him to play billiards at the palace. After a friendly game on a late October evening, as Guerra was leaving the palace, he was set upon and shot at by assassins. He escaped death, but a bullet went through his leg. Taking the almost mortal hint, the commander-in-chief resigned his command. General Monteagudo, Gómez's closest friend, was given Guerra's post. The names of the killers were said to be well known; but the guilty went scot-free. The incident, which nearly cost Guerra his life, cost Gómez only a slight temporary loss of popularity. In fact, incredible as it might seem, yet whimsically illustrative of the quick forgiveness and unaccountable fickleness of Spanish American temperament, Guerra subsequently turned his back on Zayas and embraced the cause of Gómez.

The foregoing episode is only one of many picturesque instances of Gómez's executive violence. Other men were killed "by order of the government," as the unimpassioned Carlos Trelles phrases it. Gómez used menacing pressure to influence law courts to render ruinous decisions against his critics. Through a law promulgated by Orestes Ferrara, he tried to muzzle the press. He jailed editors. He grew so dictatorial that a movement called the National Council of Veterans, headed by General Emilio Nuñez, rose against him and so nearly plunged the country into a civil war that the United States threatened intervention early in 1912. The veterans were moved primarily by a sincere desire to stamp out the evils that had arisen during the Gómez administration, and secondarily by political considerations—or, primarily and secondarily vice versa. However, the government at length reached a peaceable agreement with the veterans. But Gómez was not able to avoid a race war which flared in 1912, bringing about serious consequences.

In 1907, under the leadership of Evaristo Estenoz, Negroes, claiming that too few political plums had been handed the blacks, had formed an Independent Party of Color. It is true the Liberals had been lavish with promises to the Negroes to get them to revolt against Estrada Palma. They fulfilled the rich promises in meager measure. Some of the black leaders demanded political jobs in such violent terms that they were imprisoned. Later Gómez released Estenoz, and permitted him to agitate in completing the organization of his party. Gómez's opponents say that he shrewdly decided to use Estenoz to further his own nomination for a second term, that Estenoz worked under Gómez's protection, and that his agents and orators were given money and Pullman tickets by the President himself. They say

Gómez, promising villas and whatnot to Estenoz, plotted with him to stimulate a black revolution, so that he might win a grateful nation's plaudits for suppressing it, and thence gain the nomination and election. Certainly nothing could have been so calculated to compel Gómez's candidacy as the squashing of a formidable-looking uprising the year of the nominations. At any rate, political maneuver or not, the outbreak commenced on May twentieth, 1912, Cuba's Independence Day. In a few days it became so serious that the whole island was alarmed. Even Havana trembled with panic, and had to be pacified by 3,500 volunteer guards. Terrified foreign plantation- and mill-owners howled for American protection. Disregarding Gómez's protest that he could control the disturbance, American marines were landed May thirty-first on the historic shores of Daiquirí and were distributed to protect foreign-owned mines and sugar estates.

If the war was a hoax, it got dangerously out of hand. On June second a Negro leader named Carrera burned the La Maya sugar mill. Gómez found himself with a real civil war on his hands. He declared martial law, and was forced to fight in earnest. Perhaps the blacks were carried beyond themselves by the savage excitement of burning and yelling. Gómez now cried out bitterly against the "ferocious savagery" of the traitors. General Monteagudo could not quell them without battle. By July eighteenth, however, the last of the rebels had been cut to pieces or captured. Three thousand blacks were dead. The race-war had stirred up unnecessary bitterness that smoldered dangerously for years to come.

Although the revolution's sudden fury gave Gómez quite a turn, it did not give him the presidency. Zayas secured the Liberal nomination. Gómez, much irked, threw his support by indirect means to the Conservative candidate, General Mario Menocal. The elections of November 1912 went off with reasonable fairness. Only in Oriente was dishonesty claimed, and here Gómez is supposed to have "urged electoral arts of military intimidation to swing the balance for Menocal." Though Gómez claimed that he had aided Zayas, it is fairly obvious that he turned traitor to his party and delivered the presidency to Menocal.

The record Gómez left was indeed nothing to be proud of, yet it was far less iniquitous than that of his next three successors. The principal evil of his administration, as Chapman says, was that it put the bad Spanish traditions again in the saddle, and so opened the way to a recurrence of old corrupt political practices.

On May twentieth, 1913, Gómez relinquished the presidential chair with wistful reluctance. He is much praised by adherents for not having clung to power through the bloody force of his army, for not reëlecting himself in the face of public opinion. "I glory in having been the first ruler in Latin America to establish such a precedent," he proclaimed nobly. And the people felicitated him on his self-abnegation as he set up housekeeping in his new quarter-million-dollar mansion on the Prado. They were almost sorry they had not let him stay in the bigger palace. Today after twenty years, they willingly admit his "improprieties"; but "Ah, Miguel, he was a fine man," they say ardently. *"Simpático!"*

4

THE DANCE OF THE MILLIONS

The better elements had every reason to breathe happily at Mario Menocal's inauguration. They looked to four constructive years of intelligent leadership and fair play. Menocal was by birth a gentleman; by his war record, a hero; by his business record, an excellent executive and administrator. He had the friendship of the United States and the respect of Europe. Sydney Brooks, the English publicist, called him the most distinguished and experienced man of affairs in the island. To the press he seemed to possess in 1913 every quality which might augur a brilliant rule. When he relinquished the helm in 1921, his local and foreign prestige had tobogganed into a slough of outraged contempt; and Menocal, sullied with political iniquities, swaggered out of office, pathetically like a mangled shadow of his promised self.

At his entrance into Cuban politics, Menocal (although today certainly no friend of America) was called more American than Cuban. He had been taken to the United States at the age of two when his father was forced to leave Cuba at the beginning of the Ten Years' War. He received his preliminary education at one of the best preparatory schools, studied at the Maryland School of Agriculture, and at twenty-two received a degree in engineering from Cornell, where he made many close friends among future prominent Americans. After practicing his profession in Nicaragua, he returned to Cuba. At the outbreak of the war of 1895, he enlisted as a private, saw fierce service under all three of the great generals—Máximo Gómez, García, and the mulatto Maceo—and rose to the rank of major-general. During the military governance of the United States, he became chief-of-police of Havana. Shortly afterwards, he accepted a post with the Cuban American Sugar Company, and subsequently managed the Chaparra sugar plantation, which became under his direction the largest sugar estate in the world. He handled laborers as skillfully as he dealt with corporations, and his flair for business was crowned with outstanding success. A hard worker, yet finding time for sports and social intercourse of which he was extremely fond, he was moderately popular among all classes of Cubans, although not possessing that irresistible, expansive magnetism of José Miguel Gómez. When in office he lacked "the perception to gain the esteem of his people," says Pérez, who further comments illuminatingly: "In disposing of the funds of a nation it is necessary to respect liberties even though it may be by debasing consciences as Zayas has done."

On accepting the nomination, Menocal had made fine promises of reform and achievement. But having gained his high office, he shortly seemed content to rest on the laurels of former diligent work, to subsist pleasantly drugged with the lotus-fruits of victory. Apparently he concentrated his major energies on providing good governmental jobs for partisans and flocks of relatives; brothers, nephews, cousins, nephews-in-law, cousins-in-law. Indeed his term of office developed into one prolonged nepotic banqueting. A contemporary American correspondent pointed out Menocal's strong "family sense" as the grave defect in his typically Cuban character. While the President may have been honest as far as his own trousers pockets were concerned, he gave the appearance of handing over the keys of the national treasury to relations and cohorts to help themselves. When a kinsman was caught in an act of embezzlement by an American military attaché, Menocal would not hear of the guilty man being punished.

Up to 1915, although he did no substantial good for the public, he seemed still disposed to heed the constitutional limitations of his power. Then Cuba was precipitated into sudden astounding prosperity by the European War. The price of sugar began to soar, and the sugar crop of 1915-16 augmented to over three million tons (far greater than any in Cuba's previous history). Foreign capital flowed into the island. American business set up factories and began extensive mining projects. Cuba traded fast and furiously.

But with all the money surging into the government, Menocal had no substantial accomplishments to show at the approach of the presidential campaign in 1917. Besides establishing a Cuban monetary system, by which American money might pass equally as legal tender—a measure most beneficial to business—he did little more than make a few recommendations to Congress which were never carried out. (For instance, the building of nine hundred schools authorized by Congress was left undone, because no funds were assigned for the purpose.) Menocal squandered his talents in the field of political maneuvers and spent far more time in making political capital out of the short-comings and evidences of graft of his predecessor, Gómez, who had been the chief instrument in electing him, than in working for the good of Cuba.

Perhaps the most praiseworthy achievement in Havana at this time—and one with which Menocal had nothing to do—was the erection in 1915 of El Centro Gallego at a cost of two million dollars on the site of the old Tacón Theatre, incorporating as an integral part of the new construction the present National Theatre. This event was not so much notable because it provided a whole city block which faced on Parque Central with a beautiful building of harmonious Spanish baroque style, but because of the social and charitable features appertaining to the Galician Club. Founded in 1879 as a meeting place in Cuba for Galicians and including wealthy exporters, clerks, waiters, laborers, bootblacks, and the deposed King of Spain among its 50,000 members, the organization took on philanthropic ramifications of the highest character. Flourishing today it operates a modern hospital costing $3,000,000, a savings bank, and a school for teaching languages, sciences, medicine, and crafts. For dues of two dollars a month, members are provided not only with card-rooms, billiard-rooms, bars, and a ballroom for 5,000 dancers, but are guaranteed expert medical attention, including skilled surgery and hospitalization. This Spanish workingmen's club and its elaborate, larger counterpart across the Parque Central (El Centro Asturiano, constructed in 1926) have had an incalculably salubrious effect upon the happiness, well-being, and prosperity of their combined 110,000 members. The organizations have also been of great assistance to the government in keeping order.

On the whole a state of order existed during the first three years of Menocal's administration, despite the fact that he became increasingly dictatorial and abandoned himself to the intrigues of his henchmen. Because of the general prosperity, the Cubans stood for his high-handed methods with little protestations. However, one notorious scandal in high circles foully muddied the waters and provided the world with a most unpleasant sample of the proverbial unreliableness of Cuban temperament. Havana's chief-of-police, General Riva, had threatened to close the fashionable Prado gambling house of Ernesto Asbert, Governor of Havana Province, unless it was conducted with less notoriety. One afternoon, as Riva was driving with his two little sons on the Prado at the hour when the "world" was promenading according to its old Spanish custom, Governor Asbert and Representative Arias stopped the General's carriage and after a heated argument shot him. To save the boys, Riva, wounded, sprang from the carriage and managed to get to the sidewalk where he began to return the fire. But in a moment he dropped down mortally wounded. Two passers-by had been hit by stray bullets. Within sixty seconds the crowded Prado was in an uproar. Horses became unmanageable; motor cars jammed; ladies fainted; the little sons of Riva yelled in terror at the sight of their father's blood. The next day Riva died. The furor extended to the limits of the island. The United States pointedly assured Menocal of its vigorous support in bringing the perpetrators of the crime to justice. Asbert was "suspended" from his governorship; but although the affair spoiled his chances for the presidency, it did not destroy his political influence. To an Anglo-Saxon, particularly to an Englishman, that "excessive disposition to leniency in Cuba in the aftermath of crime" is appalling, if not totally incomprehensible.

Menocal, like Gómez, had made a forceful one-term promise full of resounding rhetoric. He lived to chew and swallow his noble words with relish. Indeed, to gratify his appetite he was not only willing to perpetrate outrageous frauds but was prepared to immerse his country in as much bloodshed as was necessary to gain himself the presidency.

By a slick political maneuver he secured the Conservative nomination with Nuñez (whom he had committed himself to back for the 1916 presidency) standing for vice-president, on a further promise of the presidency in 1920. After various splits and switchings, Zayas was again the selection of the Liberals. Swiftly Menocal began to throw Liberal officials out of office in the provinces and to replace them with military supervisors. The Liberals took up the campaign cry of "Zayas or Revolution." Riots and desultory deaths marked the agitated preëlection weeks: two killed here, three there, twenty-eight wounded in another place. The voting lists swelled to a million names. (There were about 400,000 legitimate eligible voters.) When the elections were held on November first, 1916, more riots and shootings occurred, and three Conservative presidents of electoral boards were killed. 800,000 ballots were cast. Despite Menocal's manipulation, the early returns pointed to a large Liberal majority, and that night he was ready to concede defeat. Then someone was inspired with a way to falsify the count by illegally diverting incoming returns from the telegraph office to the Secretary of Government, who issued doctored figures. Menocal won. It is undoubtedly obvious, as Carleton Beals says, that the election was stolen.

The Liberals brought charges before the Supreme Court, which accepted evidence that ballots had disappeared in strong Liberal centers in Santa Clara and Oriente. The court ordered new elections in various precincts. Zayas's victory seemed guaranteed. But Menocal marshaled troops threateningly against the Liberals, pardoned criminals to increase the Conservative votes, located booths in the woods, and made it so difficult for Liberals to approach unmolested that even the vice-presidential candidate, Carlos Mendieta, was hindered in getting to the polls. The best Conservative leaders like Varona, Freyre, and Maza wanted to concede the election to the Liberals. Varona deplored the Conservatives' methods, and said that in respect of "inegalities" both sides were equal. Freyre declared the Liberal victory was indisputable. Gómez sent a letter written by Zayas begging Menocal out of patriotism to give the Liberals a fair chance in Santa Clara. Menocal now had no intention of doing anything of the kind.

Plans for a Liberal revolution were drawn up on February fourth. The election farce in Santa Clara was solemnly conducted on Valentine Day. The Liberals made no pretense of voting. In a certain Liberal district the results recorded 2,427 Conservative votes to 31 Liberal—more votes being cast than the total number on a padded list, with Liberals *not* voting! Shortly Menocal muzzled the Liberal press. Then he began to arrest Liberals on charge of conspiracy against his life. The Liberals oiled their rifles. The United States, with sugar on its mind, sent warning notes which implied the government would back Menocal. It would give its confidence and support only to "constitutional" governments. Menocal announced that he had purchased from the United States ten thousand rifles and five million rounds of ammunition.

On February tenth Gómez put himself at the head of the revolutionary forces in Santa Clara. Zayas gave the expected signal and the revolution was on, though not with a bang. Menocal, no neophyte in the field of war, personally directed the military movement of the governmental forces during the revolution. In Washington, Secretary of State Lansing's desk was piled high with telegrams begging protection for the United Fruit Company, Bethlehem Steel, and numerous American-owned sugar companies in Cuba. On February twenty-sixth marines were landed at Guantánamo and other coast towns in Oriente. A batch of them was sent inland to protect the El Cobre mines twelve miles from Santiago.

After a series of quick engagements in the three western provinces, in which the government was successful, Menocal turned his full attention to Santa Clara and his old rival Gómez. On March seventh Gómez and the majority of his command were caught in a trap and made prisoners. This victory was decisive, although Camagüey and Oriente remained to be dealt with. The Liberals still had hope of continuing the war in Oriente until the United States would intervene and conduct honest elections.

On March twenty-fourth the United States government informed the rebels that they could and would hold no communication with them until they laid down their arms. (How different from Taft's stand in 1906!) There was some back-talk in the way of cane-burning and property destruction. But on March twenty-seventh, the Menocal forces won two victories in Oriente. On the twenty-first of April the Liberals were routed in Camagüey. By May the revolution had reached the spluttering-out stage, degenerating into desultory looting.

The real back-breaking straw was Cuba's declaration of war against Germany on April seventh, the day after the United States had made its formal declaration. It was a shrewd, swift move on Menocal's part. For now the Gómez-Zayas revolution was played up in the light of a Liberal-German plot. Menocal could condemn the rebels as pro-German. And the United States pointed out in emphatic messages that any disturbance tending to obstruct the sugar crop—sugar being so important a factor in winning the World War—would be considered a hostile act. If the rebels did not submit to the Cuban government at once, the United States would have to treat with them as enemies.

The sly Zayas had early seen how the cat was going to jump and had made his private peace with Menocal at the cost of leaving his revolutionaries in the lurch. After starting the outbreak, he had disappeared. Later he turned up in Havana to live in luxury at the eccentric Madame Abreu's famous villa, where she "also maintained the only chimpanzee born in captivity." Though Zayas's slipperiness destroyed his future Liberal support, he dexterously improved his position by flopping to the Conservatives.

In the meantime, Gómez sweltered in a crowded room in El Principe Prison, not even being allowed the consolation of tobacco. Throughout the summer his supporters lived in daily terror that Menocal would execute him. In the end, however, Menocal proved generous to his enemies and shot none of them. Doubtless America was in some measure responsible for his leniency, for Lansing insisted there be "no blood."

On the eighth of May the "vindicated" Menocal and Nuñez were proclaimed elected. Twelve days later at the inaugural ceremonies, Menocal solemnly swore to "respect the law and the institutions of the country." His second term, though skyrocketing to a phenomenal prosperity such as few countries have ever experienced, has left Menocal's reputation stained indelibly. He did not accomplish one praiseworthy act; in fact every worth-while governmental activity degenerated woefully under his rule, and he was successful only as a waster of public revenues.

Retaining the extraordinary powers granted him because of the February revolutions and the declaration of war against Germany, Menocal ruled single-handed until 1921, an irresponsible, arrogant dictator, surrounded by sycophants who kept him well filled with cocktails and flattery. Friends of Menocal declare he did not do any personal grafting; they say he was too befuddled with drink to know what was going on about him. He knew enough, however, to turn "war measures" in Cuba to back up his own imperialism.

Menocal's military service law enacted in the summer of 1918 was utilized primarily as a protective measure against Liberals. And to make sure sugar production was not interrupted, the United States in 1919 stationed 1,600 soldiers in Camagüey and 1,000 in Oriente. The troops remained for five years, long past the signing of the Versailles Treaty—serving in a measure as additional support to Menocal's unfruitful autocracy.

Carlos Mendieta, the present President of Cuba, in an article entitled *Adios, dictadura!* published in 1918, summed up Menocal's rule as "a classic and vulgar dictatorship." He denounced the president as having almost completely abandoned public services, including education and highways. "Menocal has converted Cuba into a factory that is a theater of caprices, dilapidations and madness. . . . His work of decomposition is almost impossible to repair."

Cuba's paramount activity during the World War revolved about the sugar crop, its production and marketing. Sugar being an indispensable product for the allies, the Cuban output was vastly increased. This world demand for sugar opened a new period in Cuban history. In the generation from 1834 to 1867, just preceding the Ten Years' War, the sugar industry had come largely to dominate the island. During that period Cuba had flowered into the richest colony in the world, and in many factors of material and artistic culture had surpassed the Mother Country. Such another period, on a more extravagant scale, had its beginnings in Menocal's first term and reached dizzy heights in his second. It came, however, with such meteoric swiftness that it proved little more than a money-mad debauch. "The Dance of the Millions" this flush period in Cuba was called. If money did not actually grow on trees, the silver-green leaves of sugar cane fluttering in fields held a strong figurative resemblance to bank notes.

As the price of sugar soared from three to five, to ten, to twenty-two and a half cents (in 1920), people lost all sense of proportion. Bank deposits increased a thousand per cent. Expenditures became fantastic. Fabulous prices were paid for gew-gaws without a breath of haggling. Luxuries became necessities. Narrow little Obispo Street became the Rue de la Paix of the Western Hemisphere. Prosperity cried out rapaciously for supplies. Foreign trade with the United States alone passed the billion mark in 1920. To facilitate trade, the United States established many and varied new businesses in Cuba.

A new self-conscious society was inaugurated in which American winter residents were invited to mingle with Cubans. The Havana Yacht Club, the Country Club, the Havana Biltmore Club, and the more exclusive Vedado Tennis Club became focal points for fashionable society. The Gran Casino Nacional, the Jockey Club, and a prodigious number of gambling rendezvous sprang up to satisfy gaming instincts, and to provide outlets for new minted gold that burned pockets. In efforts to spend money fast enough Cubans became a nation of show-offs. Private marble palaces, as well as elaborate office buildings, were reared on city streets; extensive subdivisions were opened in the suburbs. Real estate values increased ten-, twenty-, fifty-fold. Building sites in former ill-considered outlying districts sold for $100,000. The vast scraggly Vedado section became many-mansioned. Like an Aladdin's Lamp story, great houses of pink, azure, buff, and mauve arose, drenched with violet bougainvillea, surrounded by clipped lawns, ornamented with parterres of flowering shrubs, and protected by wrought-iron fences twice as high as a man. Here from the city moved the society (or would-be society) set to be nearer those pleasure clubs and exclusive bathing beaches, which were reached by a parked avenue seven miles long, adorned with marble, luxuriant with brilliant flowers, blossoming trees, and immaculate green turf. In the late afternoons, folk from the new villas would descend on the admiring city. With the coming of six o'clock, motors poured into the Malecón, superb with its sweep of paving, its stretch of royal palms, its flanking of glittering marble houses on one side and the eternal blue sea on the other. Like flooding tributaries seeking an already swollen river, the broad white surface of pavement became darkened richly with limousines: Rolls-Royces, Hispano-Suizas, Minervas, Isotta-Fraschinis, and occasional less impressive Packards and Cadillacs. The cars were filled with the ladies of Havana, opulently beautiful with luminous dark eyes and shining hair. They wore semi-evening dresses designed in Paris and many billowy scarves of chiffon or lace, which made those who were not already a little plump look as if they might be by next season. Jewels sparkled, as the gleaming ladies flashed by with amiable set expressions of beauties on parade.

Besides the chauffeur, in each car with the ladies, invariably sat one proud-looking male: a father, a brother, or a son, the head of the house or his representative. Cuban family life appeared very uncomplex on the surface. The ladies stepped from the seclusion of the patio to the semi-seclusion of the closed motor. An hour's daily outing with a male of the family, where all might be seen and see—down the Malecón, around the bandstand, and up the Prado; down the Prado, around the bandstand, and up the Malecón—this same routine repeated and repeated again seemed cause enough for calling forth those spots of joy that dimpled the rosebloom cheeks of the ladies of Havana. The bland expressions on the bronzed faces of males among their pink-and-white

enameled females were amusing in their paradeful respectability.
The gentlemen were so ostentatiously doing their family duty,
as was every Cuban of position at that same hour. After the drive
they would all most likely dine at home, but shortly following
the serving of coffee they would make their polite *adios* and depart to their respective clubs and/or mistresses. If the evening
were an especial occasion, these husbands or fathers or brothers
might take their womenkind to the opera or to a ball. But although a few advanced ladies played golf at the Country Club
and bathed on the coral beaches of the Yacht Club, the essential
life of the Cuban woman in 1920 still belonged as definitely behind high walls and slatted jalousies as in the days when the
grace of a mantilla stirred the air romantically about a high-
hanging balcony.

But American women in plenty cluttered the golf links, dotted
the club buildings' terraces at cocktail hours, and danced tangos
deliriously with sleek young men who looked like gigolos but
who carried wads of hundred-dollar bills for pocket change. For
the fashionable and sporting world of the United States and
South America, a winter season in Havana became the vogue.
The Ward Line and the United Fruit Company built luxurious
new passenger ships to accommodate the tourist trade. Magnificent hotels were erected to cater to the foreign guests and they
charged colossal prices: forty cents for a demi-tasse, forty dollars
a day for a room. Houses of sin were decorated with the golden
lavishness of sultanic opulence. The most famous opera stars sang
in Havana, world-champion boxers fought there, record breaking
horses ran for staggering purses, jai-alai players became social
lions. Continental countesses and Brooklyn demimondaines sat
thigh to thigh at the crowded roulette-tables. Cuban music, Cuban
food, and especially Cuban drinks, were the rage. Greek Pete
"Sazarac," who invented the Sazarac cocktail, moved from Pro-
hibition-dampered New Orleans to achieve new fame in Havana.
German Otto Precht, with his winning personality, arrived from
New York to assume charge of the Sevilla-Biltmore wine cellars.

Sloppy Joe's became an international by-word. Honeymooners spent the price of a suburban home on a fortnight's Cuban gayety. Doddering multi-millionaires came for a last fling before the grave. Spinster schoolmarms, trembling and giggling, came for a first fling, and ecstatically threw away a life's savings. To visit Cuba in the dazzling winter and spring of 1920 was to have memories of extravagance and daring to sigh over forever.

By no means did sugar prosperity affect only the cities and the business centers of the island. Like a good angel and a nemesis, like a double-edged sword which the Cubans lacked the skill to handle, the sugar boom also penetrated the civilization of the *bohio* and the very depths of manless jungle. Everything bowed before the royal decree of sugar. "Clear more land to plant cane," was the incessant cry. And the magnificent primeval forests, bowing beneath the dread command, assumed a prominent but sorrowful rôle in the Cuban pageant. No country on earth is more rich in the blessings of its woods, both beauty-making and utilitarian, than the Pearl of the Antilles. In the scarcely penetrable jungle, out of a sea of interlocked vibrant undergrowth, towering trees valiantly struggle for breath, almost stifled in the coils of giant lianas. Pale silver mosses, draped idly from defenseless boughs, temper the tropical serpent-green, and mauve orchids burst into enchanting bloom on their caressingly parasitical vines. Forty excellent cabinet and building woods are grown in the Cuban forests: mahogany, rosewood, logwood, ebony, the fragrant cedar, and the more fragrant Spanish elm, among them. In clearing up land to make way for sugar, Cubans felled and burned these valuable woods as relentlessly as they did worthless species. They burned to the roots phalanxes of century-old royal palms whose smooth-skinned trunks like slender columns of unpolished platinum-green marble rose skyward a hundred feet. Acres of coconut palms, which yielded food, milk, rope, and numerous other necessaries of peasant life, were sacrificed to the Great God Sugar.

And with more subtle significance the coming of the sugar

industry on a large scale changed the world of the peasant. Formerly the rural Cuban had squatted so contentedly on his square of land which produced about everything he wanted, that a disgusted German peddler coined the immortal phrase: the "damned wantlessness" of the Cuban countryman. Now with his land sold to sugar corporations, he found himself a part of a great industrial enterprise, which provided him with a house and wages on its own terms. Temperamentally he was unsuited to this stream of modern industrial progress in which he found himself. And as Mr. Jenks quotes from a sympathetic American: "He has no part in directing this industrial giant; he has no voice in its management. Yet to it he must look for education, recreation, and bread. He has, willy-nilly, exchanged a simple life, ignorant but virtuous, for a vassalage to a foreign colossus. His future is not his own. It is determined for him in a directors' room in New York." Alas, poor *guajiro!*

As wealth accumulated and the Cubans indulged their pleasure-loving instincts in an orgy of extravagance, men decayed, and education and worth-while activities degenerated. Although teaching positions had doubled since Wood, they were now hardly more than sinecures for the shiftless, and schools descended to a new low level of neglect. In the time of Estrada Palma far more was done for education and public service with a revenue of $15,-000,000 a year (eight dollars per inhabitant) than when Menocal squandered $182,000,000 in a fiscal year like 1920-21. In 1919 he increased the army to 18,000. On highway construction he spent as much as Estrada Palma, Magoon and Gómez combined, but the average number of kilometers a year was only 57 as compared to Magoon's 304, Gómez's 125, and Estrada Palma's 82. Where Estrada Palma had spent $6,000 a kilometer, Menocal spent $42,-000 a kilometer.

With half a billion dollars collected in taxes during his presidency, Menocal might have proved a Cosimo de Medici to the city and a Voltaire at Ferney to the countryside. But about the only signs of progress he left after seven flush years was a bronze equestrian statue of his old chief Antonio Maceo and a presidential palace costing $3,750,000, supplied with $100,000 worth of linens, and containing a painting (depicting the battle of Las Tunas in which he had fought) which he commissioned a cousin Menocal to paint for $60,000.

As if Cuba were the only spot on the globe where sugar cane could be raised, more and more cane land was put into cultivation. At the peak of the prosperity delirium, in the summer of 1920, economic reports revealed an overproduction of sugar in various parts of the world. The market, satiated with sugar, turned sick with nausea and fright. The price of sugar began to slide. It shot precipitously from twenty-two and a half cents to three and five-eighths (in 1921). In April, just before Menocal left office, the United States Emergency Tariff Bill raised the duty on Cuban sugar from 1.0048 to 1.60 cents. Coming at the most critical moment of Cuba's economical history this was indeed a stinging blow from a best friend. Speculation was in a frenzy of dismay. The fabric of business crumbled. The banks, which had made enormous loans to finance the sugar crop on the basis of high prices, found themselves with their security wiped out. Virtually all the Cuban banks collapsed. The bottom had dropped out of the island. Millionaires by the score became bankrupts. True to that inherited doctrine of *mañana,* Cubans had greeted each day as if there could be no tomorrow and had spent their all. Many men could still laugh with Latin philosophy; but some blew out their brains, and others hanged themselves. The finale of the mad Dance of the Millions was sadly draggle-tailed.

Wall Street stepped into the breach, and almost as swift as a feat of legerdemain, American capital dominated Cuban economic life. Cuba woke from its hangover to find itself in the hands of absentee landlords. (American investments in Cuba had risen in ten years from $200,000,000 to $1,200,000,000.) Three-fourths of the sugar industry was owned by American stock holders. During the next decade the railways, the public utilities, the tobacco industry, and the mines came under the control of American corporations.

The conduct of the elections of 1920 offered Menocal an excellent last chance to retrieve his degraded reputation. The decent people of the country, pained to witness the personal ruin of a man of such superior gifts, hoped against hope that Menocal would prove honest at the finish and provide fair elections. When he double-crossed Nuñez, his vice-president, to whom he had again promised support for the presidency, and offered his dictatorial influence to Zayas, his despised former rival who had switched parties, their hope perished.

In the midst of economic ruin, Menocal turned whatever abilities he had left to devising trickery and coercive methods to elect Zayas and defeat Gómez, the Liberal candidate. The Liberals demanding assurances that they would not be robbed this time, felt that help from the United States would be necessary; so, Menocal, seeming to concur, invited General Enoch Crowder to Cuba to assist in drawing up a new election law. He came in March. A new census was taken which brought all former frauds to light. Then a law was formulated purposing to avoid such recurrences and to strengthen the power of the judiciary. Menocal listened to Crowder with feigned politeness. But hardly had his simulated thanks died in the air, when he "flagrantly disregarded Crowder's safeguards" and went his own practiced way of winning elections.

The voting took place on the customary November first. Gómez had threatened in August not to go to the polls, thereby implying that he would provoke American intervention to secure fair play. Washington had told him imperatively that the Liberals should cast their ballots, and promised that official observers would be on hand to avert intimidation and fraud. So the Liberals had gone to the polls—when they could get there. American official observers did observe. With their own eyes they saw every sort of fraud, intimidation, and violence. Doctor Herbert Spinden, one of the observers, witnessed mayors of Liberal towns shorn of executive rights and supplanted by military supervisors, backed by the forces of the army. These armed men, he noted, "shot to kill." There were other forces abroad in the election which, he said, were "sinister in the extreme." For instance, Menocal in the nine months preceding the elections, had pardoned three hundred and thirty-five criminals, including forty-four murderers "in order to use them as gunmen and bullies and to get the value of their family influence." Further, in an endeavor to split the Negro vote, which was overwhelmingly Liberal, the Conservatives had revived a feud between hostile factions of Negro secret sects; and on their promise of espousing the Conservative cause, they had allowed the *ñañigos*—a vicious voodooistic hangover from African slave days—to parade publicly and even to dance *congas,* their orgiastic sexual dances, in the streets.

The observers being powerless to act against Cuba's armed forces, Zayas naturally won, though by a very small margin. The atmosphere was feverish with bitter excitement. The Liberals entered formal appeals in accordance with the new electoral law. By the New Year no adjustment had been made, and the country was rapidly drifting towards civil war. On January sixth, 1921, Crowder arrived unexpectedly as President Wilson's special representative. Menocal was furious. The existing financial crisis, however, forced him to heed Crowder's long communiqué. The Supreme Court bestirred itself and annulled the results of two hundred and fifty voting precincts. The new partial elections were set for March fifteenth. Menocal agreed not to employ military supervisors. Crowder remained to see that all went squarely.

As the date for the partial elections approached, the usual suspicions of governmental improprieties waxed. A week before elections a battle between the two parties took place at Colón, Mantanzas. Hatred rose to a crescendo. At the last moment, after all Crowder's efforts, the Liberals stupidly refused to go to the polls. Perhaps they recalled the United States' backing of Menocal's dishonesty in 1917. At any rate they feared they would not get a fair deal, and they believed the only way to compel justice was to refuse to vote. Under the circumstances, Zayas, not at all the choice of the Cuban people, won—the one time he did not win.

Crowder was convinced that the Liberals would have won if they had not withdrawn. Gómez's precipitate, ill-advised Hispanic American decision put the United States in a powerless position. The Liberals' only chance of success had lain in going through the elections and relying on the United States to see justice done. Gómez went straight to Washington and appealed to the State Department for a United States provisional government to supervise new elections. But the United States had no basis whatever for intervention: they could scarcely act on the possibility, or probability, that the Conservatives would have stolen the March election if the Liberals had won.

On April seventeenth, the United States formally recognized Zayas as elected. The acrimony did not abate until there had been some prominent killings on both sides. The Liberal candidate for Mayor of Havana was killed. Zayas's private secretary was assassinated. Zayas's own life was threatened daily. However, on May twentieth, he was inaugurated intact, and the charged atmosphere became lighter.

In the face of the United States' attitude on the elections, the Liberals recognized the futility of continued opposition. Gómez, overcome with disappointment, had bowed his head to the decision of Washington. Within a month after Zayas's inauguration he died in New York City. His death, coming so soon after his defeat, enshrined him as the foremost Liberal martyr. He had died, they said, of heartbreak. In Havana his funeral procession was two miles long. The streets were strewn with summer flowers and sprinkled with Latin tears. A fight among his emotional admirers for the honor of bearing his coffin caused a riot in which one man was killed and scores had their heads split open. No Cuban has been so beloved by the masses as José Miguel. All his peccadilloes were forgiven, because he was so *simpático!*

To the reverberations of the crashing of banking houses, which had been occurring with frightful repercussions throughout the

early months of 1921, Menocal, surrounded by a horde of relatives and flatterers, had departed from the three-million-dollar
palace he had built to shelter his family. He had made his farewells with arrogant, well-born head erect, his once keen eyes
bleary from high living, his gait affectedly like a conqueror who
had just dismounted from a white warhorse. The retiring president had one paramount consolation: his relatives and friends
were all provided with rich and downy feathers to make their
nests ostentatiously comfortable. He himself had seen his personal
fortune swell in eight years from a million dollars to some thirty
or forty millions. To still any self-accusing memories or to shut
out black whispers, he could luxuriate in foreign travel. And
never a niggard in according himself his full due, Menocal did
travel abroad in a splendor that made Europe gasp. De luxe
hotels, accustomed to housing royalty, salaamed profoundly at the
approach of such greatness.

5

THE ARCH-GRAFTER

In the campaign eight years previous to Zayas's election, one of
the Liberal newspapers had said "the election of Dr. Zayas would
be a disgrace to the country." The political parasitism and corruption during the last two years of his administration made the
prophecy come true. Zayas's astute, praiseworthy messages of program and promise proved to have come only from the tip of his
tongue. His not inconsiderable intellectual gifts were largely absorbed in the diligent pursuit of graft.

Utterly lacking any of Estrada Palma's solid idealism and integrity, with no trace of Menocal's aristocratic bearing, and without
an iota of Gómez's disarming, out-of-door likeableness, Cuba's
fourth president was an insignificant looking little man with dis-

figured yellowish complexion, grotesque teeth, and a shrewd and cunning eye. In manner he was courteous to deprecation: he could shrivel in conciliation. Lacking in physical courage, he was yet tenacious as an octopus. In his private life he was said to be a man of morbidly sensual proclivities. Like Menocal he had a strong Latin family sense, and never neglected to further the interests of his "endless and insatiable relatives," who were more numerous even than his predecessors. An admitted atheist, he did not hesitate to stand sponsor at Roman Catholic baptisms. He was a turn-coat, and a traitor to his party. He would never admit he was wrong, and when cornered he was replete with adroit "saving-face" excuses. He would promise anything, but his word meant little, and he would even deny his own signature.

No Cuban has ever been called more scurrilous and opprobrious names than Alfredo Zayas. But "fool" he has never been called, and fool he never was. If only one epithet should be chosen to characterize him, "slippery" would be the word. In Havana they speak of him generally as El Chino, because of his Chinese imperturbability of countenance and a phenomenal Oriental patience, so rare in a Latin-American. A student of history and philosophies as well as of men, he regarded the world a bizarre and cynical jest. And like an ape squeezing a sponge soaked in honey, he wrung what joy he could from Cuba, and grinned to himself behind a poker-face mask at his own evil cleverness. Pérez, in condemning his government, said the only praise to be accorded Zayas was for "his impassiveness in supporting everything, his leniency in combating enemies, and the serenity with which he has confronted difficult situations that have presented themselves, always resolving them to his own satisfaction." Make no mistake about it: this man Zayas was extremely clever. If he had been as honest, he could have done great things for Cuba and earned for himself one of the highest places in his country's chronicle.

Although he had achieved a reputation for shrewdness as a politician and a lawyer, he had accumulated little money from his practice. As early as 1908 he was known as a "peseta-stealer"—a man who would not hesitate to accept the pettiest graft. In 1912 Gómez had let him taste political fruit by decreeing for him a salary of $6,000 a year to gather materials for writing a history of Cuba. By 1917 Zayas had collected $20,000, though he had turned in no documents to the Academy of History. It is often claimed that he held his post for eight years and collected $50,000 for his services. Yet even $50,000 in his pre-presidential days was but as a nibble of hors d'œuvres to the imperial banquet which was to follow. It is estimated that it cost the Cuban people around eleven million dollars in graft to satisfy Zayas's appetite for gold, which had to be appeased all in the last two years of his term. During the first two years, saddled with General Crowder, who was sent by the United States "to save the country from bankruptcy and possible intervention," Zayas bided his time, spoke noble sentiments interspersed with innumerable "yeses" to Crowder, and winked cautioningly and promisingly at his leashed, impatient subordinates.

Menocal had left the cupboard bare, with an enormous floating debt and tainted contracts which assumed obligations far in excess of Cuba's ability to pay. Zayas pretended to be pleased to receive America's admirable schemes for setting Cuba's house in order, for the Crowder moralization program was an obligatory preamble to securing a fifty-million-dollar loan from the United States. In Zayas's first message to Congress on May twenty-first, 1921, Crowder's ideas of reform were all recognizable features, including the request that the first year's budget be cut approximately in half. Throughout 1921 Crowder continued to study various phases of Cuban affairs, to bring to light precise evils of corruption in public office. The newspapers, economic associations, and Rotary Club lent him their assistance. In 1922 Crowder presented a series of communications containing his suggestions for the renovation of public life. Because there were fifteen in number they are known as the "fifteen memoranda."

Among the evils shown up were graft in the lottery, the De-

partment of Public Works, and the administration of the custom-
house, which was conservatively estimated at fifteen per cent in
collection of revenues and twenty-five in disbursements. Sixty-odd
"imaginary" jobs were discovered existing in the bureau of telegraph operators alone. Leading politicians were drawing in pleasant revenues for "protecting" houses of prostitution.

Crowder saw that nothing could be accomplished beyond mere
recommendations unless the majority of existing Cabinet members, who were notably corrupt and in the public's bad graces,
were removed. When pressure was brought on Zayas, he dismissed his secretaries. With Crowder's assistance, he selected what
is known as the "Honest Cabinet." These new men did unquestionably good service. Unnecessary employees were cut off. A vast
number of tainted public works' contracts were scrapped or made
wholesome.

With the Honest Cabinet in prime working order, Crowder
decided the time was about ripe for the fifty million dollar loan.
Zayas humbly asked if anything else was necessary. Therewith
Crowder submitted the famous "memorandum thirteen," which
got into the hands of *Heraldo de Cuba* and was published. The
communication was not long, but it was loaded with "musts" and
"shoulds," implied or stated. Cubans in general denounced the
memorandum as an unwarranted interference in the island's affairs, "worse than the Platt Amendment." A contemporary car-
toon depicted Zayas pausing with inked pen to ask, "Which name
shall I sign, Crowder or Zayas?" One cannot help but admire
Zayas for his almost superhuman tact in submitting to Crowder's
rigid dictation. Crowder, with all his admirable qualities (he possessed uncommon executive ability, enormous energy, and was
"so honest he leaned backwards") was not only deficient in tact,
but lacked subtlety, intuition, imagination. Never having learned
to speak Spanish, he never fully caught the spirit of the people.
He had little sympathy with Spanish character and temperament,
and no patience with their undisciplined individualistic traits. He

refused to learn that "all the laws in the world mean nothing to an Hispanic-blooded person, if it does not fit his convenience."

Although beyond question Crowder was sincere in his desire for Cuba's welfare and threw body and soul into his regeneration work, he was a most unpopular man with both Cubans and Americans. Many American business men opposed him because he would not "use his office as a collection agency for their contracts." But the *Diario de la Marina,* Cuba's most conservative paper, editorially came to Crowder's defense against the charge of "intervention despot." It listed his substantial achievements. It called him a friend of Cuba, who was there to take steps to avoid civil wars and the necessity for intervention. But the Cuban people regarded their good angel coldly.

Zayas got his fifty million dollar loan early in 1923. Straightway seven million was paid to clear Cuba's war debt to the United States. Six million was turned over to the Department of Public Works for sanitation. The remainder was used on the floating debt. Virtually every dollar was used to satisfy obligations not incurred by Zayas. The politicians, who got nothing, began to howl that the debt had been forced on them.

But now the economic prospects had brightened. The price of sugar was good and the 1922-23 crop large. The next two years promised well. Zayas, seeing the rosy light ahead, decided to break with Crowder and to share plums with the patriots. Not only had politicians in general become excessively restive under Crowder's dictatorial meddling, but many of the high-class Cubans, who desired Cuba to work out her own destiny in her own way, openly said they preferred the worst Cuban government to the best foreign government. The Cuban Congress had already reminded the United States government of Root's interpretative letter of 1901 denying the privilege of interfering in the affairs of the island. An amnesty bill which passed the Senate on October ninth, 1922, but failed the House because of the United States' objection, declared that graft should not be punished as crime "since it had been introduced during the Magoon Administration and was now become customary."

Zayas, taking advantage of the turn of the tide, made much use of the word "nationalism." In throwing off the Crowder yoke, he set himself up as the savior of Cuba. It is often asserted, and is certainly quite probable, that the clever cry of "nationalism" was inspired in New York by American business interests which hoped to get Crowder sacked, so that they might profit on improper concessions in cahoots with Zayas. Certainly at the time Zayas was spouting loudest about "Cuba for Cubans," he was dealing secretly and thickly with foreign corporations, and giving them excessive privileges in his beloved fatherland.

Under cover of this new spirit of nationalism, the President prepared to dig swiftly and deep into governmental moneys, for he had only two years left in which to make his fortune. The presidential palace became a family hotel for hordes of Zayas's relatives, who so gorged themselves on the fat of the land that the bill for chickens alone for one month was $10,000. Fourteen male members of the family, placed in strategic administrative positions, assisted the chief executive most efficiently in his raids on the treasury. Alfredo Junior was given the director-generalship of the lottery, the juiciest plum of all. A brother was made head of the Department of Public Instruction. Cousin Carlos Portela was Under-Secretary of the Treasury, and later, Secretary. One son-in-law was made Comptroller-general. Another son-in-law got a notarial post worth fifty thousand annually. Step-son Willie became major-domo of the palace and was allowed to make pocket change by installing a perfumery shop in the marble halls, where politicians felt obligated to buy.

On April thirteenth, the President got rid of his main impediment to fortune, the Honest Cabinet, and substituted tar-fingered politicians in their places. The refrain of "nationalism" continued to throb throughout the island with the insistence of tom-tom beating. And doped with the hypnotic patriotic rhythm, the country gaped while Zayas put through his major grafting schemes.

One or two may be mentioned. First came the purchase of Santa Clara Convent by the state for the astounding price of $2,350,000, involving graft estimated at considerably more than a million. Next came the notorious Taráfa Law, which would take a volume to describe in its various manifestations. In 1923, thirty-one per cent of the sugar crop was being shipped to nearby ports direct from plantations over private railway lines belonging to individual sugar companies. Forty-seven private loading ports were being used. (Some had been in service for a quarter of a century and the government had acquiesced in their employment.) When the National City Bank of New York had to foreclose and take over sugar estates in the crash of 1921, they incorporated their new holdings in Camagüey as the General Sugar Company, and now they proposed not to patronize the public service railroads but to use the more economical private port method. The American Sugar Company also purposed now to ship by private line and port. Colonel José Taráfa, president of the Cuban Northern Railway, known as the Taráfa Line, devised a bill known as the Taráfa Bill and got it brought before Congress. It declared for closing private docks and wharves and forcing all sugar companies to ship sugar by the public service roads. There was much Cuban flag-waving in the process. Though the Congressmen themselves had little idea what the precise terms were, they were assured the bill was a "thoroughly Cuban measure." The President and Congress were bought for a sum estimated between a half and a full million. (The Veterans and Patriots Association asserted that Zayas's share was half a million and that no representative got less than six thousand dollars nor a senator less than twenty.) The bill was introduced suddenly at two o'clock in the morning and passed the House by eighty-eight to nine.

A storm of protest was raised all over Cuba, not only by American directors of sugar companies but by the great Cuban landholders and planters of Oriente and Camagüey. A large number of important individual Cubans, as well as the sugar companies, were to suffer by the law. Washington was besieged. American

newspapers played up the affair and denounced the law as iniquitous. Undoubtedly the original draft of the Taráfa Bill meant confiscation of valuable properties in ports and railway lines. Elihu
Root himself took the case of the sugar companies and presented
their claims. On the opposing side, American stockholders of the
Cuba Railway sent representatives to Washington. At length a
new bill was drawn up, not affecting the private ports in use prior
to 1923, but providing against the creation of any new ones. The
benefit of all further development of the sugar industry was thus
to accrue to public service railways. Cubans in general were heartily condemnatory of the restrictions of the bill even as finally presented and passed. The railways feature of the bill hinted at the
consolidation of the three great interconnecting roads. One had
strong reason to suspect that the measure was American-made,
and that the Cuba Railway (an American corporation) would
eventually get control of the United Railways and the smaller
lines of Cuba. Chapman says, "To many Cubans, it seems that
the formation of the much boasted national company has in fact
resulted in turning over a Cuban line to a foreign corporation,
which may in time monopolize the railway facilities of the island.
And for this they blame the 'nationalistic' Zayas!"

The newspapers shortly began to attack Zayas vehemently.
With an air of injured innocence, he let them have their say without molestation. According to *Heraldo de Cuba,* the President's
son-in-law "protected" a gambling house for seven hundred dollars a day. And Zayas himself did not scruple to go at midnight to
another house on Zulueta Street to collect his share of gambling
graft. He made left-handed money on Chinamen whom he allowed to enter by thousands, although there was a rigid Chinese
exclusion act and he himself stated before Congress that only ten
had entered in the last three years. (The Cuban Consul at Canton
was alleged to have made $200,000 on passport visas in three
years.) Henry Kittredge Norton in *World's Work* gave a vivid
example of how another minor graft was manipulated. "A foreign engineer, interested in comparative costs on bridge-repairing,

took a list of seven bridges that the records showed had been recently repaired at a cost of $367,000. He found not only that the
repairs had not been made, but that not one of the bridges had
ever existed!"

As the stench of corruption rose to heaven, the decent Cubans—
really remarkably long-patienced in supporting governmental
abuses—at length were roused to protest. On April first, 1923,
arraigning the government, the Cuban Committee of National
and Civic Renovation met and the next day published a manifesto
denouncing the evils.

The Veterans Society, which had kept out of politics for several
years, again became politically active. It appointed a committee to
ask Congress to repeal the Taráfa Law, the patently scandalous
lottery law, and later it made twelve recommendations which
were virtually the reforms of Crowder's original moralization program. After several months' absence, Crowder had returned as
the first United States Ambassador to Cuba, but his new position
carried no authority for intermeddling, and he was now somewhat like a Brutus without a play. However, he was strongly
allied in principle with the Veterans Association, and the im-
pending issue was said to be between his policies and those of
Zayas.

Despite the general Cuban lack of sympathy for Crowder,
Cubans themselves began to stigmatize the "nationalism" of Zayas
as a farce. Carlos Mendieta publicly stated that Crowder was a
better friend of Cuba than Zayas, and that the latter's nationalism
was synonymous with corruption. Late in September, when the
air buzzed with threats of revolution, for the moment Zayas lost
his imperturbable calm and had twenty leaders of the Veterans
arrested. Characteristically, however, within a few days he released them and then proclaimed that the aims of the Veterans'
program were precisely his own.

The Veterans were in no wise deceived. For half a year the
controversy continued without overt outbreak. Sugar planters
among the Veterans would certainly not have countenanced the

starting of a revolution before cane-cutting season was over. On the last day of April 1924 a revolt under Colonel Frederico Brú broke near Cienfuegos and spread to twenty towns in Santa Clara. The real leader, García Vélez, son of General Calixto García, was in the United States at the time buying arms, and, according to later accusations of his confrères, squandering ammunition money on New York night life. The rebellion proved a ridiculous fiasco. Skillfully and with little noise, Zayas suppressed the revolt. He straightway forgave his enemies. With the Veterans Association a dead issue, he was free to resume corruption, and Congress made no further effort to do anything of a really useful character.

Although Zayas had gone into office on a one-term platform and had five times asked Congress to pass a law forbidding re-election, when the time came, he schemed to get the nomination of the Popular-Conservative combination. Menocal, however, secured it. Zayas made another flop and allied himself with the Liberal candidate, Gerardo Machado, for an alleged consideration of $80,000 and the right to name three Cabinet Secretaries if Machado won the presidency.

The campaign for nomination within the Liberal Party had developed into a close fight between Carlos Mendieta and Gerardo Machado. Mendieta, known for his unimpeachable honesty and his bitter opposition to Zayas's corruption, was the favorite of both the regeneration element and the rank and file of the party. Machado was looked upon as a shrewd business man, but as one seeking office to increase his private fortune. Closely connected with American electrical interests, Machado declared that Cuba's future must go hand in hand with America's. A vigorous man of agreeable manners and a far cleverer politician than Mendieta, he went everywhere, making friends, making promises, and winning additional support by dispensing "liberal lobby funds, derived from Power Trust friends and other foreign business interests." It was a matter of general surprise, however, that he won the nomination over Mendieta. The latter, although pressed, declined to contest the nomination or to run on a separate ticket. But knowing the real character of Machado, which lay hidden as the body of a cuttle-fish lies concealed in the profusion of its ink, Mendieta refused to support him.

With the country normally Liberal, with President Zayas's backing and that of American business interests, Machado's victory over Menocal with his ruinous record was assured. Despite falsifications, bribery, and official coercion, Machado was "honestly" elected. Beyond doubt he was the people's choice for president at his election in November 1924.

With the presidential succession settled, Zayas and his cohorts had six uninterrupted months in which to indulge in an orgy of looting; and more, Zayas had virtually been assured of immunity from prosecution when Machado assumed the chief office. A series of sensational deals, like the notorious Cárdenas Bay dredging appropriation, were now affected, involving a prodigious amount of graft. In the sacking of the public treasury, Zayas presented "a new and tragic dance of the millions."

Leland Jenks, though admitting that Zayas's administration is considered the high spot in corruptness, pays the devil his due. "His total achievement in the face of probably justified vituperation on the part of Havana newspapers," Jenks says, "bespeaks political talents of no mean order." And whatever Zayas may have stolen, it is true that he "maintained the credit of his country, funded most of the floating debt, and left the treasury with a surplus; he averted intervention, removed the incubus of Crowder's extraordinary mission, and brought the United States Senate to sanction the Isle of Pines treaty after twenty years' delay; he foiled two threatened revolutions, and maintained his own authority intact."

One of Zayas's last acts while still in power and before too much was discovered was to erect a statue to himself in enduring bronze and marble. In November, after the Machado election, he issued a decree appropriating $36,000 to prepare a park facing the presidential palace as a suitable setting for his image. Politicians subscribed to the statue fund. Indignant University students staged a demonstration before the palace and threatened to destroy the statue if it was erected. Zayas politely asked to speak with the leaders. The boys entered the palace sullenly belligerent. From behind a curtain, Zayas regarded them, learned their names, their family connections. Then with a deprecating cordiality he came forward, talked to them one at a time, inquired solicitously of the health of various members of their family, flattered them on their interest in public affairs, insisted that he was their servant and wanted to please them in everything, urged them by all means to destroy the statue if it displeased them, and even promised them immunity for depredation. The boys, calmed by his conciliatory suavity, dispersed the crowd. On May sixteenth, four days before the end of his administration, the Zayas statue arrived just in time. It was hastily set up on its pedestal the same day. On its base a tablet proclaimed for future generations' elucidation that the monument was erected by a "grateful people" to the "restorer of the liberties of his country." Dominating Zayas's Park today, the heroic figure stands, holding its left hand against its trousers pocket and pointing with the right hand towards the palace. The passing people joke about it and say the gesturing statue means: "With this hand I filled my pocket with money and there is where I got it."

PART V

Only Yesterday and Today

I

AMERICA'S CHOICE TOO

ON the strength of being an *Hombre del '95,* General Gerardo Machado had become a politician, attaching himself in 1906 to that beloved old rascal Gómez. But having been unsuccessful in politics after 1912, he had become a business man. By his notable efficiency in managing his own electric power company and later a big sugar company he had attracted the attention of American money interests. When he felt assured of the latter's support, he had again entered politics. Nicknamed *El Gallo* long ago, because of his characteristic strut and ways, he crowed loudly and convincingly against political corruption and governmental inefficiency. He pledged himself to give honest government and to retire from office at the end of his term without seeking a second one. The Cuban populace believed him, and American capital believed him thoroughly pliable to its purposes.

Self-made, without any distinction of family background, Machado possessed little culture. His heavy, six-foot frame suggested strength and power, and he did not lack a certain animal magnetism. Like Miguel Gómez, he had learned the value of smiling. The sensuality of his pock-marked face was somewhat disguised by ever-present tortoise-shell-rimmed spectacles, which gave him that thorough-going efficient look seen on the typical American-business-luncheon-clubman. What he lacked in formal education, he made up for in astuteness. He had profited greatly by his lessons in political trickery a decade and a half earlier. He had shrewdly noted the preceding presidents' mistakes and blunders, both with their own people and with the United States. He knew the two potent weapons for keeping himself in power were American financial interests and his own well-paid, well-fed army. He knew too that if he borrowed great sums of money from American banks, they would do their utmost to help him retain his office.

The first two years of Machado's administration were ostensibly constructive and gave little cause for alarm either to his Cuban or American admirers. Yet two events occurring shortly after his inauguration might have been taken as omens of the bloody consequences that followed. Within three months after he had taken oath of office, Machado had Armando André, the editor of *El Dia,* an opponent of his election, murdered on his doorstep by hired thugs. (A few days before the killing the new president had expressed himself at the Union Club as regretting "the necessity of having to kill him.") At about the time of the editor's murder, Machado restored the garotte, that barbarous instrument of execution which had not operated since the early days of the republic. The job of executioner was conferred upon a confessed murderer with the resounding official title of Minister of Executions. Though Machado's minister was to function only a dozen times officially, some twelve hundred inhabitants were to die by official murders unofficially performed. Sawed-off shotguns, revolvers, knives, and ropes were found to be just as effective and far less bother than the cumbersome garotte, whose screws could not be twisted without red tape delays.

Under Zayas there had been an inspiriting recovery from the bankruptcy following "the time of the fat cow" in 1920. The price of sugar had risen and the market was generally good at the time of Machado's election in 1924. In the first year of his administration, however, the market dropped again, and although there were brief interludes of recoveries, the economic situation never really righted itself. The Cuban depression may be said to date from 1925, having commenced four years before the world-wide depression. In 1930 the sugar market completely collapsed—the price of sugar dropped to a cent and three-quarters cents a pound.

In 1920 the value of Cuban raw sugar exports had been nearly $1,000,000,000. In 1930 the annual total fell to $64,000,000. Since approximately 80% of the national income is dependent upon sugar (a comparison of the above figures revealing a shrinkage of $936,000,000) it was natural that poverty and discontent should have gripped the island. The Hawley-Smoot Tariff of 1930 (devised to protect American sugar-beet interests), which imposed a duty of two cents a pound on Cuban sugar (Puerto Rico, the Philippines, Hawaii, and the Virgin Islands enjoyed duty immunity), dealt the knock-out blow to the ruined market of Cuba's main product.

Adding to the hardships of the times, Machado, instead of practicing economies, began his extensive public works program, which doubled the public debt of the depleted country and increased the taxes.

In 1927 all was still well on the surface in Cuba. The rich were able to borrow enough money to keep up appearances, to live sumptuously in their marble villas, to tour Europe luxuriously, and to educate their sons in the United States, England, or Spain. Though the models of Continental motor cars in the afternoon parades were not the latest, they were still impressively elegant. And though the ladies were less bejeweled, they were beautifully gowned, and the young women, who had enjoyed social seasons in Europe, revealed an unwonted look of dawning independence.

On February 19, 1927, Machado secured his first loan of $10,-000,000 from the Chase National Bank. In July of that year, he borrowed $9,000,000 from the house of Morgan. In June of the following year, the Chase Bank arranged a revolving credit loan of $60,000,000. This issue was later converted in February 1930 into an $80,000,000 loan at 5½% due in 1945. In 1927 Machado's son-in-law, José Obregon, nicknamed the "Wood Louse" because of his manner of handling shiploads of lumber donated by the American Red Cross after the Cuban hurricane of 1926, had been made manager of the Havana branch of the Chase National Bank. For arranging one of the Chase loans Obregon received a little good will commission of half a million dollars.

On June 21, 1927, amendments to the Constitution, voted by Congress, and approved by Constitutional Convention May 9, 1928, provided that the president's term should be for six years and that he should be ineligible for reëlection. The office of vice-president was abolished; in case of death or disability, succession devolved upon the Secretary of State, a new election to be held within sixty days. The number of senators was increased to thirty-two, their term of office to nine years; representatives to one hundred twenty-eight, and the term increased to three years. The franchise was extended to all males over twenty-one without restriction. Despite increased taxes, the populace had been well enough pleased with Machado up to this time. Now murmurs of criticism from the more intelligent were listened to by the people, who began to suspect a betrayal. Cubans bitterly resented the amendment—they felt that their constitution had been violated. As his secret plans for reëlection became more obvious, Machado had to give offices here, bribes there. In order to gain support of enemies he offered fat jobs to Conservatives. He thought his Liberal friends would remain loyal for the sake of their party, but that he must buy his enemies. When criticism commenced openly, because of its justness, Machado feared it might cause him to lose power, and he determined to nip it in the bud. Shortly he began to arrest his critics. Some of the more vehement were secretly killed.

In 1928 President Coolidge himself came to address the sixth Pan-American Congress held in Havana in February. In his speech Coolidge proclaimed that Cuba's people were "independent, free, prosperous, peaceful and enjoying the advantages of self-government." He declared that the stability of their government and the genuine expression of public opinion by their ballot-box "commanded universal respect and admiration."

Coolidge was either as ignorant of Cuba's present and past as

he proved to be of Texas's Alamo, or he was being diplomatic
with unnecessary hypocrisy. The preceding November palpably
unfair elections had been held. In 1927 Chester Wright, editor of
International Labor News, had come to Washington with the
account of one hundred and forty-seven killings of workers by
the Machado régime. The affair had been given widespread publicity by the press. As early as 1925 Machado had begun his policy
of driving all labor organizations underground. Many laborers
were in military prisons. Many had been deported. Some had
mysteriously "disappeared."

The day before Coolidge's arrival a Spaniard named Brouzon,
together with two students and a fellow named Yalob, was arrested for tacking up anti-imperialistic posters. The families could
obtain no information about them; but after the foreign visitors
had returned home, undigested parts of Brouzon's body were
found in a shark's belly. Brouzon's widow identified her husband's initialed cuff-links and his shirt and coat. *El Pais* reported
on March fifteenth the discovery of Yalob's decomposed body,
which had been washed up by the tide. The prison chains were
still attached to the remains, half-consumed by fishes. On the
same March fifteenth was printed an order from the port-captain
prohibiting shark-fishing. Presumably the old Spanish custom of
releasing prisoners from a trapdoor or chute in Morro Castle to
meet their death at the teeth of obliterating sharks had been revived. People recalled the older tradition that the sharks which
infested the warm seas surrounding the island first came there
following slave ships from African waters to devour the scores of
victims who were flung into the sea when overcome by the tor-
ments of the frightful voyages.

In Fraternity Park, in soil gathered from each of the twenty-
one republics represented at the conference, grows a ceiba tree
within a bronze protective railing. Above the door leading to the
enclosure are the words *La Paz* (Peace). Encircling the enclosure
are bronze shields of the different nations and a guiding inscrip-
tion from Martí in Spanish: "It is the hour of the recount and

united march, and we must move together in a square as tight as the silver at the roots of the Andes. People are united only by the bonds of friendship, fraternity and love." Machado also had his own name immortalized on the door. Thousands came to read the words of Martí, to behold the name Machado. They were not much fooled.

On the surface, the conference, replete with banqueting and with Yankee compliments vying with Latin flattery, was a smile-making success. But the people, suspicious of the exuberant camaraderie between the high officials of Cuba and the United States, knew that something extraordinary was brewing. Yet they hardly suspected that an agreement was reached to permit Machado to remain in power for another six years.

From May twenty-eighth, 1928, when Colonel Blas Masó was officially murdered while enjoying the air on his balcony, to August sixth, when Deputy Bartolomé Sagaró was blackjacked to death, sporadic assassinations by Machado police occurred to silence those who might utter tongue against Machado's seizing power for another six years.

On All Saints' Day, at the points of the requisite number of guns, actual and figurative—no one dared run against him—General Machado was reëlected President of Cuba for a term of six years. There was great rejoicing in certain corridors of American Halls of Mammon. The Electric Bond and Share Company—which had boosted Machado into office in 1924—was particularly elated, for with its subsidiary, American and Foreign Power, it had been granted extraordinary favors by the Cuban government in the way of tax-reductions and legislation. It was allowed to charge an exhorbitant price for electric current—seventeen cents per kilowatt hour in Havana, approximately twenty-two cents in the rest of the island—and when consumers struck, it was afforded effective barbarity to force people to turn on their lights.

The President now began to decorate American business men with orders and medals. American firms made gifts to Cuban government officials through lawyers. Soon many firms found it

simpler to fire their lawyers and deal directly with senators and
representatives face to face, hand to hand. The government lottery
became more and more venal as a means of corrupting congressmen. A gentleman running for senator did not hesitate to spend
a hundred thousand dollars to buy votes and influence, for he
knew he could make it back with handsome interest from the
privilege of selling lottery tickets at illegal profits. Pornographic
movies and shows with naked rumba dancers were notoriously
operated for gain by several high officials. Yet the insatiable politicians, contemptuous of the depression, cried out for more graft.

As business grew worse, Machado, himself losing his vast income from interests in various concerns in the island, looked to
the depleted government to supply the money he desired. His
critics complained that other presidents merely stole the money
from the Treasury, but that Machado put the country into debt to
get his fortune. The President became as able a grafter as he had
been a man of business. Against the will of an impoverished people, he instituted an extravagant public works program, including
the construction of an east to west highway across the island and
a new National Capitol. These projects were made realities by
the financing of the Chase National Bank. A large share of the
money was immediately diverted into the pockets of the Machado
administration. The Capitol, originally bid out for $3,500,000,
finally cost between $18,000,000 and $20,000,000. It is true the
plans were considerably enlarged over the original, ostentatious interior ornamentation was added, some lavatories were fitted with
gold soap dishes, an enormous diamond was sunk under glass
in the pavement to mark the highway's direction. But even so,
investigators put the graft to the politicians as high as $12,000,000.

The construction of the Central Highway would have been an
excellent project if it had been carried out economically, in normal
times. But the Treasury was depleted, the people in a desperate
condition, and Machado was holding his position by reason of
usurpation and violation of the constitution of Cuba. The Chase
National Bank and other organizations which made loans to

Cuba after Machado began his last term as President knew they were trusting money to an unofficial government which did not have the will of the people. By the Platt Amendment the Cuban government was required to secure approval from the United States before it could float any foreign loans. The State Department permitted the President to borrow money from the bankers to build these memorials to his vanity and corruption, and then it sent experts to devise schemes to protect these bankers, who had full foreknowledge of the country's bankrupt conditions and were not ignorant of the gambler's chance they were taking. Since the presidents of various American interests and their lawyers stated again and again that they would do everything in their power to keep Machado in office and prevent any criticism of his methods, the United States government chose to turn a deaf ear to complaints against Machado's dictatorship. Under President Hoover, who was so closely allied to big business, a hypocritical "hands off" policy was strictly maintained.

When Hoover sent to desperate Cuba an ambassador who was a very princeling of vast capital interests himself, Harry Guggenheim, it was not unnatural that some Cubans should regard the amiable Mr. Guggenheim as a Greek bearing gifts. And as the months went by, it was claimed that the economic and financial schemes put into operation during Guggenheim's incumbency (over which he had no control) seemed devised mainly to protect the international bankers and to have small regard for the welfare of the Cuban people. The opposition to the Machado administration struck back at the United States by making the new ambassador the target of censorious attacks. Mr. Guggenheim's diplomatic bed was indeed strewn with thorns which stuck him every way he turned.

As incomes and wages declined, a food-consumption tax and sales tax were added to the poor man's burden. To carry on his public works program Machado outrageously increased taxes on necessities. For instance, in 1925, his first presidential year, the duty on pure lard was $2.43 per 100 kilos (certainly high enough at that figure). By 1933, Machado's last year, the duty had been raised to $19.32 per 100 kilos. Since the value of pure lard at shipping never exceeded $8.00 per hundred, the rate of duty amounted to almost 225% of the value of the article taxed, doubtless as cruelly high a rate on a needed commodity as any tariff ever maintained.

Although Machado has been duly praised for keeping Cuba internationally solvent, the money which was paid annually as interest to banks was desperately needed to nourish the Cuban people. School teachers and government clerks were forced to go unpaid, so that the foreign bankers and the soldiers could be paid. The maintenance of the army, used mainly as a personal bodyguard, became the heaviest drain on the Treasury, next to payments on the foreign debt. Orestes Ferrara, devious Secretary of State, expressed the spirit in which the administration regarded its obligations to American bankers: "In the name of the government I ratify the proposal to fulfill its international obligations even if the economy of the people leaves them naked." When Mr. Guggenheim said his farewells to Cuba in 1933, he saw with his own regretful eyes that the forced economy of the people had left thousands of them not only naked, but houseless and faced with death from starvation. Moreover, when the citizens, ground down by taxes, began to complain and to whisper of throwing off oppression, Machado resorted to iron-fisted tyrannies recalling the Dark Ages.

In the fall of 1930, with much éclat, T. L. Chadbourne arrived to devise a plan for rehabilitating the sugar industry. Indirectly, and probably incidentally, Chadbourne was tied up in half-a-dozen ways with Chase National Bank interests. During the decade following 1920 when the sugar market crashed, Cuba had made various legislative attempts to control sugar. None of the schemes had been successful enough to warrant its continuance. The wise and estimable Dwight Morrow had pointed out to Machado in 1926 the folly of sugar restriction for Cuba. Just before Chadbourne came, the economist, Leopoldo de Andrade (later murdered by Machado), had stated: "The only partisans of restriction left in Cuba are those individuals who have sugar because they did not sell it in time at speculative prices and a few banks which shortsightedly prefer to collect their debts quickly even though they lose their non-sugar investments which they undoubtedly will if the country is definitely ruined by restriction."

Chadbourne's plan was an international scheme supposed to be devised by those interested in the Cuban industry. It was accepted by Cuba, Java, the sugar producing countries of Central Europe, and Peru. (The United States and the island possessions were left free to raise an unlimited quantity of cane and beets.) It was, as Mr. Guggenheim explains, an attempt under the capitalistic system to establish an international control over an agricultural product grown in many parts of the world. "Regardless of the merits or demerits of the Chadbourne plan," says Guggenheim, "under a policy of laissez faire, American ownership in Cuba's sugar production would have become nearly complete." Before the World War Americans owned about one-third of the sugar properties of Cuba. Today they own seventy per cent.

Chadbourne himself thus described the plan:

> "First, we have segregated surplus stock for orderly marketing over a period of five years. Second, we have placed a rigid restriction upon output with chief exporting countries of the world so that the future output plus annual sales of segregated surpluses, will equal and not exceed consumption. Third, we have secured governmental sanction to control the arrangements made, so that recalcitrants can have no opportunity to take advantage of their fellows."

Hopes and predictions as to a rise in the sugar price did not materialize. On the contrary, the price of sugar reached a new low level for all times, dropping from an average of one and a half cents a pound in 1930 to less than one cent a pound in 1932 ("based on price of 96° centrifugal Cuban sugar on New York market, cost and freight"). In all fairness, one must be reminded that during this period, the price of all commodities suffered progressive declines in price "with the deepening of the world depression." However, any thoughtful youth might have seen that an international plan which did not have the full coöperation of the United States' domestic and island producers could hardly be effective. According to Carleton Beals:

> "Chadbourne proceeded to take Cuba for a ride on a scheme differing little from its predecessors and which has since proved ruinous. . . . The famous plan created a corporation to be responsible for the expenses of the sugar producers—in reality for the bankers' loans—through the emission of $42,000,000 in bonds to be used to buy 1,500,000 tons of sugar from existing supplies, largely impounded by the banks, and retire it from the market. The final agreement between the Republic of Cuba, the New National Sugar Exporting Corporation, the Chase National Bank, was signed December 16, 1930. . . . The whole scheme was devised apparently to permit the large foreign Centrales to break their contracts with the growers. In addition, it benefited American beet-sugar growers and cane-growers in Hawaii, the Philippines and Porto Rico."

The plan did temporarily benefit the banks, but it was disastrous to Cuba and the Cubans. Besides causing serious deterioration in the idle cane fields, the scheme severely hurt the railroads and threw many of their employees and the port-workers out of work, as well as laborers on plantations and at centrales. It lost millions of dollars of revenue to the government. Finally, it was admitted a momentous failure by even its warmest original supporters. The Chadbourne plan—however well-intentioned it might have been, however urgent as a temporary relief measure— proved a tricky weapon for economic suicide. It was perhaps one of the worst of America's "good offices" ever bestowed upon the island.

By 1933, only twenty per cent of the sugar industry was Cuban owned, and that heavily mortgaged. Ten per cent was Canadian and British owned, seventy per cent American. As to other degrees of ownership in Cuban industry at the present time, the common carrier railroads are about sixty per cent American, forty per cent British. The street railway system and the electric light and power and gas works are American. Banks are predominantly American owned, with Canadian interests second. Americans control about two-thirds of the oil business, the British, the other third. Cattle-raising remains in Cuban hands, but the packers are American. Fruit and vegetable farming are conducted by Cubans, but the Chinese are rapidly coming to dominate the business, and they control the city markets. The small merchants, the restaurateurs, waiters, bartenders, and domestic servants are largely Spaniards. In colonial days Cubans complained that the Spaniards had all the political offices while they held only the land. Today the Cubans possess all the political offices, but foreigners possess the land—by ownership or mortgage—and control most of the business.

2

REIGN OF TERROR

On May twentieth, 1929, the celebrations of Cuba's Independence Day shared honors with the inauguration of the usurping Machado and the completion of the $20,000,000 National Capitol for which, they say in Havana, the children of Cuba go hungry and the children of these children will be long in paying.

In this fateful 1929, the year of the Wall Street crash, Cuba entered a four years' tragic period of strife, turmoil, and repression with its president clinging to office by inhumanly cruel methods. The beginnings were more or less secret, undercover, but as the months passed the tyrannies became increasingly bold. By Machado's decree Cuba was placed under martial law in 1930, and except for the intervals of revocations, remained so, off and on, through the climax of the revolution of 1933. After 1930 economic, social, and political conditions in Cuba went steadily from bad to intolerable.

Since 1922 (under Zayas), gangster elements had increasingly become candidates and office-holders. Men with penal records entered the Senate and the Chamber of Deputies, and when demanded by the courts for subsequent crimes, they were protected on the ground of congressional immunity. In amnesties advocated under Machado, hardened criminals were favored in preference to political offenders. Because criticism was becoming universal, Machado resorted to outrageous tactics to bring his people to toe the line of slavish obedience. Pardoned criminals were made chief police officers of towns. A military censorship was superimposed on the press. Not only were judges terrorized, but their very authority was taken away in 1932 and 1933, and relayed to drumhead army courts. To convict a political enemy was simple enough; to convict a criminal friend of the government, all but impossible. To frighten oppositionists into submission by beating, shooting, Machado established the Partida de la Porra, the Party of Bludgeon. This strong-armed gang was honey-combed with male and female criminals. Torture as well as terrorism was encouraged.

The University was first closed by the government in 1927 because student publications criticized Machado's excesses. It was reopened later in the year and again closed in 1928 after certain professors refused to continue teaching with soldiers on guard. From the end of 1930 through 1933 it was closed continuously.

The first student to fall foul of Machado was the brilliant radical, Julio Antonio Mella, who possessed the face and figure of a young god and a magnetic gift of oratory. He was an idol among his fellows. In 1925 he was imprisoned by Machado on a false murder charge, and later exiled. Going to Mexico City, he became the acknowledged leader of Cuban exiles there, and helped to publish a magazine dedicated to liberty. On January tenth, 1929, hired assassins of the Cuban government shot him in the dark. The death of the students' idol enshrined him as the foremost martyr of the rebellion against Machado.

Official terrorism followed in the wake of Mella's death. On November eighteenth, Harry Guggenheim arrived as the new American ambassador. For the hour, the uncertain populace took heart. But before a month had passed, Luis Blanco Newman was murdered by the police for attempting to present a petition to the American Embassy. It was a telling warning.

In January 1930 on the anniversary of Mella's death, students demonstrated. Shortly afterwards official murders occurred. Opposition to Machado increased momentously during the spring. Despite press muzzling, criticism of Machado was leaking out in America. On Cuba's Independence Day, Mr. Guggenheim arranged a friendship celebration. United States Marines paraded up the Prado to martial music. Cubans interpreted the affair as a patent hint that the United States would back Machado to the limit. Mr. Guggenheim thereafter discouraged American battleships' dropping in on courtesy calls.

On September thirtieth another parade ended with significant disaster. University students and various professors prepared to march to the home of the aged philosopher, Dr. Varona, to felicitate him on his fiftieth anniversary of teaching. Because of Varona's critical attitude to the President, any mark of esteem shown him was frowned upon by the administration. Machado's police broke up the parade, rode down upon the marchers from ambush, shot into the crowd. Rafael Trejo, a medical student, was shot in the back and killed. Although several students had mysteriously "disappeared," Trejo was the first one to be killed in Havana by Machado's men. In the fight, the youth, Pablo de la Torriente, had his head split open. (He recovered sufficiently to be sent to the Isle of Pines penitentiary, where he was treated brutally.) Professor Mariello, who protested against further beating of the insensible boy, was arrested and thrown into El Principe Prison. As a protest against the Trejo killing, three hundred professors met in one of the University buildings and pledged themselves to support the students in their fight for constitutional government. For this action the faculty members were dismissed without trial.

To teach the five thousand University students a lesson for questioning his infallibility, Machado turned the lot of them into the streets, nailed up the doors, placed soldiers on guard. Shortly the high schools and normal schools throughout the island were also closed. Cuba's youth was turned loose to make what devilish workshops of idle brains it pleased. Visitors wonderingly remarked smooth-cheeked boys with faces of stone and mouths of sin and yet other lads with eyes lit like rapt Isaiah's "with wild seraphic fire." The students did not forego their education in dumb submission. They continued to hold meetings, to protest, to plan. They distributed manifestoes. By means of a contraband newspaper they spread "the message of revolt" to every hamlet of the island. They swore to die rather than desist in their purposes. Secretly they armed themselves. In the withered, disillusioned Machado era, a large untapped fund of hope and faith was found in these youths, who were willing to risk everything for ideals. In bloody reprisals many lost their lives, many were tortured inhumanely, many emasculated. Out of Machado's violence was begotten their self-protective, retaliating violence.

In the two years following 1930 a large number of professors fled into exile. Sixteen found refuge in the United States. Among those put in jail were Dr. Carlos Finlay, son of the famous scientist, and the popular physiology professor, Dr. Ramon Grau San Martín (later President of Cuba from September 1933 to January 1934). To maintain themselves and their families, professors and teachers had to seek any and every kind of employment. An anthropologist became a baker. Those unable to find work were forced to live on public charity.

Due to the general unrest in 1931, a revolution was attempted in August, under the leadership of Mario Menocal. To try to prevent such an outbreak Ambassador Guggenheim had conducted a long negotiation at the request of both the government and the opposition. He found one of the major difficulties in Cuban politics was the reluctance to compromise. He pointed out to Menocal that in the event of an attempted revolution at the time, whichever side might win, Cuba would be the loser. Immediately after the revolution (which proved abortive, partly because the people had little confidence in Menocal) Guggenheim urged Machado to take advantage of his victory to enact drastic and liberal political reforms. He emphasized the fact that although the physical conflict had been checked, there remained the far more difficult task of establishing moral peace, without which exhausted Cuba could not recover her equilibrium. At first Machado seemed to accept the ambassador's suggestions, but later through the influence of certain political advisers he changed his mind, and instead of instituting reform, he sharply "lessened" political liberties. On December fourth, Guggenheim said to Machado, "Since the revolution, the government politicians are determined to have all or nothing, and it remains to be seen whether they will continue to have all or nothing." Throughout the following year, Guggenheim told Machado again and again that his policy was suicidal, and that he must meet the opposition on a basis of compromise which would satisfy their principal demands. The ambassador's instructions from Washington, however, were strictly "hands off." Officially he did keep his hands off, and they all disliked him for their individual personal reasons.

When the revolution failed, Menocal fled the country, and many another better man than he went also into exile to escape routine prison, *ley de fuga,* or "disappearance." New York, Miami, and Merida, Yucatan, became the three chief centers for Cuban exiles. In the fall of the year, from among the reformers and students remaining in Cuba, the famed organization known as the ABC was established to cope with the violence of Machado's methods. It was in no sense a Red organization, although it contained radicals in its ranks and was organized on "traditional nihilist and terrorist lines" in units or "cells" of eight members—cell A, cell B, etc.—no one of whom knew more than one member of any other cell. (Blood brothers often did not know of each other's affiliations.) Despite its external anarchistic methods, it was motivated by the patriotic and idealistic purpose of purifying national life.

The ABC, made up primarily of young men, recruited its members largely from the intellectual and professional classes, who were heartily sick of the generation of '95 veterans—the politicos, who had betrayed their country consistently and shamefully wasted its revenues since Estrada Palma's time. Among the important reforms on its program was the discontinuance of the government lottery, which was a pool of corruption, the scrapping of the Platt Amendment, and the breaking-up of the extensive American-owned plantations and those vast untaxed areas of idle lands belonging to Cubans. Foremost in its program was the unalterable determination to remove Machado from power as quickly as possible. The organization grew rapidly in numbers and strength. Each new police atrocity not only brought a reprisal but swelled the ABC membership. (The ABC's first reprisal, however, did not take place until July 9, 1932, many years after Machado initiated his policy of terrorism.)

On December 30, 1931, one of the government's most inhuman outrages was perpetrated. In El Principe Prison a long gallery contained seventy political prisoners, many of them young students. To get rid of a student who had witnessed the governmental assassination of another student, the prison authorities armed several dozen criminals with knives and blackjacks and set them upon the defenseless prisoners with a vociferated order of "Finish them quickly. Kill the whole bunch of them who have dared oppose Machado!" As the prisoners were knocked down, stamped upon, slashed, yells of horror reverberated through the narrow chamber. One fellow had his intestines and kidneys cut open and died. Blood streamed from knifed shoulders, backs, chests. The scene resembled that slaughter of young alcatras which Humboldt had witnessed a hundred and thirty years before on the honey-scented southern coast. Three hours after the attack, ambulances entered the castle courtyard and began bearing the broken, bleeding men to the military hospital. Doctor Gonzálo Freyre de Andrade (later assassinated) protested against this infamy in Congress.

Citizens began seeking protection at foreign legations and embassies. Virtually every one except that of the United States sheltered political prisoners. Guggenheim, it was claimed by his enemies, interceded for fair trials only when stung by censorious criticisms of his indifference to the horrible injustice manifested under his nose daily. Guggenheim himself insists that although officially the American ambassador had no right to ask the Cuban government to protect a Cuban citizen, in the name of humanity he interceded "time and again to request a fair trial for political prisoners." A letter from Dr. Miguel Riva to his chief, Carlos Mendieta, substantiates the ambassador's statement regarding his intercessions and enumerates many specific instances of his requests, together with the names of individuals concerned. Whatever Mr. Guggenheim must have felt personally, however strong his protests may have been, he had no moral encouragement from the existing government at Washington, which remained smugly insistent on preserving the "hands-off policy."

The President of the Supreme Court of Cuba, in desperation at his helplessness to see justice done, committed suicide. His successor resigned, when Major Arsenio Ortiz, military supervisor of Oriente Police and most brutal of all killers, was "forgiven" and promoted by Machado after the Circuit Court of Santiago had indicted him for forty-four gruesome murders. This Ortiz (a huge fellow, part Negro, with deep-sunk, hoggish eyes), who was favored by Machado, possessed a formidable criminal record. In 1914, he had been sentenced on convictions of robbery, homicide, and swindling, to serve terms of seven years, twelve years, and four months respectively. A typical Cuban amnesty had released him. He entered the army and rose rapidly to a majority. To save him from imprisonment, which was ordered by the judge in Santiago, Machado transferred his minion to Havana, secured full pardon from Congress, and vindicated him by making him chief of the military police of Havana, which really meant that he was in charge of all police, because Cuba was under martial law. In the capital, his killings were so degenerately brutal that the "mark of Ortiz" upon dead bodies became a ghastly byword.

The ABC's, who up to this time had merely protested by words, effected their first retaliation on July 9, 1932, when they killed Calvo, inhuman officer of the secret police. From the date of Calvo's death to the coming of Sumner Welles, the ABC's and the students combated violence with violence. The explosion of bombs in Havana became a sound as familiar as the curfew gun of Morro Castle.

Standing out from the customary horrors, September 29, 1932, was a particularly dreadful day for Havana. In the morning Machado had retired to his bed at the news of the death of his old friend Henry Catlin, former president of the Cuban Electric Company and a legal adviser of the Chase National Bank—the man who arranged for the money which put him in power. Before luncheon Machado received word that Vasquez Bello, President of the Senate, had been assassinated by sawed-off shot guns fired by unknown parties. In a rage of grief and vengeance, Machado "paced the floor in his underclothes giving out orders."

That afternoon many estimable citizens became the victims of Ortiz. Among them was Gonzálo Freyre de Andrade, former professor of the philosophy of law at the University. Freyre was one of the most brilliant and admired of Havana's barristers. He was so beloved and trusted by the students that they went to him for help when they were forced to appear before the unjust court martial. And veritably he took his life in his hands to assist them.

(It was exceedingly dangerous to attempt to argue cases for political prisoners before either civil or military courts. For doing so, lawyers had been exiled, held incommunicado, threatened with death.) While sitting in the study of his home, working on the defense of three students facing a death charge, Gonzálo was butchered by seven of Ortiz's men, who forced their way into the house. In the same room with him at the time was his brother Guillermo, a sugar chemist. The Porra mowed him down too. In a room across the hall, they finished off the other brother, Leopoldo, a graduate of Cornell and an expert economist, who had fought the ruinous Chadbourne plan. Thus the three admirable scions of the distinguished Freyre de Andrade family were wiped out in a brief moment. The police from the station next door waited a quarter of an hour after the sounds of firing before entering the house to find the brothers lying dead in pools of blood which stained the pale floor-tiles of the Freyre home and the sanctity of all Cuban homes.

Ricardo Dolz, rector of the University, who was also working on a defense case, escaped a similar fate by fleeing to the sanctuary of a foreign legation. The murder of the Freyres was peculiarly terrifying because it showed that Ortiz and his men finally dared to go directly into homes and do their killings there without the formality even of military trials. Individual rebellion of a terrorist nature was the only weapon Cubans had left now. The Republican administration at Washington smugly reiterated its hands-off policy, and Guggenheim was bound by the decrees of his superiors.

Such hideous occurrences as the Freyres' murder did not halt the students. Even girls became bold in their protests. Cultured and beautiful young women of the privileged class were now ready to kill, "to carry the bomb which would put an end to Machado," and if need be, themselves. To intimidate women, Machado formed a female Porra, composed of stalwart prostitutes gathered from various parts of the island. These Porristas were provided with tobacco knives, razor blades, and gloves tipped with steel claws, to rip the clothes off wives and daughters of anti-Machadoans on the streets. Once when a delegation of upper-class women came to the palace bearing a petition begging clemency for students under trial, the Porristas set upon them and not only cut their clothes from their backs, but severely lacerated their shoulders and breasts.

A courageous Machado official, the Mayor of Havana, Miguel Mariano Gómez, son of that popular José Miguel, protested against the perfidious barbarity. He pointed out to the Secretary of Interior "the deplorable condition that affronts our civilization." "Such ignominious acts," he said, "were never registered in our history, not even during the excess, hate, and drunkenness of the colonial volunteers." For his temerity in opposing Machado, Gómez, whose administration had been conspicuously upright in midst of corruption, suffered exile.

Although the government had installed a rigid censorship commission headed by Ferriera, chief of secret police, the truth of the murder of Juan Gonzáles Rubiera leaked out flagrantly in the last week of 1932. Three hours after he was arrested on a charge of attempting to kill a secret service sergeant, Rubiera was found dead on the roadside. The police claimed he had been shot when trying to escape. *El Pais* of Havana printed on December thirty-first a picture seven columns wide by four and one-half columns deep at the top of the first page, showing the dead, bullet-ridden body of the boy lying in the roadway *with his feet and hands bound*. There had been a stupid slip-up somewhere in police circles: they had neglected to remove the ropes. The night managing editor, Enrique Pizzi, who had dared to print the picture, rushed into hiding at the Uruguayan Legation, but was subsequently arrested through treachery and thrown into El Principe. Salvador Diaz Versín of the *El Pais* staff, who had written of the Gonzáles Rubiera assassination, fled on a ship, when "one of the government agents detailed to murder him telephoned him a prior warning."

In early January 1933, despite the fact that Guggenheim begged for a fair trial in the case of the student, Ángel Álvárez Fernández, who was accused of complicity in the assassination of Vasquez Bello, the youth was mortally wounded by the police in an Havana suburb a few hours after the ambassador's intercession and the assurance that his life would be respected. After this murder the ABC issued the order: "Shoot it out with the police if they attempt to arrest you—they will kill you anyway."

On January 15, 1933, the dead body of Mariano Gonzáles Gutierra, an engineering student, was found several hours after he had been taken to secret service headquarters. Before he was shot to death, his wrist veins had been severed, his wrists broken, his abdomen slashed. The Spanish Embassy protested on the ground that the murdered youth was a Spanish subject and demanded punishment of policemen responsible for the crime.

In February 1933 Machado had the effrontery to insist to a New York *Times* correspondent that the student killings were all "bona fide applications of *ley de fuga.*"

The dreaded *ley de fuga* (law of flight), which means that the victim is shot while trying to escape, was employed with increasing frequency and most casual boldness. Even in prominent residential sections in the daytime, Cuban police would stop their automobile, throw a youthful prisoner out of the door, command him to run, and shoot him down. From his own balcony in the Vedado, J. D. Phillips, correspondent for the New York *Times,* witnessed such a shooting of a fifteen-year-old student at 2:45 P.M. on April 14, 1933.

> "Sharp shooters, mostly Negroes, posted on a high cliff, which overlooks both sides of the street at this point where escape was absolutely impossible, opened a withering fire. . . . The first fusillade missed the boy and he started running and shouting, 'Don't shoot any more!' Despite his cries for mercy a second volley followed. The victim, hit in the head by bullets, staggered, ran some twenty feet and collapsed as a third volley poured into his body. . . . The ununiformed Negroes

who had done the fatal shooting came down the side of the
cliff with rifles and revolvers in their hands to inspect the
body, after which they sauntered off, unmolested by the
uniformed national police, who arrived on the scene immediately."

Such an event as Mr. Phillips saw was merely a daylight episode in that blood-stained cavalcade sponsored by Machado, in
which men disappeared in the night never to be heard of again,
and a steady stream of prisoners was sent to the Isle of Pines,
some never to arrive there. (The New York *Times* had stated on
March 12, 1931, that only sixty-seven of one hundred and eighty
prisoners who went to the Isle of Pines penitentiary were reported
to have arrived there.) As early as 1927, according to Carleton
Beals, Ferriera, the chief of secret police, had admitted with pride
that he had initiated "the practice of disappearances, for this
eliminated investigation, scandal, and even burial of victims." "I
arrest them," he said, "when they are alone and no one sees it,
and then they disappear and there are no disputes or bother."

In January 1933, in the United States House of Representatives,
Hamilton Fish—the name had been significant in Cuban history
during the administrations of Grant and McKinley—rose to his
feet to plead for some sort of intervention to protect the Cuban
people from what he called "this reign of terror." Later in the
spring he denounced the backing of the Machado dictatorship by
United States banks and utility companies as "an outrageous example of dollar diplomacy." Twice Senator Borah spoke out
boldly in the name of humanity. "At our very door," he said,
"we have one of the most cruel governments in the world; it is
government by assassination. . . . I am unwilling to have the unspeakable outrages which have been perpetrated in Cuba continue indefinitely, at a time when the United States has the con-
sent of the Cuban government itself, according to the Platt
Amendment, to put an end to them."

When Franklin D. Roosevelt was inaugurated President of the

United States in March 1933, the reign of terror in Cuba was at its height. Doubtful of where he stood with the new United States government, Machado redoubled his efforts to terrorize the undercover insurgent movement to speedy obliteration. His foes, on the other hand, organized more secret groups of bombers and killers, with the idea of breaking down the morale of the governmental forces. Although Machado, fearing an outbreak, forbade the usual Holy Week processions, twenty youths under twenty-five lay dead after the reprisals of Easter. Anarchy and confusion prevailed. Police continued to parade the streets in pairs, "carbines crooked under their arms." Cuban newspapers were firmly gagged. American periodicals carrying true recountals of affairs in Cuba were banned or confiscated.

In Washington, President Roosevelt, confronted with a hundred major problems in the first weeks of his administration, paused to listen to the accusations from Cuba: "Machado stays in power only by virtue of support of American financial interests which profit from his favors and which fear repudiation if he is displaced." In the midst of the red haze of terrorism, Roosevelt recalled Mr. Guggenheim, and appointed as new Ambassador to Cuba, Assistant Secretary of State Sumner Welles.

Cool, lean, erect, handsome, youngish Mr. Welles had been chief of the Latin American division of the State Department under Secretary Hughes and he had acted as mediator in Honduras, Santo Domingo, and Nicaragua. For a decade, however, he had been out of public service, living the life of a scholarly country squire on his Maryland estate, gaining knowledge of Cuba from a prolonged study of the island's problems. And because he was known to be *persona grata* to the Roosevelt government, the spirits of the Cuban people lifted, as if they had been promised a miracle. The populace looked forward to Welles's arrival as the catalytic that would purge the country of its terror, a feat indeed nothing short of miraculous, for Machado had sworn to retain his power if he "had to drown the island in blood."

Versed and practiced as he was in Spanish American affairs, the task before the new envoy was one of most complex difficulties. It required an extraordinary understanding, courage, forcefulness, tact. As American ambassador, Mr. Welles was asked to restore a government "adequate for the protection of life, property, and individual liberty," and yet not impinge on the sovereignty of Cuba. He had to keep one eye on Latin American reactions to his work and another on United States investments in Cuba, which involved more than a billion and a half dollars.

Mr. Welles's first duty was to act as mediator and to bring together the various factions of the opposition; to try to reëstablish a state of normality, or temporarily at least, a state of artificial normality; to bring about the release of political prisoners; and to secure a restitution of constitutional guarantees. His rôle on the surface was merely that of mediator, but in sounder reality he was sent to rid the island of Machado by the swiftest diplomatic means which would involve the least criticism from Latin American countries,—without the removal of Machado there could be no bona fide restoration of Cuban liberties or any economic reconstruction. He was to hint that Machado take an extended leave of absence. He was to prevent an armed intervention, which would have been very awkward indeed in face of the approaching Montevideo Conference, and which might easily have taken on the aspect of an effort on the part of the United States to keep Machado in power. And—though of course the matter was kept secret—he had up his sleeve all sorts of New Deal benefices for the Cuban people.

On that bright May morning of the ambassador's arrival on the United Fruit liner *Peten*, Cuba was at as low an ebb politically, economically, and socially as at any period of her history. All look of self-reliance seemed to have been plucked from the faces of the populace, except for the students, in whose eyes shone the light of indestructible courage, and except for the ABC's, who more cleverly concealed their rage and their determined purposes.

There was a fearsome silence in the air. The people of Cuba, from the highest to the most humble in estate, had lived in an atmosphere of increasing anxiety, ever since the killing of the first student in the street three years before. From whispered words circulating about the streets one could pick up as little or as much meaning as he wanted to. "Any discerning tourist could see the horror that lay just under the veneer of civilized life in Havana." Waiters, bell-boys, chamber-maids, taxi-drivers, or even guides at the Capitol would eagerly relate stories of the terror, if they could get a sympathetic foreign ear. In fact, almost everybody one met was pitiful in his eagerness to tell.

A visitor to Havana, who had known the city in previous years, was bound to be somewhat shocked at the change. The famous Prado was still lined with its clipped laurel trees; but its facing rows of carved marble seats, fit for judges of Hellenic tragedies, were filled with hollow-eyed unemployed. Few dandies strolled its mosaic pavements. The glittering Malecón, sweeping along the sea's edge, remained clean as a new silver pin; but instead of a vast procession of Rolls-Royces and Minervas, there was not enough traffic of the few Chevrolets and Fords, which had superseded them, to necessitate a policeman to direct it. Rarely one might catch a glimpse of the tortoise-shell-bespectacled President dashing through the streets in his armored car, accompanied by a formidable bodyguard in cars fore and aft, bristling with protective guns. On the five-mile showy Fifth Avenue, leading through the Vedado to the Miramar, weeds choked the flowers and shrubs in the parkways, and deep ruts in the paving lay unrepaired.

Hungry mothers with small children huddled in the doorways of vacant houses under the stone porticos and begged with the pitiable, sick-animal humility of *reconcentrado* days. In the winter tourist seasons of previous years beggars had been provided for and kept off the street. In 1933 the situation had gone entirely beyond the control of the tourist commission. Out of the island's population of four million, an estimated five hundred thousand were without employment. Those who did have jobs were deplorably underpaid.

On the sugar plantations cane-cutters were given ten, fifteen, and twenty cents a day (twenty maximum for most expert cutters) for wielding a machete from dawn to dusk under a cruel tropical sun. For the most part the cane-cutters were Haitian and Jamaican Negroes. The white peasant could scarcely survive such work. The Cuban living near a *colona* (sugar cane plantation) made his living by renting ox-carts to haul the cut cane. For the use of his yoke of bulls, his cart, his services as a driver, and hire of a boy to prod the beasts, he received about thirty cents a day *in toto*. For sewing a dozen shirts a day a girl received a wage of ten cents, or she became a domestic servant at three or four dollars a month, or she hired a room to trade in prostitution. With some the latter became the easiest course. But the depression of the last six years had increased the number of prostitutes so enormously that the profession was thickly over-crowded, business was dull, prices had tobogganed, and many girls had barely enough spare money to pay for combating diseases to which they were daily a prey.

But it was not the poor alone who suffered. Employers for the most part had been paying wages out of their fast diminishing capital or from borrowed money. There was hardly such a thing as a dividend in Cuba. The rich had sacrificed one security after another. Plantations were mortgaged, homes mortgaged. (In their homes, it is true, the well-to-do lived almost as comfortably as formerly, because servants were so cheap. A man-servant who acted as houseboy and butler, cleaning the rooms and serving the meals, and in the afternoons "spreading the lawn with water," received five dollars a month.) Once-affluent professional men went back and forth between their Vedado homes and downtown offices by street car. Many were forced to move their families into their fathers' houses, most likely along with a brother's family and a sister's family. This forced doubling-, tripling-, quadrupling-up of households was the rule rather than the exception and was as common with the wealthy as with the middle classes.

In a sense the middle classes had suffered more than the proletariat. As long as they had a little food, the Cuban poor did not let their minds become tainted, for pride was not involved. If they had a few cents in their pockets, the crowds, sleeping on beds of thin newspapers spread under the portico of the closed Sevilla-Biltmore Hotel, on the floors of open markets, and in church doorways, did not bother to be bitter. And thousands of the poverty-stricken preferred to beg a few pennies in Havana— where they could beat time to music, blink at bright lights, and join the kaleidoscope of passing throngs—than to plow fields, tend oxen, and live remotely in their own thatched bohios.

Before he left Washington, Sumner Welles was thoroughly cognizant of these sad conditions. He came keyed to use his faculties to face the naked truth. He gave hundreds of interviews, he observed, he listened sympathetically. He received delegations of each faction of the opposition. Individual Cubans, no longer afraid to appeal to the American Embassy, came by the scores, bringing complaints, some bearing marks of torture on their bodies. The ambassador was soon convinced beyond doubt that "well over a thousand" had been killed by Machado's agents. He discovered that the murders were often of sadistic brutality, accompanied by previous torture and mutilations. Some had been buried alive gradually, others beaten to death or ripped open. To wrench confessions from men, innocent of incriminating knowledge, pins had been driven under their nails, their feet burned with white-hot irons. Bodies had been bent backwards between heavy rifles until the bones were dislocated. Youths had had their organs of generation crushed to pulp. A peasant boy of fourteen from Pinar del Rio came to the embassy to exhibit his mutilated hand. Because he would not reveal the hiding place of his father whom the police wanted to kill, they had gradually cut off his fingers with a pair of scissors, and then in disgust had thrown the lad into a prison pit and left him in the blackness alone with pain and without medical attention.

The Cuban newspapers (all strictly under military censorship) had given smallest possible space to the new ambassador's arrival.

Machado had declared himself to Russell Porter of the New York *Times* as "unequivocally opposed to any intervention of the United States to straighten out the tangled situation." But he had received Welles with a show of friendliness, and because he was not certain how extensive was the ambassador's power, he tried to win his good will. The press was unmuzzled to a degree. Murders and terrorism abated for the time. To carry out peace negotiations Machado promised to free several hundred political prisoners. On June fifteenth, the powerful ABC announced that it would coöperate with the ambassador's efforts to reëstablish peace. The releasing of prisoners commenced shortly. Exiles in Miami and New York began preparations to return home.

A look of self-reliance and hope came back into the eyes of the populace. From one end of the island to the other there was heard a curious little sharp, staccato, metallic sound, as people began snipping photographs of Sumner Welles from magazines and newspapers. They enshrined his printed image on the wall beside colored lithographs of favorite saints or over their prized-above-everything white electric refrigerators.

3

FLIGHT OF THE BEAST

During the last fortnight of June and the first week of July, a semblance of peace descended upon Havana. But it was not an easeful peace. It was like the false lull between onslaughts of the hurricane. On Tuesday, July eleventh, just before the luncheon hour, a bomb shattered the tall windows at the American Club. Hurtling missiles went clean through the lobby and smashed the glass case of the stuffed spread-winged eagle, suspended on the back wall of the dining-room. Other bits of lead tore out holes as large as baseballs in the portico across Virtudes Street. The explosive had been disguised as an air mail package and left on the mail box at the door of the club. It was believed to have been placed there by Machado agents to stir up antagonism against the opposition. Due to the vigilance of the policeman on the corner, who had noticed the suspicious package (with only a ten-cent air stamp) and had roped off the sidewalks, awaiting the arrival of experts in explosives from headquarters (they were careful to delay coming until after the explosion), no one was killed. The Machadoans claimed the ABC's were guilty of the outrage, but since one of Machado's police had had his hand blown off while placing a bomb in a public toilet, no one took much stock in the accusation. Sporadic bombing in various parts of the city, however, did begin again and continued for the next fortnight.

On Tuesday, July twenty-fifth, occurred a seemingly insignificant event, which led to the sudden downfall of the Machado government. The chauffeurs of the Omnibus de la Habana struck on that day, refusing longer to tolerate the graft exactions of Havana's Mayor, José Izquierdo, who demanded $2.60 for each bus running. When the street car motormen and the taxi drivers struck sympathetically, the affair began to develop into a city-wide transportation tie-up. Shortly stevedores, ferrymen, longshoremen promised their adherence.

On Thursday, August third, two conferences between the oppositionists and the governmental officers were held, with Ambassador Welles presiding. Limitations of the powers of the president and a form of decentralization of the government were finally agreed to.

On Friday Machado issued an edict that he would declare martial law and a state of war unless the "seditious" transportation strike was promptly ended. He was answered by a preparation for a general strike that affected virtually every industry, trade and profession in Havana. On that very day all dock workers quit. Foreign ships in port remained unloaded. No ferries or launches chugged across Havana Bay to Regla and Guanabacoa.

No fishing boats put out to sea. By midnight Thursday, street vendors had already parked their carts indefinitely.

A state of war was declared. The streets became strangely empty of people. From behind closed doors and shuttered windows one heard the sibilant sound of low whispers.

After Friday the doors of even the private garages remained locked. Gasoline could not be obtained. No hired family chauffeur dared drive a car for fear of being mobbed. An owner driving his car risked having it turned over by the protesting citizenry. The streets were strewn with broken glass, nails, tacks, so that the few venturesome fellows who drove forth to their offices had to tie house-brooms before their front wheels to sweep their way for them. Tourist-hotel bellboys living in the suburbs came to their work on roller-skates.

The Unico Market, from which Havana obtained virtually all the vegetables consumed in the city, closed. The corrugated iron façades of the small butcher shops were rung down, their proprietors refusing to buy beef from the grafting government-controlled slaughter houses. Bakers let their ovens grow cold. There were no milk deliveries. Garbage piled up uncollected. Bars closed. Restaurants stopped serving food. A few hotels harboring tourists scraped up meals from canned goods, and served them clandestinely behind closed shutters. Every shop of every kind was barred and bolted. Only a few bodegas did business when policemen kicked open the doors and forced shopkeepers at the point of a gun to wait on customers. As food supplies diminished, people borrowed from neighbors, or went hungry without resentment. The strike spread from town to town like a forest fire in midsummer, until it gripped the smallest hamlet in the island. Virtually all communication was cut off. Newspaper presses stopped. No trains ran after Monday. There was no post, no telegraph.

An ominous silence pervaded the island. The paralyzing strike had resolved itself into a nation-wide protest against the tyranny and corruption of the Machado government. It had no other meaning. It was by no means merely a mouthing of underpaid garment-makers, cane-cutters, stevedores, or of the unemployed whose living conditions were degraded beyond belief. The lower and upper classes, and even the rich were body and soul for the revolution. Cuba had never before known such unanimity of purpose. Only a fraction of one per cent of the nearly 4,000,000 population were in sympathy with the Machado administration, which was good only for the politicians, the government office-holders, the army, the police force, the lawyers retained by politicians. Except for that small fraction of the Cuban people and the few foreigners who had found Machado pliable, the whole nation, from the capitalist in his marble villa in the Vedado to the unhoused beggar who made his domicile where night caught him, was unanimously in sympathy with the strikers. In fine, Cuba Libre, backed by the moral support of Ambassador Welles, had struck against an intolerable situation, brought on by tyranny, greed, and corruption topping the economic depression.

The strike was profoundly harmonious in its direction. It was carried on with dignity and elation. There was no bitterness between employer and employee. Even the encroaching starvation was faced with amazing fortitude. Machado tried to blame his troubles on Communism, but to attribute the revolution to the Red flag was a rash and silly distortion of truth. Notwithstanding the desperation and misery, communistic leaders from Russia and Spain had had a strenuous job inoculating the proletariat with their doctrine. Communism as Communism, its principles and ideals, meant little enough to Cubans. But too long they had been playing touch and go with death in various ways. They did desire a little security. So when leaders said Communism would give them security, they were in such a desperate situation they were naturally willing to ally themselves, at least temporarily, with any organization which promised them relief for their hurting stomachs.

As the situation grew increasingly critical and the various foreign legations became seriously concerned for the well-being of their countrymen, the withdrawal of Machado seemed hourly more imperative. The President was in a panic. Clever as he was, he had not anticipated this negative kind of opposition. To stir up some sort of action, to give him an excuse to prove his necessity for resorting to strong military measures, the Machado forces resorted to a desperate strategy, which proved ruinous.

On Monday afternoon at the hour of the promenade, word came over the radio: "The beast has resigned. Go into the streets and shout." The voice pretended to be speaking for ABC but in reality it was that of a government agent. The people surged forth. The Prado, Central Park, Zayas Park facing the Palace became thronged with rejoicing citizens. Suddenly the police and the Porra swooped down like vengeful fiends. They turned machine guns on the unarmed crowds, which broke and ran in pandemonium before the murderous fire. A hundred and sixty were wounded, twenty-eight killed. For five days after the deliberate massacre terror reigned. Frightened inhabitants remained behind closed doors. Shots were heard from hour to hour. New murders were reported daily. The drunken chief of police, Ainciart, tore up and down the avenues in an armored car, taking pot-shots at people as the notion struck him.

Chill horror gripped the hungry city from that bloody Monday of August seventh through Friday. Low-voiced people lined the seawall along the Malecón, and others leaned against the parapets of house roofs with field glasses to their eyes, scanning the northern horizon for a sight of American gunboats. Many had relatives in hiding for whom the Porra was searching to wreak hideous vengeance. The atmosphere of Havana was like that of a besieged city, hourly fearing to be blown up and vainly looking for succor.

Mr. Welles, in constant telephonic communication with President Roosevelt, was working day and night for a conciliation that would avoid intervention. The ambassador urged Machado to ask for an indefinite leave of absence to take effect immediately, and to appoint a Secretary of State agreeable to everybody.

(Orestes Ferrara, the incumbent Secretary of State, being an Italian by birth, was disqualified for the acting-presidency. Besides, because he was as notoriously unscrupulous as he was brilliant, he would have been satisfactory to none but unconscionable scoundrels.)

The Executive Committee met to consider the formula of peace presented by Ambassador Welles which entailed the immediate withdrawal of Machado. On Wednesday, Machado considered the mediators' proposals that he withdraw immediately. His followers raised a cry of nationalism and independence. They knew they were ruined if he left. Heeding the serpent whispers of Ferrara, who had arrived speedily from a vacation in The States, Machado began to block and double-cross the mediation of Mr. Welles at every turn. He proclaimed before Congress that the ambassador did not represent Washington. Swelling out his chest, El Gallo crowed that if he chose he could rid the island of Welles within five days.

On Thursday, August tenth, the President of the United States sent this word to the Cuban government: "The problem of starvation and of depression are of such immediate importance that every political problem should be met in the most patriotic spirit in order to improve conditions at the earliest possible moment." Once again Welles begged Machado to resign on the grounds of patriotism. In a fury of desperation, Machado went to the radio microphone and proclaimed the United States ambassador *persona non grata,* one who threatened Cuba's sovereignty. The megalomaniac declared himself the salvation of Cuba, the symbol of her hopes!

When he flatly refused to treat further with the ambassador, the army officials, scenting how the wind was blowing, called on Mr. Welles, and after a conference, gathered that it might be best to force the resignation of the President, both for their country's sake and for the sake of their own jobs. They gathered that if they refused, American intervention would ensue and troops would be landed within forty-eight hours. They knew America would not support a Cuban army. Besides, many of them had already talked secretly of revolting.

While Machado was catching a few hours of troubled sleep, the army decided to save their country from further bloodshed by deposing the President. Just before midnight on Thursday they learned that Mr. Welles's ultimatum would expire by midnight Friday. Early Friday afternoon Battalion Number 1 of the Cabaña Fortress trained its guns on the yellow-domed presidential palace.

General Herrera, Minister of War, was informed by subordinate officers that he had been chosen to break the news to the President. Refusing, he was arrested and forced to his mission. Despite the guns pointing threateningly at the palace, the thunder-struck President refused to believe that his well-paid, pampered soldiers had turned against him. He sent a hurried command for a troop of armed cavalry from Atares Fortress Prison. Commanded by Captain Crespo, assassin and executioner, the cavalry arrived in a sweat. Machado hastily got into his armored car, and, surrounded by his formidable escort bristling with guns, dashed to Camp Columbia to confront the rebellious officers. Before a line of set, sullen faces, he begged support. Brave little Captain Lorres Menier, the aviator, walked with steady resolution up to Machado, and—standing very close to him so that Crespo would not risk firing at him—boldly asked the President to resign. "If you do not," he said, "the men of the air corps will join the revolt as one man."

Machado could not believe his ears. He threatened, promised, stormed with rage. The men regarded him with cold defiance. At a conference of higher officers immediately afterwards, Colonel Sanguily told him authoritatively that he must resign before noon of the morrow. Dumbfounded, he was convinced the end had come. "All right, my boys, I'm through!" he said. Without the army's aid he knew he could not have the satisfaction of attempting to drown the island in blood. He returned to the palace with Crespo. Part of the night was spent feverishly in packing. At half-past two in the morning Machado handed in his resignation.

Not long after sunrise Saturday morning, before the shops were open, the proprietor of the Parkview Hotel, stirring about, preparing to receive a Ward Liner excursion party, was surprised to see a truck load of baggage from the palace pass his hotel, which was a block to the west. Then came a green car bearing the President's daughters. Close behind followed Machado's armored car. After an interval, soldier guards from the palace went by in trucks, waving their hats and throwing a party of just disembarked excursionist ladies into confusion by jocularly leveling rifles at them.

The creamy-marble palace was deserted except for a solitary blue-bloused policeman left on guard at the south door. Two unemployed stragglers went by. The policeman beckoned them. "Want a stem of bananas?" he asked with casual cordiality. The tramps entered shyly, bewildered. They came out with two enormous bunches of ripe bananas. They spread the miraculous story. Machado was gone! There were things to eat in the palace! A third man walked by. At the policeman's friendly nod he went in. A few moments later he staggered out with a huge sugar sack of specimen limes from Machado's farm. He sold the lot for twenty cents to the Parkview's proprietor and went back for more valuable booty. In a few minutes a swelling mob began to emerge from the avenues and side streets. Cautiously at first, then boisterously, deliriously, the people came, shouting the good news. Pell-mell they rushed on to the palace grounds and into the building itself.

While hundreds of singing, yelling citizens were bearing palm fronds and long-stemmed yellow cannas torn from the palace gardens to wave triumphantly as a tribute of gratitude before the façade of the American Embassy, other groups, more grimly ecstatic, looted the palace's lower floors of food supplies. The main thought of many whose bellies had been unpleasantly pinching them for weeks, months, and even years, was to carry off the large quantity of food stores which Machado, as if in anticipation of a siege, had ordered brought within the walls. In the patio, con-

spicuous in a crate and grunting uncertainly, squatted a razor-
back hog, which had been fattened on far better ration than most
of the looters. Swooping down on the prize, invaders wrenched
the crate apart and lugged off the porker, upside down and
squealing with terror. This was no gesture *pour le sport,* nor was
the hog stolen in the spirit of revenge, nor with any symbolical
significance. Men were hungry. Bearing the noisy beast across
Zayas Park fronting the palace, without ceremony they slit its
throat at the foot of ex-President Zayas's statue—even as Cæsar
was stabbed at Pompey's. Then with knives flashing from half-a-
dozen eager hands, the razor-back was butchered into small
pieces, and distributed among eager bystanders, who rushed off
with bloody joints and hunks of meat into the side streets to seek
diverse charcoal fires for the cooking.

Many of those who were not hungry let off the steam of years'
pent-up hatred by smashing and pillaging. Typewriters were
hurled from windows; avocado pears flung at tapestries. A ne-
gress tore Machado's sheets from his bed. Some mercenary fellows stole silverware and fine china. Others bore off potted plants
for souvenirs. Lieutenant Cesar Lorrie himself, one of the leaders
of the army's coup, looted the wine cellar of eight quarts of cham-
pagne, "for celebration." When a sign "To Let" was hung on the
palace door the crowd broke into hysterical shrieks of laughter.

From the balcony of the American Embassy two blocks away,
Mr. Welles promised "continued mediation," declared that Cubans were solving their own problems, and urged "control and
calm."

But the Cubans could not be calm. They did not want control.
They wanted revenge. On the Prado, across the street from the
American Club, someone recognized Jiminez, the murderous
chief of the Porra. "Kill him!" the people yelled. Jumping behind
a pillar, Jiminez drew his revolver and began firing into the
crowd. Lieutenant Villalon happened to dash up in a car with
several soldiers. Jiminez tried to escape into a closed drug store.
Whizzing bullets shattered the glass front. Jiminez crawled under

a stone bench. He and Villalon shot it out. Jiminez was mortally wounded. The crowd finished the dying man off with kicks.

A man-hunt for Porristas began. Cabinet members, senators, lawyers of politicians, scurried into hiding. Some fled the country by launches; those who could, by planes. The houses of Machado's henchmen were set upon. Furniture was smashed; pianos were split with axes; books and paintings, thrown out windows. Sacrificial pyres were made of limousines drenched in gasoline and set on fire. The beautiful yacht of the thieving Secretary of Public Works was burned in its basin. The offices of *Heraldo de Cuba,* Machado's subsidized newspaper, were gutted with fire. Every stone lamp post of the long Avenida del Presidente Machado was smashed with crowbars. The mistresses of politicians were hunted out in their apartments, their jewels taken, their crystal scent bottles shattered, their lace negligées and Parisian gowns torn to shreds. They were hustled out on the streets in whatever clothes they had on their backs at the moment of intrusion. By sunset, which was particularly lovely that evening, eighteen persons were dead and nearly a hundred wounded, twenty-eight houses had been sacked, eight houses reduced to smoldering ashes and crumbling walls. In the early evening a sudden torrential rain with brilliant electrical display burst upon the excited city. The squall quickly cleared the streets of demonstrators, cooled the fury of the mob, and doubtless prevented an all night vandalistic celebration.

The orgy of revenge extended to the far corners of the island. In Camagüey, Pinar del Río, Santa Clara, the houses of politicians and the shops of Machado adherents were rifled; goods and furnishings were hurled into the streets, piled in heaps, turned into bonfires. The bodies of a former mayor of San Luis and an army sergeant were dragged up and down the hills of Santiago, and human blood ran in rivulets over the terraces of the Casa Granda Hotel.

At two in the afternoon, while the looting was at its height in the capital, Machado, who had first rushed from the palace to his *finca,* twenty miles from Havana, was at the General Machado Airport, fifteen miles from the city in a different direction. With four cohorts he had chartered an amphibian plane. But officials at first refused to let it take off without a permit from the Cuban War Department. After more than an hour's nerve-straining delay, Avaroff, Secretary of the Treasury, telephoned Ambassador Welles to say that they had a plane and could escape, and to ask if they should wait for a permit. Welles dryly advised him to forego formalities under the circumstances and fly while the flying was good. The propeller was twirled. The one suit case among them—it contained a great sum of money, no change of clothes—was placed aboard. At the last minute Machado refused to take Captain Crespo. But the killer whipped out a revolver threateningly. At the point of the gun Machado relented, and Crespo was not left behind. The plane took off in the direction of the Bahamas at two minutes after half-past three. Within three months after Ambassador Welles's arrival, the beast had fled.

Thus the main feature of the mediation plan, the retirement of Machado—sponsored by Ambassador Welles and approved by Roosevelt and the opposition political groups in the Cuban republic—had been accomplished.

The resignation of all members of the cabinet except Secretary of War Herrera had already been accepted in the forenoon. Herrera, being regarded by the army, the civil opposition, and the American Embassy, as a small edition of Machado, remained president only about half an hour—just time enough for him to appoint another president pleasing to the military chiefs and the various political factions. To succeed Machado, they agreed upon modest, highly cultured, wealthy Dr. Carlos Manuel de Céspedes, son of "Cuba's George Washington," that patriot-soldier who launched the Ten Years' War and became Cuba's first revolutionary president. De Céspedes had served his country admirably in the diplomatic corps, holding the highest posts in the United States, Spain, and Mexico. Having retired from public life several years previously, he accepted the present difficult position only for supremely unselfish considerations. Scholarly, aristocratic, impeccably honest, he was the only other President of Cuba who possessed many of the attributes of Estrada Palma. Perhaps he lacked initiative. Perhaps also there was too little iron in his fist. At any rate the public was lukewarm to him.

At nine-thirty Sunday morning on the garden terrace of his home, before eight black-robed members of the Supreme Court and a select group of ladies and gentlemen, de Céspedes was quietly inaugurated Provisional President of Cuba. The American ambassador was not present, nor was any foreign envoy. After the ceremony, changing from hot, formal morning attire to white linen, the new President talked briefly to newspaper correspondents. At eleven-thirty he received Ambassador Welles. Twice again during the afternoon the President conferred with the ambassador.

Throughout the Sabbath the looting continued. The soldiers and police made no effort to restrain the crowd. They let them wreak full vengeance on their enemies. Armed members of the ABC hunted Porristas from house to house, and when they found one they killed him with thorough execution. Only when a communistic group gathered to destroy the shops of some person who had not joined the strike did police interfere. The burly Ainciart, chief assassin at the massacre of August seventh, was discovered disguised as an invalid old lady, his face half-veiled by a black lace mantilla. Caught like a rat in a trap, he committed suicide under a kitchen sink. His corpse was mutilated and dragged through the streets.

Like French revolutionaries moving upon the palace of Versailles, a mob from Havana marched to assail Machado's *finca*. They were far more destructive than the Citizens, however. They looted the house, smashed windows, dug at the jade green walls with crowbars, until the very roof tumbled in débris. In the gardens, they hacked at the mosaic fountains, uprooted rare plants and flowers. Country people joined in the celebration. Slaughtering the blooded cattle, they held an impromptu barbecue, fed the multitudes. And that night prize-winning cocks worth hundreds of dollars (Machado had been a chicken fancier) went into guajiros' stew-pots. For days after the fiesta, on the rural roads, men would offer for sale to astonished tourists an after-dinner coffee-cup of filigreed gold or a porcelain soup tureen with the Machado monogram.

By nightfall Sunday, the new government consisted solely of the modest Dr. de Céspedes. Obviously some support more substantial than that of the demoralized Cuban army was needed. After a telephone conversation with Roosevelt, Welles calmly assured the new President that three U. S. destroyers were steaming posthaste to Cuba. De Céspedes announced the news publicly, declaring, "The order was issued with my full knowledge and approval. It carries no implication of intervention." At one-thirty in the morning while most of the city was sleeping off its nervous debauch, the destroyers quietly slipped into Havana's bottle-necked harbor.

4

THE SERGEANT KING-MAKER

Automobile horns tooted hysterically as the general strike ended Monday morning. The iron shutters of shops were raised, wagons rattled cheeringly as they brought in heaping loads of green vegetables for the markets. At noon trams began to clang again and cross country busses started from Havana east and west into the hinterland.

After another conference with Ambassador Welles, the Provisional President selected a Cabinet, which virtually ignored the claims of the old political parties. Members of the ABC received four posts; its leader, Dr. Joaquin Martinez Saenz, being made Secretary of the Treasury. On the whole, it was probably the most honest cabinet Cuba had ever had. The men possessed a high average of intelligence as well as integrity and imagination. For the most part, it is true, they were untried, without political experience; their strength and their worth were yet to be proved. Certainly no cabinet in Cuba ever faced a more colossal task; for the life of the island was still utterly demoralized, labor disturbances widespread, and political enmities ready to take advantage of the social and economic disorder.

One could not be sure of the army. The young leaders among the officers seemed completely loyal to the new régime; the lower ranks were definitely doubtful. The attitude of the students was one of suspicion. "The students, vital and headstrong, are a grand lot," Hubert Herring wrote with a prophetic hint, "and if the new government gives them enough to do and plays fairly with them they will make a robust contribution to the housecleaning of Cuba." The more radical students were by no means pleased with the cabinet selections. Some of them demanded the right of sanction on each cabinet minister appointed. Their emphatic Leftwing tendencies were threatening and foreboding. However, the new government began to function, without the aid of the students or a congress—most of the congressmen were in hiding.

The bankrupt economic situation confronting de Céspedes was desperate, if not hopeless. According to statistics furnished by that reliable Cuban periodical, *The Import and Industrial Record,* the debt of Cuba on June 30, 1933, six weeks before Machado's flight, was as follows:

Foreign (Consolidated) $48,000,000
Interior (Consolidated) 7,000,000
Public Works (Interior) (Consolidated) 80,000,000
Sugar Bonds (Exterior) (Consolidated) 24,500,000
Floating Debt (Interior) (Consolidated) 85,000,000

The last three debts, aggregating one hundred and eighty-nine millions, were solely due to the Machado administration.

In Washington, Secretary of State Hull canceled his vacation and plunged into a study of measures for the relief of Cuba's economic troubles. He announced that the American-Cuban policy had choked Cuba's commerce and that steps would be taken immediately to remedy the situation by hastening work on the proposed reciprocal trade agreement to stimulate American trade with the island.

The excessive sugar duty designed to aid the beet sugar industry, but actually failing to do even that, had brought with it destruction of profitable trade in Cuba for other American industries like the automobile, radio, typewriter, etc. American goods imported into Cuba during 1920 had amounted in value to $404,386,000. For the year 1933 imports from the United States dropped to $22,674,000. In 1902, the first year of the republic, with a population of one and three-quarter million, Cuba imported $10,000,000 worth more of goods than she did in 1932, with a population of approximately four millions.

Cuba's exports had fallen off almost as much proportionately as her imports. In 1933 the total value of her exports, which had reached over $700,000,000 in 1920, had dropped to $84,391,000. The character of the exports varied little, though the diminution in amount was significant. The tobacco trade had all but been ruined by the world-wide depression. Although the actual cultivation of the tobacco plant is still in the hands of the Cubans and Spaniards, the manufacture of cigars for American trade has largely been transferred to the United States, and the Cuban tobacco industry is almost entirely American-controlled. Fresh fruit is the only article of Cuban export which has remained approximately at its usual level. (In aggregate value, the fruit export ranks in this order: bananas, pineapples, grapefruit.)

In 1930 the United States obtained considerably more than three-fifths of her sugar from Cuba; in 1932 only a little over a third. In recent years, the tourist trade has become, after sugar, the second largest income-making business for Cuba. In fact, the tourist industry, although severely curtailed by the social unrest and the sounds of bombing, has been less affected than other income-bringing agencies. In 1930, the number of tourists and excursionists who entered ports of Cuba was 163,152; in 1932, 114,127.

By 1933, the United States' sixth largest market had been virtually wiped out, and Cuba's trade had fallen lower than it had been before the War of Independence. The root of the evil lay largely in the excessive tariffs decreed by Republican administrations. As an example of the degree of loss in business to the United States, comparative figures for 1926 and 1932 on three articles imported by Cuba are impressive. In 1926, Cuba imported from The States 4,754 passenger automobiles (value $3,110,700); in 1932, 550 automobiles (value $298,345). In 1926, 3,879 typewriters were imported; in 1932, only 23. In 1926, Cuba imported 1,921,433 pairs of shoes from the United States; in 1932, only 11,074 pairs. This last figure does not exactly mean that Cubans were forced to go barefooted (though that is partially so) but that the island had set up her own shoe factories, Machado owning one of the largest.

When Cuba could no longer afford to import articles from America because of the high custom duties, Machado invited American manufacturers to erect plants in Cuba, and he himself set the example to local industrialists by building various kinds of factories of his own. His experimental scheme was admirably constructive, but not entirely altruistic, because he forced retailers to buy his goods—whether first rate or low grade—at his own figures. (For instance, good shoes were turned out, and an inferior grade of a paint.) His critics say that if merchants refused to buy his wares, he would have a sanitary inspector fine them $1,000 on some trumped-up charge.

Whether the charge is false or true, Machado deserves the highest credit for wisely aiming to make the island more self-sufficient. Because of the terrorism of his last years, constructive elements of his régime are likely to be entirely discounted or forgotten. The reviled President did one particularly fine service: he strongly encouraged the people to raise their own food stuffs. A telling factor in his encouragement was, it is true, the exorbitant custom duties put on necessities. But regardless of his methods there was resultant good, for in 1933 the island raised several times as much of what it consumed as in 1924, the year of Machado's first election. Cuba no longer imports vast quantities of beans, coffee, eggs, milk, butter. She can today successfully produce almost everything she needs for her stomach, except wheat flour, rice, and pure lard. With comparative ease, Cuba raises an abundance of green vegetables and fruits of various sorts throughout the year. In 1926, eggs to the value of $3,104,438 were imported; in 1932, the importation of eggs had shrunk to $74. The import of bacon in 1932 had dropped to one-tenth of its total for 1926. In the last six years butter imports dropped from $364,405 to less than $2,000. The importation of condensed and evaporated milk, which amounted to more than two million dollars in 1926, has virtually ceased. This development in native dairy products has had its esthetic value too. It used to be peculiarly depressing to enter an exotic Chinese restaurant in Havana and find a can of Carnation Condensed Milk gracing a table at which you were shortly to savour a divine Oriental concoction of chicken breast and fresh almonds.

President Roosevelt, Secretary Hull, and Ambassador Welles clearly saw that the tariffs of both countries were the stumbling blocks hampering a two-way maximum of trade between Cuba and the United States. They knew that to achieve a two-way maximum would be to reach the goal of true reciprocity. America could supply Cuba with wheat flour, cotton cloth, steel products, automobiles, etc. Cuba, on the other hand, could give America sugar, tobacco, fresh fruit and vegetables in winter. If such a maximum exchange of goods could be achieved, employment in both countries would be benefited and bring a return in the national buying abilities of the two nations. The President was convinced that there should be a reciprocal and drastic lowering of duties. He was determined to give forgotten Cuba a New Deal, one which would grant a double blessing to the island republic and to the United States. To de Céspedes aid, Roosevelt decided to send one of the most valuable members of his Brain Trust, the brilliant, soft-spoken, young Adolf Augustus Berle, Jr., an expert on Caribbean law and economics.

On August eighteenth, Washington announced that Ambassador Welles would be recalled from his Havana post to resume his former position as Assistant Secretary of State. (He was slated to take a leading part in the forthcoming Pan-American conference at Montevideo.) He had done the work in Cuba he was sent to do—"with the maximum of wisdom and good taste, with the minimum of affront to the pride of Cuba," as Hubert Herring aptly stated. By and large, Cubans were profoundly affected by this news and were very loath to have Mr. Welles go. In overthrowing Machado, the ambassador had revealed himself an excellent diplomat. If he had left the island immediately he would have been generally considered one of Cuba's greatest revolutionaries. But he was held up by another unexpected revolution which overtook Cuba in a swiftly accomplished, bloodless seizure of power on September fifth.

Within twenty-four days of his inauguration President de Céspedes yielded to the radical opposition, which effected a coup d'état under the leadership of Top-Sergeant Fulgencio Batista, a court-stenographer. For three weeks the army's non-commissioned officers "had whispered out of the corner of their mouths to the enlisted men that many of the officers were still loyal to Machado, that Provisional President de Céspedes planned to cut the army's numbers and pay." On September fourth a group of sergeants walked into the quarters of the same officers who had demanded Machado's resignation. With a revolver in his hand and with the same suavity he assumed when taking down dictation, Batista informed the chief-of-staff that he was relieved of duty. Other sergeants entered the various offices of local commanders and demanded their arms. The dismayed officers yielded and retired to their respective homes. The insurrectionists promptly seized all barracks in and about Havana, took possession of the forts and

ships. Machine guns were deployed in strategic points throughout the city. Every military and police unit stationed in the interior of the island joined the mutinous movement with celerity.
Automobiles filled with youngsters armed with rifles and pistols
dashed about the streets. The ABC quarters on the Prado was in
an uproar of vociferated argument—only the extreme radicals
had joined the revolution. The uprising was swift, startling, but
there was no bloodshed. Batista saw to that. When the day was
done, the little stenographer was master of Cuba. The shorthand
notebook and pencil had been dropped for the revolver and a
scepter.

The amazing leap of Sergeant Batista to the position of the
most powerful man in Cuba was as sudden and dramatic as the
rise of Mussolini or Hitler. Ingratiating, accommodating, ever-
smiling, the stenographer had been particularly well known to
the officers for his energy, his accuracy, his dependability. "Leave
it to Batista!" had been a byword, which meant that whatever
the business was it would be thoroughly done. He was always
on the alert to be of service. The society officers, often too busy
with personal affairs to bother, turned over secret state documents
to him to attend to. Nothing was too much trouble for him.
On every side he won good will and admiration for his abilities.
But he was realist enough to know that diligence would not take
him into the high ranks, or raise his pay from $60 a month to
$600. Commissions for officers were by social or political favor.
Batista's origin had been most humble. Of mixed blood, he was
born the son of a small truck gardener. From his Chinese grand-
father he has inherited his flat nose and his ability to disguise his
designs behind a cryptic mask, to make his eyes volcanic, dancing,
or blank as he chooses. A bantam in size, with a body of steel and
a jaw of bronze, his crowning glory is a glistening comb of coarse
black hair, which he tosses about in eloquent gestures. Snappy,
quick, forceful in movements, he has the inherent dramatic sense
so essential to demagogues, to dictators like Mussolini and Hitler.
Besides, he possesses a rallying sense of humor, which does not

belong to the pure-blooded Italian or German. Backing a fatalistic fearlessness, he is gifted with a super-keen intuition, which shows him whom to trust. In hatching his secret plot, where one unguarded whisper to the wrong person would have meant disaster, the firing squad, and most likely torture, Batista made not a single mistake in the coup which involved thousands of private soldiers and hundreds of students. It was all done by words spoken under the breath, not one scrap of evidence was set down on paper.

A commission of five was selected by the soldiers and students to take over the government as a "governmental executive commission." It was composed of a lawyer, a banker, an editor, and two university professors, one of penal law, the other of anatomy. All five men were under fifty-five. Batista had the good sense to refuse the presidency of the republic when he could so easily have taken it, if he had wanted. By breaking the tradition of the typical Latin American revolutionary system he gained the admiration of powerful forces.

Courtesy marked the fall of de Céspedes. The commission of five waited on the President, who had just returned from inspecting the damages in Santiago from the preceding week's hurricane. The narrow-faced, calm, high-minded anatomy professor, Ramon Grau San Martín, quietly informed the President that the commission bore a mandate from the revolutionary junta, which asked him to turn over the power of the republic to them. Radiant Fulgencio Batista stood at his elbow, and by the "refulgent Baptist" stood four soldiers with machine guns. Taken completely by surprise, de Céspedes paused momentarily to ponder the significance of the words. "Gentlemen," he said, "I am more revolutionary than any of you. My government has carried out faithfully the will of the people. In twenty days we have got well along with the work of reorganizing every government department." The commissioners courteously reiterated their request. Much moved, de Céspedes signed his resignation. Offering his services at any time in the future, he said, "I see you are all Cubans, and I trust your work will be a success." He shook hands with each member of the commission and therewith left the palace. From the second floor balcony, Commissioner Sergio Carbo, the volatile thirty-nine-year-old editor, climactically addressed the milling mob below. "For the first time in history," he roared, "the Cuban people will rule their own destinies."

As provisional president the junta selected Dr. Grau San Martín. At his inauguration on the palace balcony at noon Sunday, the crowd was surprisingly small, and the only important non-junta supporter with him was Miguel Mariano Gómez. The de Céspedes administration, which was regarded as an American-made affair, had not had the unity of public opinion behind it, but the new administration had even less. Taking advantage of the upheaval, communists assailed the new régime, distributed handbills attacking Señor Carbo, who had been understood to be powerful in labor circles. Disgruntled laborers created disorders in Cienfuegos, Santiago, and at the Matahambre asphalt mines in Pinar del Rio. Two American executives of the Delicias sugar mills in Oriente were forced to flee for their lives and take refuge on a British freighter.

Ambassador Welles reported to Washington the dangerously disturbing disquiet that existed. The government ordered a cruiser and three destroyers sent to Cuba to protect American property threatened by Red agitations. A regiment of marines was mobilized at Quantico for foreign service. Making an unprecedented and thoroughly commonsense move, President Roosevelt called in important Latin-American diplomats and took them fully into his confidence on his Cuban policy. Armed intervention, he made clear, was the last thing he wanted. In the meantime, precautionary plans for military action went ahead, in case the United States would be called upon to exert force. Within three days a dozen destroyers encircled Cuba.

The demoralized soldiers were about to get out of hand, when Sergeant Batista assumed the rank of colonel and chief-of-staff of the army. With shrewdness, tact, and phenomenal energy he began to whip them into shape. On September seventh the terra-cotta, twin-towered National Hotel, located strategically on its cliff-walled hill, was designated as a rallying point and refuge for American citizens in case of an outbreak against them. Ambassador Welles was already making his home at the hotel, and Mr. Berle, Roosevelt's financial adviser who had arrived simultaneously with the fall of the de Céspedes government, was registered there also. Several American families moved in that day. Shortly after midnight on the morning of September eighth, while Mr. Welles and Mr. Berle were in conference at the embassy, the ambassador received a frantic message to come to the hotel as quickly as he could get there—a frightful thing was about to take place.

At the hotel in the evening had foregathered about four hundred of the deposed Cuban army officers to hold a meeting. From the presidential palace, orders had been issued to search the hotel for arms. The officers protested vehemently against the search. While guests in evening clothes wandered somewhat nervously about the reception rooms, the soldiers under the command of a sergeant set up a row of machine guns at one end of the huge lobby, and the four hundred officers armed with revolvers banded themselves at the other end. The hostile groups were facing each other menacingly when Mr. Welles and Mr. Berle entered. Mr. Welles talked with the sergeant in command. The latter insisted on carrying out the search. The officers threatened to open fire on the soldiers if they made the first move. One shot, and the place could have been a shambles! The ambassador explained to the sergeant that the hotel housed American citizens, as well as America's ambassador, and that most unhappy international complications might ensue if a fight occurred. He urged sending an emissary to the palace to explain the situation to the President. The sergeant agreed, but insisted that in the meantime he would go on with the search. Mr. Welles told him he had better use discretion. The sergeant wanted to know what that was, and several minutes were consumed in definition. While an attaché was dashing to the palace, Mr. Welles and Mr. Berle proceeded to seat themselves on a long divan in the very center of the lobby in direct line between the rows of machine guns and the phalanx of well-armed officers. Mr. Berle lighted a Havana cigar and Mr. Welles began to talk of Emily Dickinson's poetry and quoted some of his favorite lines. The topic of conversation drifted to gardens in the Berkshire Hills. The simulated serenity had a sedative effect upon the animosities of the hostile camps. Instead of murdering each other—and incidentally the guests in the hotel —they merely glowered across the lobby until an order from the palace arrived countermanding the search. By sunrise the officers had decided to set up residence in the hotel, and began telephoning their wives to send their clothes. With the clothes came great bundles of arms and ammunition wrapped up in paper. Mr. Welles and Mr. Berle moved out. With them departed most of the Americans. They went to the Hotel Presidente in the Vedado, which was now designated as the rallying point for Americans, if the situation became too hot. In another day or two all the guests had left. The servants had fled too. Only the manager hung around, wondering what would happen next. Soldiers with machine guns and more formidable artillery surrounded the place.

On September fourteenth, while Yankee warships lay at anchor in Havana harbor, President Grau issued a proclamation establishing a virtual dictatorship until the meeting of the Constitutent Assembly. The proclamation voiced the principles of the student revolutionary movement, which aimed at the removal of all influence from the United States and the establishment of complete sovereignty. Because of Mr. Welles's assistance in appointing the de Céspedes cabinet and his help in guiding the financial policy of administration he was regarded by the students and the "autenticos" (Grau's followers) as a typical example of the old diplomatic system of America's meddling in Cuba's internal affairs. If, instead of aiding de Céspedes, the ambassador had just put obstacles in his way, the students and "autenticos" very probably would have backed the son of the great patriot.

The real rulers of the new régime were not the Cabinet, nor the non-commissioned officers, but thirty intense young men, known as the *Directorio Estudiantil,* who had played a brave and significant part in Machado's overthrow. It was they who sat in conference and issued orders with Latin vehemence for the Cabinet to put into effect. Even the most conservative Cubans had admiration for the courage, passionate sincerity, and patriotic zeal of *Los Niños,* but they were hourly apprehensive of the next move of The Boys, who were determined to experiment in the agitated island with the most advanced radicalism.

In Havana, despite the foreign battleships at anchor, native soldiers on the march, and the four hundred deposed officers barricaded in the National Hotel, business was resumed. But as the government of Grau San Martín approached the end of its first fortnight, harassed by labor conditions and demands for its abdication, speculation was rife as to the stability of the new régime. It had already survived longer than most people had wagered.

Because it seemed necessary to ultimate stabilization to have the United States' recognition of the new revolutionary government, the students finally agreed to talk with the American ambassador. To the conference with Mr. Welles came Mr. Berle, who had been sent to aid Cuba's rehabilitation. The thirty radical young men of the *Directorio Estudiantil* sat around a long table in a private home, like students at an economics seminar, with Mr. Welles and Professor Berle leading. The intense expressions on the young faces more than ever suggested rapt Isaiah's wild, seraphic fire. They were not easy to address. It was like speaking with youths who had returned from hell. All thirty of them had suffered imprisonment, twenty-seven of the thirty had been tortured, seven had been castrated. Courageous to the ultimate degree, having risked more than lives for an ideal, they knew little enough about practical finance and economics, a solution of which factors was as necessary to their country's salvation as martyrdom. They listened to Mr. Welles grimly, almost with sardonic contempt. Patiently, sympathetically, with persuasive sincerity, the ambassador recounted his own earlier efforts to talk out a solution of Cuba's basic economy, and he assured them of

Roosevelt's good faith and his strong disinclination to intervene. He promised the recognition of Washington as soon as the Cuban government could give "proof of ability to maintain public order, obtain public support, and meet obligations." When the conference broke up, the students sent representatives into the interior to make speeches urging public order and support of the new government.

Shortly Mr. Berle returned to Washington. "It is not a government, but a shell," he reported. "The situation is a kind of passive anarchy. . . . There are no laws, no courts. Nobody pays taxes because he cannot be sure they won't be collected a second time by a new government. There is order without law because the Cubans are a friendly people."

But the interior was not entirely passive. Rampaging proletarians egged on by communist leaders had seized more than a dozen American-owned sugar mills in Oriente Province alone and had incarcerated some mill executives and their families in their quarters and cut off water and electricity. Warships stood by, waiting to land rescuing marines if the worst came.

On October second, the focus of attention was dramatically shifted to the National Hotel, where the four hundred army officers had been beleaguered since September eighth, surrounded by machine gun squads ready to repulse any attempted sortie. Batista had ordered them to return to the army as privates. They had refused and Batista had declared them deserters. The officers, in various stages of undress, but with big revolvers dangling handy at their belts, had been doing all their own menial tasks, making up their beds, running the elevators, washing dishes, cooking their own stews out of the scraps of fast diminishing stores. For the last ten days they had had only one meal a day—boiled rice and beans. At a few minutes past six on Monday morning a single shot fired from the hotel by one of the officers started a bloody battle that lasted until mid-afternoon. The entrance to the hotel of a truck carrying ammunition caused the army to force the issue and bring up reënforcements. Colonel Batista personally conducted the attack. One shell tore away a balcony on the sixth floor, another shattered the main entrance. Auxiliary guns blazed at the hotel windows from the roofs of Havana University buildings three blocks away. Two hundred shell holes dented the walls of the building. Stray bullets peppered near-by apartment houses. Slugs whizzed into the rooms of private families, who flattened on the floor for safety. An American, the local agent of Swift & Company, was killed while leaning over a terrace balustrade of his apartment. The Red Cross established a first-aid station half a block from the hotel. Ambulances tore through the distracted streets, their sirens wide open.

The officers, heavily armed with machine guns, rifles, and revolvers, returned the soldiers' fire with far more deadly precision, for they were the crack marksmen of Cuba. Soldiers dropped like ducks in a shooting gallery. Some of them lay for hours in agony before they could be removed. Frantic wives of the officers beseeched the American ambassador for intervention. Ammunition in the hotel began to run low.

At four o'clock in the afternoon the officers surrendered— tricked, they alleged, by a fake message that American marines would be landed immediately if the carnage was not stopped. They opposed intervention at any price, they maintained.

Soldiers trooped boisterously into the hotel and began to raid the wine cellars—to guzzle vintage champagnes. Such bedlam resulted that officers on the top floor thought the truce had been violated and began firing again into the streets. For twenty more bloody minutes the battle raged and then the exhausted officers gave in peacefully. The streets became choked with a gawking populace to watch the long stream of sweat-stained, prideful men wind down the hill and march off to prison. That evening the cool slabs of the morgue were impressively spread with corpses of colonels, lieutenant-colonels, majors and captains. An official check of casualties among the defiant officers were seventeen dead, twenty-odd wounded, one hundred seventy-eight imprisoned at El Principe Fortress, and one hundred ninety, at Cabañas.

The soldiers' losses reached fifty-three dead and some two hundred wounded. On Tuesday night through the wind-whipped streets of the capital seventeen black hearses bore the bodies of officers to the cemetery. Services for the dead were held briefly, almost stealthily, so that the hearts of the living might not be inflamed.

The noisily staged Punch-and-Judy show was over. But as the manager of National Hotel went about the now deathly silent, empty building, estimating the damage, remarking the blood-soaked carpets, the shattered mirrors, the bullet-pricked walls, the looted wine cellars, a new turmoil of unrest broke over the island. Communists seized upon the distraction as a golden opportunity to spread propaganda. Batista the revolutionist, however, stood vigorously for law and order. With an iron fist he squashed outbreaks relentlessly.

The students turned to blame the whole slaughter of the National Hotel on the American ambassador. In their publication they proposed that he be straightway returned to the United States. "The bitter attack of the students in this case was symptomatic," said their friend, Hubert Herring. "They are quick to scent conspiracy when the facts point to a coincidence. The fact is that Mr. Welles was living at the National Hotel; that the officers moved in without his invitation. It was not Mr. Welles's conspiracy; it was his bad luck."

The United States continued to refuse to recognize the Grau government, and Mr. Welles still managed to avoid intervention. Weeks of passive and less passive anarchy went by. "Intervention by inertia," President Grau called America's attitude. At length, at the end of November, Mr. Welles went to Warm Springs, Georgia, to confer with President Roosevelt. Shortly it was announced that he would be recalled from his post to resume his former position as Assistant Secretary of State. His successor was to be Jefferson Caffery, an experienced career man from Louisiana. Mr. Caffery was to go as an unofficial "observer," free to confer with and advise politicians of all parties. There was jubilation among those Cubans who refused to believe in Mr. Welles's utterly friendly offices, but the recognition of the Grau San Martín régime seemed definitely denied. Mr. Welles returned to Cuba for another fortnight and was scheduled to leave on December thirteenth. In an effort to reach a basis of conciliation between the Cuban president and the opposing forces, the ambassador made overtures towards abrogating the Platt Amendment. But in the end the conciliation failed—according to the Uruguayan minister, because a Cuban friend of the ambassador's used too much pressure on President Grau to bring about his resignation—and Mr. Welles departed on a Pan-American Airways liner under a withering blast of criticism. Many Cubans had come to suspect him as a mere puller of strings, the old time intermeddling diplomat. Few realized that "he held in his power the adrenalin magic of loans, moratoriums, revised debt structures, increased sugar quotas, and other economic panaceas." "Five years from now," wrote Tom Petty, "Sumner Welles will be regarded as one of the best friends Cuba has ever had."

Throughout the rest of December and the first fortnight of January, the Grau San Martín government clung to power only because of Colonel Batista. As chief-of-staff of the army, Batista had revealed a genius for organization. He had whipped the disorganized army into shape. He had shown considerable military ability in putting down outbreaks of Communism and in pacifying Cuba generally. That he had kept Dr. Grau in office for four months, in view of the varied forces allied against the President, was an extraordinary achievement. In the second week of January, just before he was forced to abdicate, President Grau signed far-reaching decrees. (Already in December he had stopped interest on $60,000,000 lent by American banks to Machado.) He dismissed Thomas L. Chadbourne from his post as President of Cuban National Sugar Exporting Corporation. He put his signature to an admirable agrarian decree bestowing on every indigent Cuban farmer, thirty-three acres of land, a yoke of oxen, a plow, seed, a milch cow, and tax exemption for two years. He sent government troops to seize Cuban Electric Company's properties where a strike was in progress, put the whole system under government control, had the dynamos started, and reduced the rates 45%—"any operating loss to be made up by the Treasury." Because he sponsored the cause of the weak, the surgeon idealist had a considerable following among the lower classes in something the same way as the "Great Commoner," William Jennings Bryan. But the ABC thought he lacked a practical sense of business, and they failed to give him the proper support when he sought their coöperation, which the other political sections were about to lend. As the United States feared in recognizing the Grau régime that they would have a baby communist at their doorstep to deal with, so the ABC representing a Fascist trend accused Grau San Martín of favoring the communistic tendency. (This accusation, however, was not well founded in fact, since his government was the only one which took drastic steps to fight Communism at its most acute moment.)

Notwithstanding the marked Leftist principles of Grau San Martín and his cabinet, the communist leaders redoubled their efforts to put into practice tactics proclaimed by the Third International of Moscow as the most efficacious to upset the organization of a capitalistic nation. At the downfall of Machado which loosed pent-up, powerful energies, an intense campaign of syndicalization was initiated throughout the island, preparing to gather together and discipline the proletariat and their intellectual allies under the direction of well-known Reds. Simultaneously, the leaders put into practice the sovietic "methods of direct action"—"street demonstrations," which invariably led to bloodshed (deliberately provoked by the organizers, so that the clash of the parading masses with the public forces should inflame class hatred), "factory demonstrations" (by means of which the workers make unacceptable demands an easy pretext for revolutionary strikes, which gradually undermine the strength of the employers and weaken the economic stability of the country). Again quoting Hubert Herring, "The radicals followed their immemorial course by blocking the one man who honestly hoped to help them."

As the agitators paid by Moscow are doing in many countries of heterogeneous ethnical formation, they have preferably used in Cuba the racial topics as a basis of propaganda, fomenting hatred of negroes against whites. Cuba was selected as the Latin-American headquarters for the communistic movement sponsored directly from Russia, largely because of the island's strategic geographical position, which together with the political disturbances against the Machado régime made the work of the organization more easy than it would have been elsewhere. In addition, Cuba was selected deliberately to embarrass the United States into international complications due to the United States' obligation under the Platt Amendment to intervene in Cuba to preserve life, liberty, and property rights. The plan was to put Cuba in such a chaotic condition that the United States would be compelled to intervene, thereby incurring the ill will of the rest of Latin America.

A critical situation existed all around at the turn of the new year. Grau and Batista had to use their energies against the new-risen communists. The communists were loudly anti-American; the students were strongly anti-American. The United States was anti-Grau; the ABC was anti-Grau.

In the midst of the confusion and wrangling Mr. Caffery, Roosevelt's personal representative, had by no means been idle. He had tactfully urged Grau San Martín's resignation to no avail. Then he had turned to swart little Colonel Batista, who was the only substantial prop the tottering régime seemed to have at the moment. They conferred repeatedly, closely, and Caffery talked in underscored words. Batista, no vague idealist but a shrewd realist, who had proved his military skill, now revealed remarkable political acumen. He was convinced that the United States would withhold recognition until a president agreeable to the American government would be chosen. He knew that without recognition there could be no real stability, for non-recognition meant the withholding of credit, and without credit the sugar crop could not be harvested. It meant the postponement of increasing the sugar quota and of favorable reciprocity tariff terms. It meant doom to Cuban economic life.

5

1934

On Sunday, January the fourteenth, Batista saw the light of revelation and hurried out to Camp Columbia to meet with Cuba's leading politicians. Most of them were there except Grau San Martín himself, who remained in the vast palace, coolly alone in the single blessedness of his bachelorhood. At half-past one in the morning it was announced that President Grau's resignation had been obtained. After four more hours of dispute, the wranglers chose for Grau's successor youngish Carlos Hevia, the Secretary of Agriculture and the only Cuban graduate of the United States Naval Academy.

On Monday afternoon ex-President Grau slipped out a sidedoor of the machine-gun-surrounded palace into semi-seclusion of the private life of physician. For two and a half stormy days President Hevia held his precarious high position. The choice had not been pleasing to Latin America because of Hevia's United States military training, nor to Mr. Caffery because of his radical tendencies, nor to numerous opposition leaders on various grounds. There was excited talk of renewed civil war. At one-thirty in the morning of Thursday, the eighteenth, amid scenes of pandemonium, Hevia tendered his resignation. Carlos Mendieta, veteran of forty years in politics, yet still admired even by his enemies for his integrity, was chosen the new provisional president.

When he took the oath of office, at noon on January eighteenth, the enthusiasm of the vast crowd surrounding the palace was spontaneous, genuine, heartfelt. A calm fell upon the island—at least temporarily—and a new sense of stability. An announcement was made that Mendieta's selection had the approval of all parties. Because of his scrupulous record, his patriotism, his revolutionary activity against Machado, he was the only old-school politician who could have got the support of the Cuban youth movement as represented by the ABC and the less radical students. If Mendieta had secured the nomination in 1924, when he was defeated by Machado because of the latter's backing by American financial interests, the Cuban people would have been spared much of the misery they have undergone in recent years. Now with a liberal-minded, yet conservative, patriot at the helm, one whom his enemy Machado had called "the most honest man of the opposition," the United States officially recognized the new provisional Cuban government before it was quite five days old. Straightway, Mendieta cabled to Sumner Welles, who was reestablished in his former position as Assistant Secretary of State and in charge of Cuban affairs at Washington: "I am particularly grateful to your Excellency . . . for your noble efforts . . . I am encouraged . . . because . . . I can count on your intelligent and weighty coöperation."

Because of the Cuban people's critical, needy condition, President Roosevelt gave immediate orders to the A. A. A. to prepare ten million dollars' worth of foodstuffs and other supplies to be sent to the bankrupt island as a loan. Two million dollars' worth of rice, wheat flour, pork, and lard were hastily dispatched. Mr. Welles hoped the food proffered to the hungry multitudes would check the Negro uprisings and the probable race war reported to be perilously near breaking loose.

In Havana, Jefferson Caffery paused in his arduous work on a new trade treaty which would let more Cuban sugar into the

United States, to receive announcement of his appointment as Ambassador to Cuba. On Monday, February fifth, the New Provisional Constitution of Cuba was signed. The following day in the salon of mirrors in the presidential palace, Mendieta and the members of his cabinet took their oaths of office under the new Constitution.

On February eighth, President Roosevelt in a message to Congress urged the addition of sugar to the Agricultural Adjustment Act and the settling of quotas upon all areas producing sugar for the United States, including Cuba (the only foreign country). The President asked for Cuba a quota of 1,944,000 short tons. After long and involved hearings and negotiations, it was eventually fixed at 1,902,000 tons. On March twenty-ninth, Assistant Secretary of State Welles announced that the United States government proposed to do the following: (1) Give Cuba a fair sugar quota. (2) Arrange a new commercial treaty (reciprocity) with increased preferential for Cuban sugar, under which trade between Cuba and the United States, fallen to a record low ebb, might be restored. (3) Stimulate mutual commerce through the Second Export-Import Bank of Washington (the First was on behalf of Russian trade). (4) Revise the permanent treaty between Cuba and the United States, whereby right of intervention was established in 1902 with the reluctant agreement of Cuba.

April in Havana was marked by the death of two prominent citizens and a sudden, surprising swing of Mendieta to the Left. The Secretary of Justice, Roberto Mendez Penate, long-time close friend of the President, one who shared with him the honor of being the most popular man in Cuba, shot himself in the throat when Carlos Manuel de la Cruz was made President of the State Council, a position he was supposed to have coveted. Mendieta, overcome at the news, retired to his bed and ordered a three days' period of mourning. The next week Alfredo Zayas, the republic's fourth president, died of uremia at the age of seventy-three.

As if the funeral dirges of that clever old arch-politician, Dr.

Zayas, had sounded the death-knell of political corruption and had rung in a new era of humanitarianism looking to the needs of the masses, Mendieta made his unexpected swing to the Left. He declared a two years' moratorium on amortization payments on $52,000,000 due American bond-holders and affecting three loans floated by Morgan and two by Speyer. (The decree did not affect the $80,000,000 public works loan sponsored by the Chase National Bank in default and under investigation to determine its legality.) He had the Constitution amended to remove all civil cases from the jurisdiction of military courts, even during suspension of constitutional guarantees. He authorized confiscation of property of officials found guilty of misappropriating public funds, past, present, and future. The following week he signed ten Leftist decrees, which were more radical in certain instances than anything Grau San Martín had done. Without the slightest antagonism to the United States, Mendieta pointed four of his decrees at foreigners, with a strong "Cuba for Cubans" implication. He provided that seventy-five per cent of employees hired by any private enterprise must be either native or naturalized Cuban. He revised the land tax system, and put a stricter control over private corporations that rent land. More radically conclusive was his safe-guarding decree that foreigners be prohibited from acquiring land except by special governmental permission to establish new industries. The remainder of the new measures were purely internal. An amnesty for more than two thousand prisoners, including the officers imprisoned after the siege of the National Hotel and many communists, was declared. A civil service system for public employees was instituted. Banks for agricultural credit were to be inaugurated; plans to fight unemployment were arranged for. The property of guilty Machadistas was confiscated and they themselves were disqualified from holding future official positions. A significant homestead law, much like Grau's, granted land to poor farmers. This latter liberal decree was a particularly excellent basic move in the right direction. Thirty years ago Sir William Van Horne saw that Cuba could only reach her greatest prosperity and greatest stability of government through the widest possible ownership of the lands by the people who cultivate them. "In countries where the percentage of individuals holding real estate is greatest," he said, "conservatism prevails and insurrections are unknown."

On April twenty-ninth, at the request of Cuba's state department, ex-President Machado was sought by the United States police. The charge was murder. When United States marshals failed to find him at his New York apartment, where he resided in seclusion after living in the Bahamas and Canada, a general police alarm was sent throughout the country. The former man-hunter became a hunted man.

While the search for Machado went on in the United States and Mendieta's "Cuba for Cubans" decrees were being put into effect in the island republic, President Roosevelt signed the Costigan-Jones Bill which placed sugar by amendment in the A. A. A., setting quotas for domestic production, and providing for the establishment of insular quotas.

At the same time the President made the significant and far-reaching move of ordering a reduction of 25% in the tariff on all imported sugar. The provision for executive changes in the tariff, either up or down, to the extent of 50% without recourse to Congress but on recommendation of the Commission, had been written into the tariff law of 1923. In no major commodity, however, had there before been a reduction. Nearly all executive revisions had been sharply upward, the only exceptions being in very minor commodities. The first important exercise of this power, therefore—and one marking a reversal of America's long-held tariff policy—was made in sugar and on behalf of Cuba. It was also the most significant of retirements from a virtual repudiation of America's moral obligation to Cuba, which had grown up step by step under congressional pressure in previous administrations. It marked a reaffirmation of the economic interdependence of Cuba and the United States, which the first Roosevelt had clearly seen.

The President, in the same announcement, made note of the administration's intention to revise completely the reciprocity trade agreement with Cuba, which would still further reduce the actual tariff on Cuban sugar, while maintaining protection against entry from any other foreign country. The treaty was to contain many hundred items, each of which would bring its own special benefit.

Cuba's Independence Day, May twentieth—that triple anniversary of The Lord's Ascension, the death of Christopher Columbus, and the establishment of the Cuban Republic—passed with more peace, faith, and promise than any national holiday for many years. Nine days later, at Washington, there was signed a new permanent treaty between the United States and Cuba by which the rights of the former to intervene in Cuba under the terms of the Platt Amendment were abrogated.

The news threw the island into a fanfare of rejoicing. On May thirty-first, the new treaty was ratified by the Senate of the United States. On June ninth, Secretary of State Hull and the Cuban ambassador, Marquez Sterling, made the ceremonial exchange of ratifications. For three days Cuba reveled in official fiesta. From the palace President Mendieta addressed his people over the radio, hailing the abrogation of the Platt Amendment as the "rebirth of Cuban Independence."

Just before he was killed, Martí prophesied that after independence had been won the real liberty of Cuba would have to be fought for. Forty years later, with the symbolic setting down of two signatures and the affixing of two red seals, the island republic made a momentous advance towards the realization of Martí's dream of an ideal Cuba Libre. This year of 1934 marks a new chapter in Cuba's chronicles—a period of regeneration. It may rank as one of the five most significant years in the island's history—1492, 1511, 1898, and 1902, being the other four. It has been blessed with a revaluation of values and an unwonted inspirational light from the north. At historic Cartagena, on July tenth, President Roosevelt in speaking to the people of Colombia said: "We, the citizens of all the American republics, are at the threshold of a new era. . . . There is a growing insistence of the peaceful solution of international problems. . . . We are entering the new era also in accepting the principle that no one of our nations must hereafter exploit a neighbor nation at the expense of that neighbor. . . . All of us are seeking new ways to improve the condition of the average citizen, and we give to social legislation an interest and incentive which augurs well for succeeding generations."

On August twenty-fourth, the United States and Cuba signed the new reciprocal trade agreement, which had taken more than twelve months of "painstaking and expert study." With the completion and signing of the document, the policy outlined by President Roosevelt during the campaign of 1932 and again by Secretary Hull in March 1934 ceased to be a theory and became an established fact. Advantages accorded Cuba by the United States under the new treaty are estimated by Dr. John Lee Coulter, former member of the Tariff Commission, to give the island republic about $50,000,000 more during the first year's operation of the agreement than it realized from its exports to the United States in 1932. Sugar exports alone in the first year are expected to increase Cuba's business $40,000,000. The novel document inaugurating the new American policy of traffic-making and a new method of effecting important international agreements was signed in the diplomatic room of the State Department. Cordell Hull, Sumner Welles, and Jefferson Caffery participated in the ceremony as agents for the United States. Cosme de la Torriente, Cuban Secretary of State, and Manuel Marquez Sterling, Cuban ambassador, dipped their pens in the alchemic ink as representatives of the island republic. Immediately after the signing, President Roosevelt issued a proclamation making the schedules the law of the land at the end of a ten-day period provided in the pact. Dr. Torriente said, "In the name of the Cuban people and at the special request of President Mendieta and of his government, I express our sincere gratitude to President Roosevelt and the American people."

The United States, however, makes no claim that it was mere sentimentalism, or a neighborly desire to support the Mendieta government which led to the consummation of the Cuban treaty. It was, as Professor Berle says, "hard-headed business sense, some good Yankee trading, and an endeavor to bring back a situation out of which American farmers and American manufacturers have made money for half a century." So not only were Cuban sugar planters, tobacco growers, and rum makers and the hordes of unemployed exuberant over the terms of the treaty, but American exporters hailed the reciprocal agreement as a move of greatest importance to themselves. The reduction by the United States in the tariff on Cuban raw sugar of six-tenths of one cent a pound was held extremely beneficial, as it places the Cubans in a better position to buy goods on which concessions have been granted them, particularly manufactured textiles, automobiles, and foodstuffs. For the United States the reciprocal treaty was a step forward in the whole technique of handling international relations and international exchange. For Cuba, it was a life saver.

Often it has been said that because of her varied natural resources and the marvelous fertility of her soil, Cuba can never sink so low that two years' wise economical administration cannot restore her. Now with this intelligent helping hand from the United States—if selfish revolutions do not bedevil her—the island should be on her feet again almost as quickly as her own landscape blossoms after the ravages of a hurricane.

As to the immediate future of Cuba, a great deal will also depend upon the Constitutional Council, the legislative body which is to be elected during the winter to frame a new constitution. This body will determine the type of government to be adopted by Cuba in the future and will set the date for the presidential election. The election will most likely be prudently postponed for many months to give the country a longer respite from the recent political unrest.

It is not at all unlikely that the next duly elected President of Cuba will be someone who is totally disconnected with the past régime or the present government. None of the leaders of the various revolutionary sectors who fought against Machado could hardly be acceptable to all. There are several prominent men in Cuba, able and honest, who would be good timber for the post. Most probably in the normal reactions of political events the selection of such a man will become imperative, much to the surprise of those who consider themselves the bosses of political factions.

In the meantime, Colonel Batista, commander-in-chief of the army, continues to live modestly among his soldiers at Camp Columbia—a practical example of democracy that enables him to keep always an eye on his men. Far from being a militaristic martinet, he knows when to relax discipline and open a keg of beer. Time and again he has shown his desire to reëstablish civil government in the island, to give that civil government a free hand. Although he was largely responsible for overthrowing the de Céspedes administration, even his political enemies admit that were it not for Batista, the island today would most likely be chaos.

Again looking ahead into the future, not minimizing the brotherly gestures of Mendieta, there are many things which will have to be done to improve the condition of the laboring classes, and to establish the financial and economic independence of the country. The accomplishment of these changes will, as everywhere else, be combated by conservative elements. However, according to the weight of the best opinion, Cuba, without swinging too far to the Left, will find a happy medium to bring a new deal to the forgotten labor classes, a new sound national economic freedom, and some revivifying degree of prosperity. With the abrogation of the Platt Amendment and with the awakening in the Cubans of their sense of responsibility to govern themselves, the island, as a whole, will be far happier and better off in every way. Certainly relations with the United States will be more friendly and cordial than heretofore.

The younger men of Cuba, in looking backward at the epitaphs reared by the mistakes and greed of their elders, are saddened and somewhat bitter, but undauntedly hopeful. They have faith that their people may rise on the stepping stones of their dead past to higher and better things. With unconscious irony, the incorrigibly idealistic among them visualize their future civilization as approaching that Utopian state of happiness which the unlettered Cubeños had achieved so naturally, and which the sophisticated Europeans—the Cubans' own forefathers—wiped out so inhumanly and thoroughly that not a trace remained.

AFTERWORD

THE last time I sailed from the historic blue harbor of Havana that "slithers like a blue curved dagger" into the voluptuous, sun-ripened land, memories of revolution, political squabbles, the depression, terror, misery of the last years began to fade to nothingness like a disturbing dream, and I thought only of the delights of Cuba, the inherent kindness, the pervading beauty. The pleasant things seemed to possess a deep-veined sense of permanence, as solid as those enduring Spanish-made walls, as deep-rooted as the giant ceiba tree. The distressing things seemed transitory, like the sudden black clouds and roar of a Caribbean hurricane, like passing hours of nemesis and atonement. I forgot the detonation of bombs, the expressions of want-pinched faces. I thought of bamboos interlacing feathery branches above still-voiced brooks in the mountains of Oriente, the surrounding air odorous with aromatic herbs. I savored fresh-ground, fresh-made black coffee, drunk in a peasant's palm-thatched hut, amid hospitable smiles and friendly solicitude, and with pigs running about like members of the family. I recalled narrow, sun-drenched city streets with glimpses of fresh green patios framed in the gloom of high-arched, iron-grilled gateways. I saw again jungle orchids "flaming in a network of Spanish moss." I recalled delectable odors drifting into train windows, that of tuberoses growing in fields of green corn, mingling with those of mangoes in fruit and ripening sugar cane. And I beheld the thousands of *cocuyos,* those incredibly brilliant fireflies, which emerge to beautify and amaze the summer night-scenes, like a charming, breathtaking innovation of the Cuban pageant. I thought of a particular first hour of darkness in August on the Central Highway when we were driving down from the mountain shrine of the Virgin of El Cobre, and *cocuyos* drifted into our automobile like large migratory emeralds, moving our Cuban host to tell that lovers made subtle use of the lanterns of these toy night-watchmen by placing them in thin alabaster jars to serve as romantic night lamps.

Without doubt there are visitors to Cuba who remember nothing but the spectacular, the sportive, the raw, the exciting, the violent manifestations of Cuba's civilization. But the discriminating traveler, who has taken time to see more of the island than Havana, perceives that so much of Cuba remains gentle and to be loved by acquaintance. Ask any Americans who have lived there long to tell you about Cuba and the Cubans, and you will find what they best recall is the simple, the undramatic; some unadorned remembrance of warm kindness, some humorous byplay, an appreciated freedom, some fragment of their own household loves, the mere sparkling richness of the outdoor world. Perhaps best remembered of all will be those star-lit nights, secure in some secret and tropical knowledge which they seem not to possess in cooler latitudes, and which make the Cuban scene, both in its rustic and civilized manifestations, something elusive, miraculous, like the promise of paradise. Those glamorous nights may incline the sensitively responsive to wonder—twisting a query of Izaak Walton—what nights the Lord has provided for the angels in heaven if he affords bad men such nights on earth.

SOURCES AND ACKNOWLEDGMENTS

SOURCES AND ACKNOWLEDGMENTS

I AM under an immense debt to the more than threescore writers upon whose books I have drawn extensively in this chronicle. I have examined considerably more than a hundred magazine articles and selected bits of material from almost all of them. Some of the most significant material has come from old newspapers, both American and Cuban, and some from private letters. Perhaps the most lively material has been gathered from personal interviews and reminiscences. Of the many volumes which have been especially valuable to me, none stands higher than the works of Miss I. A. Wright, Dr. Chapman, and Mr. Millis referred to in the Introduction. I have made lavish use of their material. I have also found highly serviceable Terry's *Guide to Cuba*, Horatio Rubens's *Liberty, the Story of Cuba*, Fiske's *The West Indies*, Jenks's *Our Cuban Colony*, Guggenheim's *The United States and Cuba*.

Obviously the writing of the Machado régime and the several revolutionary governments of 1933-1934 has involved breaking much new ground. The march of events during the past two years has been so fast, and happenings are still so fresh, that judgments expressed at this time will necessarily be premature. The passage of time may reveal the short-sightedness of many of my interpretations. However, I have done my best not to allow personal feelings to influence opinions expressed.

For the régime of Machado I have relied in great measure on the files of the New York *Times*, the New York *Herald-Tribune*, *The Nation, New Republic, Time, Current History, Collier's,*

Today, and various Cuban newspapers. I am indebted particularly to the tempered and illuminating articles of Dr. Hubert Herring, to *Time's* vigorous, pungent condensations of events, to the keen newspaper accounts of J. D. Phillips, Tom Petty, and Russell Porter, to the accurate Associated Press dispatches, and to Carleton Beals's sensational exposé of American exploitation in his articles as well as in his book, *The Crime of Cuba.* I owe many of the facts about Batista to Frederick Palmer's vivid article about the little sergeant in *Liberty.* I am grateful to the *New Republic* for permission to use several paragraphs and considerable material from an article of my own called *Behind the Cuban Revolt.* I have gathered much from interviews at the American Embassy in Havana and the American Consulates in Havana and Santiago, from talks with Ministers of foreign countries, with Machado officials, with prominent non-political Cubans, with soldiers, students, Rotarians, and leaders and members of ABC. I have profited too by the "testimony and true avouch" of my own eyes in Cuba throughout the tempestuous summer of 1933, before and after the fall of Machado, and during the first fortnight of de Céspedes's administration.

I am under deep indebtedness to many of the citizens of various towns and cities of Cuba and to resident Americans for courtesies and readiness to give information. I owe a tremendous debt to Dr. Luis Machado—no relation of the President—and his wife for their kindness to me, and to Dr. Machado's profound knowledge of Cuban history and his balanced, unimpassioned, and unclouded judgments. I am grateful for the valuable assistance of Don Alcides Betancourt of Camagüey, and for the courtesies of Emilio Lopez and Dr. Chaves Milanese and Jorge Schweg y Bacardi of Santiago. For much of the material of Santiago society during General Wood's governance I am indebted to Señor O'Fallon. I wish to thank Dr. Oscar Gans y Martinez and Tirsa Mesa, former Mayor of Havana, for courtesies and for historical information. To Juan B. Suris, Director of *Cuba Importador e Industrial* and to Miguel Gonzalez Rodriguez, expert on economics, I am grateful for statistical information. To M. S. Rosich, the architect, and to Armando Roldán, Conductor of the Havana Symphony Orchestra, and to Dr. José Perrara, former Professor of Penal Law at Havana University, I am indebted for answering hundreds of questions about Cuba past and present, and for clarifying my impressions of various phases of Cuban civilization. To Don Donald, Manning Ogden, Nathaniel Heller, Otto Precht, and Pete Economides, my thanks for glimpses of Cuban night life.

I am indeed grateful for assistance rendered me by the American Embassy and Consulates in Cuba. I wish to thank ex-Ambassador Sumner Welles for helpful suggestions from the fruit of his scholarly knowledge of Cuba. I am most grateful for the kindness and hospitality of Consul-General and Mrs. Dumont and for the interesting talks of their many years' living in Cuba. Consul Edwin Schoenrich at Santiago was most kind in helping me find out what I wanted to know in Oriente Province. And George Andrews, Third Secretary of the American Legation, proved himself most obliging in arranging interviews in Havana, in making valuable suggestions, and in helping me to dig out all sorts of information. To the Chinese Minister, Dr. Ping Ling, I want to say that his delightful friendship and the varied discussions we had are among the happiest remembrances of my last trip to the island.

To Norman H. Davis, United States Ambassador at Large, who lived in Cuba for a dozen years, and to Adolf Augustus Berle, Jr., I am grateful for helpful and illuminating interviews. And to Albert D. Barker, I am under deep obligation for valuable statistical information.

To numerous friends who have been kind enough to hunt up material, scan the periodical literature on Cuba listed in *Poole's Index* and the *Reader's Guide,* and make notes, I am exceedingly grateful, and I am even more obligated to those who read and criticized parts of the manuscript. I am deeply indebted to various faculty members of the University of Alabama: to Dr. Chas. H. Barnwell, Dean of the College of Liberal Arts, to Clarence

Cason, Head of the Department of Journalism, to Elizabeth Coleman, Assistant Professor of English, to Clanton Williams, Assistant Professor of History, and to Margaret Davis and M. E. Nunn of the Spanish faculty, who assisted me with translations, and moreover to Miss Davis for her personal recollections of ten years' teaching in Cuba. I am grateful to Shaler Houser, Professor of Civil Engineering, for interesting memories of Cuban life in 1914. To Johnstone Parr and Wanda Detlie Cade I am particularly indebted for their patience and assistance in proofreading and criticizing various drafts of the text. Among others who helped me with research I want to express my warm thanks to Marielou Armstrong Cory, Barbara Way, Norwood Sorrell, Bob Gilbert, Frederick Posses, Edward Gebhard, Robert Teague, Paul Sanderson, Carroll Kilpatrick, Virginia Mosby Leland, and Denis de Lagarde Johnson. For the use of books on Cuba, some of them out of print, I am grateful to Dean Lee Bidgood, Jeff Coleman, and Louise de l'Aigle Reese.

I want to thank Owen Johnson with especial warmth for encouraging me at the outset to undertake what has proved a fascinating task, and for his valued comments on my completed manuscript.

Most of all I am indebted to my wife for her unflagging assistance in helping me plan and execute the work, for her indispensable page by page criticisms, and for her five typings of the manuscript.

THE PLATT AMENDMENT

The text of the Platt Amendment as passed by the Senate and the House of the United States Congress, and after much delay accepted by the Cuban Convention on the 28th of May, 1902, by the very close vote of 15 to 14, reads as follows:

"That, in fulfillment of the declaration contained in the Joint Resolution, approved April 20th, 1898, entitled 'For the recognition of the independence of the people of Cuba,' demanding that the Government of Spain relinquish its authority and government in the Island of Cuba, and withdraw its land and naval forces from Cuba and Cuban waters, and directing the President of the United States to use the land and naval forces of the United States to carry these resolutions into effect; the President is hereby authorized to leave the government and control of the Island of Cuba to its people so soon as a government shall have been established in said Island, under a Constitution which, either as a part thereof or in any ordinance appended thereto, shall define the future relations of the United States with Cuba, substantially as follows:

(1) That the Government of Cuba shall never enter into any treaty or other compact with any foreign Power or Powers which will impair or tend to impair the independence of Cuba, nor in any manner authorize or permit any foreign Power or Powers to obtain by colonization or for military or naval purposes, or otherwise, lodgment in or control over any portion of said Island.

(2) That said Government shall not assume or contract any public debt, to pay the interest upon which and to make reasonable sinking-fund provision for the ultimate discharge of which, the ordinary revenues of the Island, after defraying the current expenses of government, shall be inadequate.

(3) That the Government of Cuba consents that the United States may exercise the right the intervene for the preservation of Cuban independence, the maintenance of a government adequate for the protection of life, prop-

343

erty, and individual liberty, for discharging the obligations with respect to Cuba imposed by the Treaty of Paris on the United States, now to be assumed and undertaken by the Government of Cuba.

(4) That all acts of the United States in Cuba during its military occupation thereof are ratified and validated, and all lawful rights acquired thereunder shall be maintained and protected.

(5) That the Government of Cuba will execute, and as far as necessary extend, the plans already devised or other plans to be mutually agreed upon, for the sanitation of the cities of the Island, to the end that a recurrence of epidemic and infectious diseases may be prevented, thereby assuring protection to the people and commerce of Cuba, as well as to the commerce of the Southern ports of the United States and the people residing therein.

(6) That the Isle of Pines shall be omitted from the proposed Constitutional boundaries of Cuba, the title thereto left to future adjustment by treaty.

(7) That to enable the United States to maintain the independence of Cuba, and to protect the people thereof, as well as for its own defense, the Government of Cuba will sell or lease to the United States lands necessary for coaling or naval stations at certain specified points to be agreed upon with the President of the United States.

(8) That by way of further assurance the Government of Cuba will embody the foregoing provisions in a permanent treaty with the United States."

SELECTED BIBLIOGRAPHY

Frederick Upham Adams: Conquest of The Tropics. New York: Double-day, Page & Co. 1914.

Henry Adams: The Education of Henry Adams: An Autobiography. New York: The Book League of America. 1928.

Alexander Emmanuel Rudolph Agassiz: Cuba. Printed for Harvard Museum. 1910.

Russell A. Alger: The Spanish American War. New York. 1901.

Edward Arber: The First Three English Books on America. Birmingham, Edinburgh: Turnball and Spears. 1885.

William Archer: Through Afro-America. New York: E. P. Dutton & Co. 1910.

Edwin Farnsworth Atkins: Sixty Years in Cuba. Cambridge. 1926.

Maturin M. Ballou: History of Cuba. Boston: Phillips, Sampson and Company. 1854.

John Kendrick Bangs: Uncle Sam, Trustee. New York: Riggs. 1902.

Enrique Barbarrossa: El Proceso de la Republica. Havana. 1911.

J. J. Barry: Life of Christopher Columbus, Compiled from the French of Roselly De Lorgues, Patrick Donahoe. New York: Catholic Pub-lication Society. 1870.

Carleton Beals: The Crime of Cuba. Philadelphia: J. B. Lippincott Com-pany. 1933.

Thomas Beer: Stephen Crane. New York. Alfred A. Knopf, Inc. 1923

Hon. James G. Blaine, J. W. Buel, John Clarke Ridpath, Hon. Benj. But-terworth: Columbus and Columbia. St. Louis, Mo.: Historical Pub-lishing Co. 1892.

Bleyer: Main Currents in the History of American Journalism. 1927.

Stephen Bonsal: The American Mediterranean. New York: Moffat, Yard and Company. 1913.

N. Bossu: Cuba. Amsterdam, Changuion. 1777.

Edward Gaylord Bourne: Narrative of the Career of Hernando de Soto, from Oviedo's History. New York: A. S. Barnes Co. 1904.

Marcel Brion: Bartolomé de las Casas, Father of the Indians, translated from the French by Coley B. Taylor. New York: E. P. Dutton & Co.

George Waldo Browne: The Far East and the New America. Boston: D. Estes & Co. 1910.

William Cullen Bryant: Letters of a Traveller. New York: Putnam. 1851.

Mildred Stapley Byne and Arthur Byne: Spanish Gardens and Patios. Philadelphia & London: J. B. Lippincott Co. New York: The Architectural Record. 1928.

Caldwell: The Lopez Expedition to Cuba. 1915.

Theodore Canot: Adventures of an African Slaver. New York: Albert and Charles Boni. 1928.

Bartolomé las Casas: Brevissima Relación de la Destruycion de las Indias. 1542.

Las Casas: General History of the Indies.

Las Casas: History del Almirante.

Bernal Diaz del Castillo: The Discovery and Conquest of Mexico, translated by A. P. Maudslay. New York: Harper. 1928.

French Ensor Chadwick: The Relations of the United States and Spain. New York: Charles Scribner's Sons. 1911.

Charles E. Chapman: A History of Spain. New York: MacMillan Company. 1918.

Charles E. Chapman: A History of The Cuban Republic. New York: MacMillan. 1927.

Charlevoix: History St. Domingo.

William J. Clark: Commercial Cuba. New York: Charles Scribner's Sons. 1898.

Alfred Coester: The Literary History of Spanish America. New York: The MacMillan Company. 1928.

Commissioner of Public Schools: First Annual Report. Havana: Rambla. 1902.

Rafael Conte and Jose M. Capmany: Guerra de Razas. Habana. 1912.

Stephen Crane: The Red Badge of Courage. New York: Appleton and Co. 1925.

Cronicas de Santiago de Cuba, Compiled by Emilio Barcardi y Moreau. Barcelona (España): Tipografia de Carbonell y Esteva. 1908.

Samuel Crowther: The Romance and Rise of The American Tropics. New York: Doubleday, Doran & Co. 1929.

Richard Harding Davis: Cuba in War. New York. 1897.

Richard Harding Davis: The Cuban and Porto Rican Campaigns. New York: Charles Scribner's Sons. 1898.

Adolfo Dollero: Cultura Cubana. Habana. 1916.

Richard Eden: The History of Travayle in the West and East Indies. London: Richarde Iugge. 1577.

L. E. Elliott: Captain William Dampier—Pirate and Hydrographer, His Life and Times, 1651-1715, Pan American, Vol. 42.

George Edward Ellis: Las Casas and the Relations of the Spaniards to the Indians, in Justin Windsor Edition, Narrative and Critical History of America. Boston and New York. 1884-89.

Ford Fairford: Peeps At Many Lands. London: A. & C. Black, Ltd. 1926.

Amos Kidder Fiske: The West Indies. New York: Putnam's. 1899.

John Fiske: Discovery of America.

Grover Flint: Marching with Gomez—A War Correspondent's Field Notebook. Boston and New York: Lamson, Wolffe. 1898.

Flores: La Guerra de Cuba. 1895.

Forbes-Lindsay and Nevin O. Winter. Boston: L. C. Page & Co. 1911, revised 1928.

Charles Harcourt Ainslie Forbes-Lindsay: Cuba and Her People of Today. Boston: L. C. Page. 1911.

Harry T. Guggenheim: The United States and Cuba. New York: The Century Co. 1920.

Leopoldo Freyre de Andrade: La Intervencion Gubernamental en la Industria Azucarera. Havana. 1931.

James Anthony Froude: The English in The West Indies or The Bow of Ulysses. New York: Charles Scribner's Sons. 1888.

William Crawford Gorgas: Sanitation in Panama.

Marie D. Gorgas and Burton J. Hendrick: William Crawford Gorgas, His Life and Work. Garden City, New York: Doubleday, Page and Company.

Harry T. Guggenheim: The United States and Cuba. New York: The MacMillan Company. 1934.

Murat Halstead: The Story of Cuba. Chicago: The Werner Company. 1896.

Herrera: History of the Indies.

R. T. Hill: Cuba and Porto Rico. New York: Century. 1898.

Hobson: The Sinking of the Merrimac.

John Holladay: The United States and Latin America. New York. 1920.

Alexander von Humboldt: Essai Politique sur l'Ile de Cuba.

Alexander von Humboldt: The Island of Cuba. New York: Derby and Jackson. 1856.

Alexander von Humboldt: Political Essay on the Kingdom of New Spain. New York: John Black. 1811.

Alexander von Humboldt and Aime Bonpland: Personal Narrative of Travels to The Equinoctial Regions of America, 1799-1804, translated by Thomasina Ross, Volume III. London: George Bell and Sons. 1881.

The Life, Travels and Books of Alexander von Humboldt. New York: Rudd and Carleton.

Washington Irving: The Life and Voyages of Christopher Columbus. Philadelphia: J. B. Lippincott & Co. 1872.

Leland Hamilton Jenks: Foreign Relations.

Leland Hamilton Jenks: Our Cuban Colony, A Study in Sugar. New York: Vanguard Press. 1928.

W. F. Johnson: The History of Cuba. New York: Buck and Co. 1920.

Chester Lloyd Jones: Caribbean Interests of the United States. New York: Appleton. 1919.

Paul de Kruif: Microbe Hunters. New York: Harcourt, Brace and Company, 1926.

Fitzhugh Lee: Cuba's Struggle Against Spain. New York: The American Historical Press. 1899.

Joaquin Llaverias: Historia de los Archivos de Cuba. Habana. 1912.

Lodge: Letters of Theodore Roosevelt and Henry Cabot Lodge. 1925.

C. E. Magoon: Republic of Cuba: Report of Provisional Administration. Havana. 1906-08.

W. M. Malloy: Treaties, Conventions, International Acts, Protocols and Agreements Between the United States and Other Powers, Vol. 1, page 358.

George Marian: A Little Journey to Cuba and Porto Rico.

Jose Marti: Apuntes Historicos. Tampa. 1896.

Jose Marti: Obras. 12 v. Havana.

Theodore Maynard: Peter Martyr d'Anghiera: Humanist and Historian. Baltimore: Catholic Historical Review. 1931.

Walter Millis: The Martial Spirit. Boston and New York: Houghton Mifflin. 1931.

Hon. Amelia M. Murray: Letters from the United States, Cuba and Canada. New York: G. P. Putnam & Company. 1856.

Sir Charles Augustus Murray: Travels in North America During the Years 1834-1835-1836.

George Clarke Musgrave: Under Three Flags in Cuba. Boston: Little, Brown. 1899.

Navarrete: Primer Viage de Colón.

F. A. Ober: A Guide to the West Indies. New York: Dodd, Mead and Company. 1908.

Ogden: Life and Letters of E. L. Godkin. 1907.

James J. O'Kelly: The Mambi-land, or, Adventures of a *Herald* Correspondent in Cuba. Philadelphia: Lippincott. 1874.

Victor H. Olmstead and Henry Gannett: Oficina del Censo. 1907.

Julius E. Olson and Edward Gaylord Bourne: The Northmen, Columbus and Cabot. New York: Scribners. 1906.

Fernando Ortiz: Las Actuales Responsibilidades Politicas y la "Nota" Americana. Havana. 1919.

Fernando Ortiz: La Decadencia Cubana. Habana. 1924.

Oviedo: Cronica de las Indias.

Gonzalo Fernandez de Oviedo y Valdes: Historia General y Natural de las Indias. Madrid: Impr. de la Real Academia de la Historia. 1851-55.

William Belmont Parker: Cubans of To-day. New York and London: Putnam's Sons. 1919.

C. M. Pepper: To-morrow in Cuba. Harper. 1899.

Demoticus Philalethes: Yankee Travels Through the Island of Cuba. New York: Appleton. 1856.

Fernando Pizarro: Varones Illustres del Nuevo Mundo.

George Bronson Rea: Facts and Fakes About Cuba. 1897.

Albert G. Robinson: Cuba Old and New. New York: Longmans, Green and Co. 1915.

Rochefort: Hist. Nat. des Iles Antilles. Rotterdam. 1665.

Francisco de Paula Rodriguez: Sociologia Cubana. Habana. 1919.

Theodore Roosevelt: The Rough Riders. New York. 1899.

Theodore Roosevelt: Theodore Roosevelt: An Autobiography. 1913.

Ricardo Rousset: Historial de Cuba. 3 v. Habana. 1918.

Horatio S. Rubens: Liberty, The Story of Cuba. New York: Brewer, Warren and Putnam. 1932.

James Brown Scott: The Recommendations of Habana Concerning International Organization, Adopted by American Institute of International Law at Habana, January 23, 1917. New York: Oxford University Press. 1917.

Seitz: Joseph Pulitzer. 1924.

Reisendenkwiirdigkeiten und Forschungen von Jegor von Sivers: Cuba, die Perle der Antillen. Leipzig: Verlag von Carl. Fr. Fleischer. 1861.

J. Russell Smith: North America. New York: Harcourt, Brace. 1925.

Mark Sullivan: Our Times. New York: Charles Scribner's Sons. 1928.

T. Philip Terry: Guide to Cuba. Boston: Houghton Mifflin Company. 1929.

John Boyd Thacker: Christopher Columbus. New York and London: G. P. Putnam's Sons. 1903-04.

Carlos Manuel Trelles: Biblioteca Historica Cubana. 2 v. Matanzas, Cuba. I: 1922, II: 1924.

Sir Frederick Treves: The Cradle of the Deep. New York: E. P. Dutton & Co. 1925.

James Westfall Thompson: The Middle Ages.

United Fruit Company Medical Department: Nineteenth Annual Report, 1930, Made in United States of America.

United States Adjutant-General's Office: Military Notes on Cuba—1898.

United States Department of State: The Ostend Manifesto 1854. New York: Lovell. 1892.

Enrique Jose Varona: De la Colonia á la Republica. Habana. 1919.

Ramon Vasconcelos: El Gral. Gomez y la Sedicion de Mayo. Havana. 1916.

A. Hyatt Verrill: The Book of The West Indies. New York: Dodd, Mead and Company.

A. Hyatt Verrill: Cuba Past and Present. New York: Dodd, Mead and Company. 1920.

A. Hyatt Verrill: Cuba of Today. New York: Dodd, Mead and Company. 1931.

Mrs. M. H. Wade: Our Little Cuban Cousin. Boston: L. C. Page. 1902.

Charles Dudley Warner: Library of the World's Best Literature, Volume VI. New York: R. S. Peale and J. A. Hill.

West India Pilot: London. 1899.

Valeriano Weyler y Nicolau: Mi Mando en Cuba. 5 v. Madrid. 1910-11.

Wheeler: The Santiago Campaign. 1898.

Robert Wiles: Cuban Cane Sugar. Indianapolis: Bobbs-Merrill. 1916.

Winkler: Hearst. 1928.

Basil Woon: When It's Cocktail Time in Cuba. New York: Horace Liveright. 1928.

Irene Aloha Wright: Cuba. New York: MacMillan. 1910.

I. A. Wright: The Early History of Cuba, 1492-1586. New York: MacMillan Company. 1916.

CHARACTERS OF THE CHRONICLE

A

Madame Abreu, 243
Henry Adams, 111, 113-114, 166-
177, 179
John Quincy Adams, 103
Dr. Aristides Agramonte, 194
Porrista Ainciart, 308
Lord Albemarle, 59-61, 98, 191
Señor Aldama, 98
Count Almonte, 77
Armando André, 270
Dr. Angulo, 47-48
Baptista de Antonelli, 53
Ernesto Asbert, 240
E. F. Atkins, 110, 137, 173, 186
Avaroff, Cuban Secretary of
Treasury, 307

B

Robert Bacon, 219 222, 228
Pedro de Barba, 40
Bishop of Barcelona, 121
Fulgencio Batista, 314-317, 321-324,
326-327, 335
Carleton Beals, 241, 279, 291
Count de Beaujolie, 63

Vasquez Bello, 287, 290
Adolf Augustus Berle, Jr., 314,
318-321, 334
Juan Rodriguez Bermejo, 8, 19
Don Alcides Betancourt, 107-108,
190
Captain-General Blanco, 116, 131-
133, 162-163
Boabdil, 4
Senator Borah, 291
Godfrey de Bouillon, 18
General Boza, 119
Marcel Brion, 35
General John R. Brooke, 185-189,
193
Sydney Brooks, 236
Brouzón, 273
Colonel Frederico Brú, 263
William Jennings Bryan, 325
James Buchanan, 102

C

Cabrera, 104
Julius Cæsar, 6, 305
Policeman Calvo, 287
Martínez Campos, 108, 118-119,
121-122

PHOTOGRAPHERS

Frontispiece and Photograph 1
by F. S. Lincoln, New York

Photographs 6, 8, and 10
by Robert Machado, New York

Photographs 2, 4, and 9
by Lopez Ortiz, Havana

Photograph 3
by Mateo, Santiago de Cuba

Photographs 7, 11, 12, 13, 14, and 15
by American Photo Studio, Havana

I
Guajiro prodding oxen

2

Patio of the old Governor-Generals' Palace with statue of
Cuba's discoverer, Christopher Columbus

3

Upper view of Morro Castle, Santiago

4

Statues of José Martí in Parque Central, with Capitol and Gallician Club in the background

5

Patio of modern suburban residence designed by Mira and
Rosich, Architects

6
Chinese vegetable-vendor, Trinidad

7

Driveway through forest of bamboo

8
Cuban sunset behind royal palms

9

Patio of Aldama Palace, noted for its lavish entertainments
in the gala days—now the factory of Corona cigars

10

Typical scene in the market section of Havana, with street
vendors of lottery tickets and singing birds

11
Bohio, with coconut palms

12

Narrow old street, looking towards the Presidential Palace,
with spire of the Church of the Angels at left

13
Detail of Hotel Camagüey Patio, Camagüey

14
Loading sugar cane

15

Mission house, with royal poinciana tree in pod, Isle of
Pines

171